D0667144

FALLEN ANGELS

Fallen Angels

BERNARD J. BAMBERGER

BARNES
&NOBLE
BOOKS
NEW YORK

TO
EKB

Acknowledgments

Work on the studies here presented was greatly facilitated because the resources of the following libraries
were available to me: the Albany Public Library,
the New York Public Library, the New York State Library, and
the libraries of the Catholic University of America, Columbia
University, General Theological Seminary, Hebrew Union College-
Jewish Institute of Religion, Jewish Theological Seminary of America, Seminary of St. Anthony on the Hudson and Union Theological
Seminary. I am grateful for the courteous help received in each
case; my special thanks are due Dr. Joshua Bloch and Mr. Abraham
Berger of the Jewish Division of the New York Public Library,
Prof. Boaz Cohen of the Jewish Theological Seminary, and Rabbi
I. Edward Kiev of the Jewish Institute of Religion.

At the start of the inquiry I had the privilege of consulting my teacher, Dr. Jacob Z. Lauterbach of blessed memory. President Julian Morgenstern (*yibbadel l'hayyim*) has helped me throughout by his advice and encouragement. I wish also to express my indebtedness to Dr. Solomon B. Freehof, the Rev. Michael J. Gruenthaner, S.J., Dr. Leo Jung, the Rev. Kenneth Ohrstrom, Prof. Shalom Spiegel and Dr. Joshua Trachtenberg for information and assistance they graciously supplied.

Prof. Abraham J. Heschel read the chapters on mysticism and suggested many changes and improvements. I deeply appreciate his friendly guidance; in gladly acknowledging his aid, I must state that he is in no way responsible for the many deficiencies that still remain in this section of the book.

Mr. Edwin Wolf 2nd, Dr. Maurice Jacobs, and Mr. Lesser Zussman of the Jewish Publication Society family have displayed warm interest in my work, and have rendered many services for which I am truly thankful. Last but surely not least, Dr. Solomon Grayzel, the editor of the Society, has been a source of strength at all times. It is hard to find words to express my appreciation of his warm interest, sound counsel and tireless help.

BERNARD J. BAMBERGER

Contents

Acknowledgments   vii

PART ONE: **Gateway**

I Introducing the Theme   3
II The Hebrew Scriptures   7

PART TWO: **The Outside Books**

Introduction   15
III The Ethiopic Enoch   16
IV The Ethiopic Enoch (*continued*)   21
V The Ethiopic Enoch (*concluded*)   23
VI Jubilees, Testaments, Zadokite Work   26
VII The Slavonic Enoch   32

viii The Adam Books   35
ix The Testament of Job   37
x Esdras, Baruch, Pseudo-Philo   42
xi The Apocalypse of Abraham   46

PART THREE: **Crossroads**

xii Hellenistic Writings   51
xiii Where the Ways Divide   54

PART FOUR: **The Early Christian Church**

xiv The New Testament   61
xv The Church Fathers   73
    The Interpretation of Genesis VI . . . Satan . . .
    The Limitations of Christian Dualism

PART FIVE: **The Rabbis**

xvi Talmud and Midrash   89
    The Sin of the Angels . . . Enoch . . . The Frailty
    of Angels . . . The Character of Satan . . . The Evil
    Inclination . . . The Serpent . . . The Demons . . .
    The Princes of the Gentiles

xvii Interlude: The Legend in Islam   111
    Iblis . . . Harut and Marut

xviii New Paths: The Visionaries   117
    1. Apocalypses . . . 2. Mystical Writings

xix New Paths: The Later Aggada   128
    Sinful Angels . . . The Fall of Satan . . . Satan's
    Malice . . . Samael as Prince of Rome . . . Uzza the
    Patron Angel of Egypt . . . The Guardian Angels
    of the Nations . . . Enoch . . . Lilith . . . Sum-
    ming Up

PART SIX: **Medieval Judaism**

xx The Rationalists   147
    The "Sons of God" . . . Enoch . . . Azazel . . . Job
    . . . Hillel ben Samuel and the Christians

PART SEVEN: **Jewish Mysticism**

XXI	The German Cabala	163
XXII	The Spanish Cabala	168
XXIII	The Zohar	176

The Fallen Angels . . . Naamah, Lilith, the Rulers of Arka . . . The Paternity of Cain . . . Samael-Satan . . . Mystical Dualism

XXIV	The Later Mystics	186
XXV	Mysticism for the Masses	194

PART EIGHT: **Christian Theology**

XXVI	The Devil of the Philosophers	201
XXVII	The Devil of the People	208

Witchcraft . . . The Devil's People—the Jews . . . The Heretics

XXVIII	Protestant Christianity	220

Luther . . . Calvin . . . English Literature . . . The Witches

PART NINE: **The Devil in Modern Dress**

XXIX	The Century of Liberalism	235
XXX	Epilogue	239
	Bibliography	253
	Notes	263
	Index	291

FALLEN ANGELS

PART ONE

Gateway

CHAPTER ONE

Introducing the Theme

Everyone likes tales of adventure. A more mature taste finds interest in the study of character and the development of personality. This book, however, traces the evolution of an idea and its adventures through the centuries.

The study of ideas may be both interesting and practical: it is important to know, for example, how the democracy of Franklin D. Roosevelt differed from the democracy of Thomas Jefferson. But what value can there be in the history of a mythological idea, a belief in angels, and in sinful angels at that? Can such a story be of interest to anyone but a student of antiquity or a dabbler in the curious vagaries of the human mind?

An obvious answer is: The myth of the rebel angels has had a great influence on world literature. The figure of Prometheus,

staunchly defying the omnipotent Zeus, even though he is fore-
doomed to defeat, has fascinated many poets. The drama is
heightened when the rebel against Deity is not a human being,
but an angel—one of God's holiest creatures. Such a paradox was
bound to stir the poetic imagination. Its most notable result is
the massive epic of John Milton. The depiction of Satan is one of
his greatest successes—the desperate fallen angel is more vivid
and interesting, sometimes more appealing, than his unspotted
fellows. *Paradise Lost* is, as the saying goes, more famous than
widely read; but its rich music and dramatic power still reward
anyone old-fashioned enough to open its pages.

We need not mention the Faust literature, nor the countless
works of imagination in which the Devil plays a part. Our concern is not with his manifold activity, but only with his rebellion
and fall. To Milton, indeed, this was no mere literary theme. He
may have embellished *Paradise Lost* with poetic fancies; but to
him this was only the adornment of profound and literal truth.
Later authors, however, have utilized this subject matter more
freely for their own special purposes.

The romantic pessimist, Alfred de Vigny, tells in his poem,
Le Déluge, of one Emmanuel, son of an angel whose name he
bears and of a mortal woman. Emmanuel learns from the stars
that the flood is coming, and seeks refuge in the company of his
beloved on Mount Ararat. She had been offered marriage and
security by Japhet, son of Noah, but remained faithful to Emmanuel. The pair hope that his angel father will rescue them;
but no help comes and they are overwhelmed by the rising
waters.

De Vigny's longest poem, *Éloa,* is about a female angel, born
of a tear dropped by Jesus. (In the authentic tradition, angels
are exclusively masculine.) Deeply moved by the spirit of divine
pity, Éloa is obsessed by vague reports about an exiled rebel
angel. She goes forth to seek and comfort this unfortunate being.
Satan, however, is not redeemed by her good offices; Éloa is
caught in the net of his blandishments and dragged down to
perdition.

Utterly different again is Anatole France's *La Chute des Anges.*
Here much curious learning is combined with fantastic imagination and mordant wit, the whole presented in France's limpid
style, to expose the evils and follies of French society and to

advance the cause of social and spiritual revolution. The ancient legend is only the vehicle of the author's satirical aim.

The varied uses which creative writers have made of this old belief testify to its fascination. But we have to do with much more than a fantastic tale suitable for poetic treatment. Fantastic it is, sometimes grotesque; but as we trace its development, we shall find ourselves standing at some critical points in the history of the human spirit. Most of those who have previously investigated this subject have dealt chiefly with its folkloristic aspect. The present study is more properly theological, not to say apologetic. Following the fortunes of the belief in fallen angels, we shall gain a deeper insight into the character of Judaism and the character of Christianity, and into their divergences. Before we finish, we shall have to confront contemporary issues of major importance.

Our study will lead us through many and varied writings, in a dozen languages, composed through the centuries in many parts of the world. Some of our sources are queer indeed, many of them confusing. So at the start it will be well to outline the nature of our undertaking.

Man has always had to contend with physical and moral evil, with wickedness and with pain. But the existence of evil, however unpleasant, presented no theoretical problem to the primitive mind. Everyone knew that there are good, friendly gods, and also wicked, cruel deities and demons. It is the latter who cause all our woes and worries. The purpose of religion was to conciliate (and strengthen) the powers of good and to placate or defeat the spirits of evil. Of course one had to deal cautiously even with the kindest gods, for they too could be dangerous if offended. One might even utilize the powers of evil for his own purposes—that is, practice witchcraft—but this was hazardous in the extreme. The general division of the supernatural beings into kind and cruel powers was familiar to all the pagan peoples; this dualism found its most extreme and dramatic expression in Persia.

The religion of Israel affirmed that the whole world is the creation and domain of one God, who is all good. We need not dwell here on the sublimity of this conception or its liberating effects on the human spirit. But there is no denying that it posed new problems. If God is unique, and if He is perfectly good, how are we to account for the evil in the world? This question still gnaws at our hearts; it was soon perceived by Israel's more thoughtful spirits.

Originally, the difficulty was put thus: Why do the righteous suffer and the wicked prosper? The prophet Jeremiah raised the question in these terms, and his perplexity is echoed in many of the Psalms. The Book of Job states the problem with unequaled power and passion, and attempts a noble and dignified solution. But the answer which Judaism later adopted, and even made official, was that all the apparent inequities we encounter in this life are adjusted by reward and punishment in the life beyond the grave.

Yet the problem in its broader sense remained. Granted that the wicked will be punished and the righteous rewarded after death, why are men wicked at all? Why did God create a world which is not entirely good? In the centuries preceding the Christian era, so much hardship and tragedy befell the Jewish people that they were bound to ponder these questions; and many who lacked philosophic training felt the sting of the questions no less keenly. And so some of them attempted a mythological explanation.

God, they said, created everything good. But certain angels whom He made for His service were faithless to their high calling. The story of the fallen angels appears in two general forms.

One version tells that a group of angels became enamored of mortal women, succumbed to lust and defiled their heavenly holiness with earthly love. Their human consorts bore them giant offspring, violent and cruel. Having sinned first in weakness, the fallen angels went on to deliberate rebellion. A terrible punishment overtook them and their violent children; but the corruption they had wrought continued to taint all mankind.

The other form of the story concerns one of the mightiest of the angel host, who rebelled against God at the time of Creation, or, according to some, even before. His sin was pride, and he even dreamed of usurping the place of the Almighty. Cast down from heaven, he became Satan, the adversary; and out of his hatred of God and his jealousy of man, he led Adam to sin.

Both these stories appear in Jewish writings dating from the last few centuries before the Christian era. At the same time, we meet two related ideas. One is the existence of a demonic power, called Satan and also by several other names, who is opposed to God and an enemy of man, especially of Israel, but whose origin is not clearly accounted for. The other concept is somewhat different. It holds that each nation on earth has a guardian angel above, a *sar* or prince. The nations that have oppressed and persecuted Israel have done so at the instigation and under the leadership of their heavenly patrons. The redemption of Israel must therefore be preceded, not only by the overthrow of its earthly enemies, but also by the downfall and punishment of their guardian angels.

These ideas were not altogether new. They drew upon a common store of mythological notions which have spread from people to people. Different scholars have found the sources of these myths in Babylonia, Persia or Greece. It is almost impossible to decide the matter finally, for there must have been constant interchange of such legendary coin among the nations. But in recent years, a great deal of Canaanite literature has come to light—the literature of a people who were the nearest neighbors of Israel and spoke almost the same language; and we shall not greatly err if we suppose that the Jewish mythographers drew largely on Canaanite-Phoenician materials. But they did not just borrow and retail an old myth. They created something new and different: they tried to graft pagan branches on the monotheistic trunk of Judaism.

Our task will be to trace the fortunes of this belief within the Jewish religion and in the religions that sprang from Judaism.

CHAPTER TWO

The Hebrew Scriptures

The post-biblical authors who told the stories of the rebel angels believed themselves to be expositors of Scripture. They were only elaborating with greater clarity and detail what was already hinted in the Bible. Were they right in this supposition? On this point scholars have disagreed. So our first inquiry is: does the Hebrew Bible contain the belief in fallen angels?

The passages we must consider are few and brief, so we may quote them in full. The first is Genesis 6.1-4:

> 1. And it came to pass, when men began to multiply on the face of the earth, and daughters were born unto them, 2. that the sons of God (*b'ne haElohim*) saw the daughters of men that they were fair; and they took them wives, whomsoever they chose. 3. And the Lord said: 'My spirit shall not abide (? *yadon*) in man forever, for that he also is flesh; therefore shall his days be a hundred and twenty years.' 4. The Nephilim were in the earth in those days, and also after that, when the sons of God came in unto the daughters of men, and they bore children unto them; the same were the mighty men that were of old, the men of renown.

Who were the "sons of God"? Some ancient commentators have insisted that the phrase is no more than an honorific title for human beings, meaning "the sons of the rulers." But they had special motives (as we shall see) for adopting this interpretation. Both the present context, and the other cases where this phrase occurs in the Bible, compel us to explain "sons of God" as divine, angelic beings.[1] This little paragraph tells of the marriage of mortal women to superhuman spouses.

Verse 3 is obscure. The translation of the word *yadon* is no more than a guess; the whole sentence does not seem to have any bearing on the rest of the section. But certainly it is not a condemnation of the action of the sons of God.[2]

The most significant fact about the passage is a negative fact: the Bible does not suggest that these intermarriages were sinful, or the issue of them bad. It gives no hint that any punishment resulted. Ancient teachers supposed that this little tale accounts for the Flood, the story of which follows our paragraph. But the Torah nowhere suggests such a thing. The Flood was a punishment for human wickedness.

These four verses have no clear connection with the rest of the book of Genesis. They seem rather to be a mythological fragment, which accounts for the origin of the famous ancient heroes. Such mighty men, whose fathers were gods and whose mothers were mortal, are found in the lore of many peoples. Such was the Babylonian hero Gilgamesh; such was Hercules, among many examples in Greek mythology. And the Canaanite epic of *The Beautiful and Gracious Gods* tells how the great god El begot

Shahar and Shalim on mortal women.[3] Of course the Bible represents the fathers not as gods, but as angels. The *Gibborim* or
heroes—so our text seems to say—are not identical with the
Nefilim.[4] (The latter are a breed of primeval giants who are mentioned elsewhere in the Bible under such names as *Refaim* and
Zamzumim.) The *Nefilim* were on earth before the heroes were
engendered as well as later on.

Beyond question, the tale of the fallen angels was based on
this passage; it is a kind of Midrash upon it. But the Torah supplied only the starting point of the story, not the story itself.

The second passage is from a doom-song upon the King of
Babylon; it dates, then, at the earliest from the Babylonian exile,
perhaps later. It runs (Isaiah 14.12-15):

> How art thou fallen from heaven
> O day-star, son of the morning! (*Helel ben Shahar*)
> How art thou cast down to the ground,
> That didst cast lots over the nations!
> And thou saidst in thy heart:
> 'I will ascend into heaven,
> Above the stars of God (*El*)
> Will I exalt my throne;
> And I will sit upon the mount of meeting,
> In the uttermost parts of the north;
> I will ascend above the heights of the clouds;
> I will be like the Most High (*Elyon*).'
> Yet thou shalt be brought down to the nether-world,
> To the uttermost parts of the pit.

Christian tradition has regularly adduced this passage as a
proof-text for the fall of Satan—very rarely, the same interpretation appears in Jewish literature.[5] But leaving this tradition aside,
the modern scholar must recognize that the poem has a strong
mythological flavor. *El, Elyon,* and *Shahar* are now known to us
as members (the first two as leading members) of the Canaanite
pantheon. "The mount of meeting in the uttermost parts of the
north" is the abode of the gods, corresponding to Mount Olympus
in Greek myth. It is very tempting then to see in this poem an
allusion to a Canaanite or Phoenician myth concerning one Helel,
son of the god Shahar, who sought to usurp the throne of the
chief god and for his audacity was cast down into the abyss.

This would be a parallel to the Greek legend of the revolt of Zeus against Kronos, and of the unsuccessful attempt of the Titans to unseat Zeus in his turn.

But all this, though plausible, remains conjecture. No extant Canaanite source tells us about Helel ben Shahar, nor of a revolt against Elyon. It is still possible that "Shining one, son of the dawn" was a poetic phrase coined by the author of the prophecy. In any case, the writer was exulting over the fall of a human king. Even if he is alluding to a myth, we need not suppose that he believed in it.[6] English literature is full of allusions to classical mythology, but for the purposes of ornament only.

The last passage we must consider is Psalm 82:

1. God standeth in the Congregation of God (*El*);
   In the midst of gods (*elohim*) He judgeth.
      2. How long will ye judge unjustly
         And respect the persons of the wicked?
      3. Judge the poor and the fatherless,
         Do justice to the afflicted and the destitute.
      4. Rescue the poor and the needy;
         Deliver them out of the hand of the wicked.
      5. They know not, neither do they understand;
         They go about in darkness.
   All the foundations of the earth are moved.
6. I said: Ye are gods,
   And all of you sons of the Most High (*Elyon*).
7. Nevertheless ye shall die like men,
   And fall like one of the princes (*sarim*).
      8. Arise, O God, judge the earth;
         For Thou shalt possess all the nations.

Scholars have been at loggerheads concerning this brief Psalm. Some insist that it is directed against wicked earthly rulers; others are just as positive that it describes a judgment upon sinful angels. Dr. Julian Morgenstern has now brought us closer to a solution of the difficulty.[7] He points out that, whichever interpretation one may adopt, part of the Psalm will fit his view and another part will not. Look at the Psalm again: the lines which (following Dr. Morgenstern) have been indented refer unmistakably to human rulers. They have been substituted for part of a mythological poem, of which only the beginning and end have been preserved. The older verses contain the names of El and Elyon, and their subject matter is plainly mythological. It is the judgment by the God of Israel upon the wicked angels. The part of the poem that has been suppressed must, among other things, have stated the sin for which the angels were punished.

Thus far Dr. Morgenstern's analysis seems to be correct beyond question. But he has indulged in some other conjectures which are less convincing.[8]

What, says Dr. Morgenstern, was the sin of the angels? It is the sin related in Genesis 6, of marrying mortals and engendering children. The order of the universe is that celestial beings are deathless: therefore they need no offspring. Indeed, were they to reproduce their kind, the increase of the immortal population would soon overcrowd heaven and earth. Only earthly creatures who taste death need to achieve immortality in their children. The *elohim* upset this wise dispensation by begetting offspring; therefore Elyon punished them by stripping them of immortality.

Curiously enough, Dr. Morgenstern's reasoning was anticipated by the Midrash. When Hannah prayed at Shiloh—so the rabbis relate—she said: "Lord of the Universe! The celestials never die, and they do not reproduce their kind. Terrestrial beings die, but they are fruitful and multiply. Therefore I pray: Either make me immortal, or give me a son!"[9]

But the ancient mythographers were not so logical. The gods of Canaan, like those of every folk but Israel, begot children with blithe indifference to any quasi-Malthusian considerations. No one ever questioned their right to marry among themselves, or to consort with mortals. If Hera objected to the flirtations of Zeus, it was not because his lady-loves were human. Hephaestus was no less indignant when his wife betrayed him with the god of war. At her marriage to Eros, Psyche was transformed into a goddess; and Artemis was not condemned for loving Endymion.

In short: Genesis 6 tells that the angels married women, but not that this was a sin. Psalm 82 reports that the *elohim* sinned, but not that they married women. There is no biblical evidence to warrant a combination of the two items. On the assumption that these mythological materials came from North Semitic sources, the probability is all the other way. A more reasonable guess is that the sin of the angels described in the part of the Psalm now lost was an attempt to usurp the power of El and

Elyon. This would fit in with the (admittedly conjectural) interpretation of Isaiah 14.

The Bible, then, contains some of the materials of which the myth of the rebel angels was fashioned. But the story itself and the ideas it expresses are found neither in the Bible nor in the heathen sources which Scripture occasionally echoes. As for the myth of the fall of Satan, there is no hint of it in the Hebrew Bible. Satan appears a few times, but always as a member of God's entourage, an agent entrusted with special duties, never as a rebel. The serpent of Eden is neither a devil nor the agent of a devil. He is just an animal, although a crafty and malicious animal.

But the belief in guardian angels of the nations is found in a few late passages of the Bible. These passages occur in apocalypses—visions of the end of days and the last judgment, which were composed in the Maccabean period or close to it. Thus Daniel receives a revelation from the angel Gabriel after a long period of fasting and prayer. Gabriel explains that he could not come to him sooner because he had to struggle for twenty-one days with the prince (*sar*) of Persia. At length Michael, one of the chief *sarim*, came to his aid—this, presumably, enabled Gabriel to answer Daniel's call. Later, he adds, he will have to return to his combat with the guardian of Persia and then with the prince of Greece; "and there is none that holdeth with me against these except Michael, your prince." Further on, in the account of the final redemption, Michael, "the great prince who standeth up for the children of thy people," is to play a leading role (Daniel 10.13-21, 12.1).

The Book of Daniel does not say that the angelic rulers of Persia and Greece will be punished along with their peoples; but the author probably took this for granted. In another biblical apocalypse (a brief and enigmatic document which cannot be exactly dated) we read: "The Lord will punish the host of the high heaven on high, and the kings of the earth upon the earth; and they shall be gathered together as prisoners are gathered in the dungeon, and shall be shut up in prison, and after many days shall they be punished" (Is. 24.21 f.).[10]

This same little prophecy declares that in the end of days God will punish "Leviathan the slant serpent and Leviathan the tortuous serpent" (Is. 27.1). This creature is described in almost exactly the same words in the Canaanite poems discovered at Ras Shamra.[11] Leviathan, or as these poems spell it, Lothan, is the North Semitic name for the primeval sea serpent whom the Babylonians called Tiamat. Did our apocalyptic writer believe then in a mythological power of cosmic evil? Probably not. Throughout his booklet the root of evil seems to be in the pagan nations and their angelic patrons, not in the universe itself. Leviathan is most likely only a figure of speech designating the great heathen empires, not a concrete embodiment of the satanic.

This interpretation is the more probable because the name Rahab, by which the primeval serpent is also known, is twice applied by the Bible to Egypt. There are indeed several passages which speak of God's triumph over Leviathan-Rahab in the days of old.[12] They celebrate the power of God over nature, not over evil. In any case, they imply that the serpent was completely destroyed in ages past, so that God will have no new battle to fight at the end of time. The Hebrew Bible does not know an organized realm of spiritual evil arrayed against the Kingdom of God.

PART TWO

The Outside Books

Introduction

The story of the fallen angels, which we did *not* find in the Bible, appears fully in works which Jewish tradition characterizes as the Outside Books, that is, books left out of the Scriptural canon. They are writings which imitate the biblical style, usually with indifferent success. The oldest of them are contemporary with the latest biblical books (the second pre-Christian century); and the rest were written at different times down to about the year 100 of the Christian era. Most of them were composed in Hebrew or Aramaic, a few in Greek. Frequently these writings were attributed by their authors to heroes of an earlier age: Abraham, Noah, Moses. Because of this, the whole literature is often called the Pseudepigrapha.

Some of these books were included in Greek manuscripts of the Bible, and thence were taken over by the Catholic Church as sacred scripture. They are known as the Apocrypha ("hidden books"); in Jewish tradition they have no more status than the bulkier literature which was rejected by the Catholic Church as well. Some of the latter writings (such as the Book of Enoch, to which we shall come at once) exercised considerable influence on early Christianity; but then they were discarded and were preserved only in such ecclesiastical backwaters as the Coptic and Armenian Churches.

Most of these books, though written by Jews, represent a type of Judaism off the main line of Jewish religious development. In some cases there is doubt whether the book is of Jewish or Christian authorship. Few of the Hebrew originals have survived—in tattered fragments recovered from the attic of the old synagogue in Cairo. The rest are known to us only in translations and in translations of translations—from Hebrew to Greek, and thence into Latin, Syriac, Ethiopic, Slavonic, Armenian! These versions were made by Christian scribes; many contain manifestly Christian insertions. There must be other instances that have not been detected. Moreover, when a text has passed through the hands of several Christian translators, its tone and flavor may have been considerably modified.

Despite much careful scholarship, the text and interpretation of many of these writings is still far from certain; and there is often sharp disagreement as to their respective dates and their relation one to another. They are indispensable for our inquiry, but we must approach them with a somewhat skeptical humility.

CHAPTER THREE

The Ethiopic Enoch

Over a century ago the explorer Bruce brought back to England from Abyssinia three manuscripts of an Ethiopic work called the Book of Enoch. It has now been established that the original of this work was composed in Palestine, in Hebrew or Aramaic—or perhaps some sections in one tongue, some in the other.[1] It bears the name of Enoch, the ancient worthy, of whom we are to hear a great deal. Concerning Enoch, the Book of Genesis gives a brief but interesting account: He lived three hundred and sixty-five years—much less than the other antediluvians!—a figure that suggests some connection with the sun and sun myths. Then "Enoch walked with God and was not, for God took him" (Gen. 5.18-24)—a cryptic remark that was to inspire a whole cycle of Enoch-legends.

The present Enoch book (sometimes called I Enoch, for there are two others) consists largely of visions in quasi-biblical style, dealing with the end of days, punishment for the wicked and reward for the righteous, the Messiah, and similar themes. But it is far from a unit. It even contains a section on astronomy and the calendar that is almost scientific in tone. It is a collection of documents different in content, spirit, style, and date. Following the most diligent student of I Enoch, the late Canon Charles, we shall begin with some sections in which Enoch plays little or no part, and which Charles believes came from an ancient "Noah Book." [2] These sections bring us at once to our central theme.

The angels, the children of Heaven,[3] saw the beautiful daughters of men and desired them as wives; but the chief of these erring angels, Semjaza, feared that they would not dare to carry out their desire and would leave him to pay the penalty of sin alone. He therefore bound them by an oath to fulfill their resolve. They descended to earth in the days of Jared (Gen. 5.18; from *yarad*, "descend") and alighted on Mount Hermon, which was named for the oath (*herem*) they had sworn. These angels, in the number of two hundred,[4] each took a wife to whom they taught charms and enchantments, root cutting and knowledge of plants. Soon young were born to them, who grew to be giants three thousand ells high. The giants consumed all the possessions of mankind; then they began to feed on human flesh and, at last, to eat one another. They also began "to sin against birds, beasts, reptiles, and fish." [5] The earth made accusation against them and the cry of men went up to heaven.[6]

The outcry of suffering mankind reached the four principal angels, who interceded with God. In their complaint, they mentioned Semjaza, but gave first place in criminal responsibility to his associate Azazel, "who hath taught all unrighteousness on earth, and revealed the eternal secrets which were preserved in heaven." God replied to their appeal. Uriel was sent to warn Noah of the impending Flood, Raphael to bind Azazel and imprison him in the desert place Dudael. The fallen angel was placed on jagged rocks and covered with darkness, to abide till the final judgment when he shall be cast into fire. "The whole earth has been corrupted through the works that were taught by Azazel: *to him ascribe all sin.*" Raphael was also bidden to heal the earth, which the angels had corrupted, that all men might not perish through the secrets revealed by the "Watchers"—for it was to this high order of angels, who never sleep, that the backsliders belonged.[7]

Gabriel was directed to incite the giants to mutual slaughter, disregarding the prayers of their fathers who had hoped that their children, if not immortal, might live at least five hundred years. Then Michael was ordered to bind Semjaza and his companions; after seeing their children slain, they were imprisoned in the valleys of the earth for seventy generations. When the final judgment comes, they will be led off to the abyss of everlasting fire. Michael was further instructed to destroy all the children of the reprobates and the Watchers who have wronged mankind, yea, to destroy all evil from the earth. The passage ends with glowing predictions of a future purified and redeemed from all wickedness, and dedicated to righteousness and holiness.

This is the substance of I Enoch 6-11. Before examining the story in detail, let us look at some fragments which Dr. Charles has also assigned to the cycle of Noah-legends.

One section tells how Noah, terrified at the approaching Flood, appeals to Enoch (already translated to heaven) for guidance. In a vision Enoch tells Noah that the end is coming because men have "learnt all the secrets of the angels and all the violence of the satans, and all their powers—their most secret ones"—as well as sorcery, witchcraft, idolatry and metallurgy. In a burning valley of the west, which Enoch shows Noah, the wicked angels are tortured by subterranean fires. Hot springs on earth result from the heat thus generated; human rulers should look on this phenomenon as an awful warning, not as a medical resource. When the angels are removed from this place (to permanent hell fire?), the hot springs will become cold again.[8]

Several other lists of the fallen angels are given; one in particular is puzzling, for it contains names we have not encountered before. Those who led the angels astray through the daughters of men are here called Jekon and Asbeel. Then there was Gadreel, who taught men to make and use weapons and who lured Eve to sin. Penemue taught men "the bitter and the sweet" and all the secrets of their wisdom. Worse still, he introduced the art of writing: for men were created in a state of innocence and had no need "to give confirmation to their good faith with pen and ink;" but "through this knowledge they are perishing." Another of these angels, Kasdaye, taught a variety of ominous, demonic practices, including abortion.[9]

Lastly we learn of an angel who possessed the secret of a powerful oath by which the forces of nature might be controlled. He wished to learn from Michael the "hidden name" (probably the ineffable Name of God), so that by pronouncing it in his oath he might still further enlarge his power. But the end of the story is lost.[10]

It is impossible to say just how old these stories are; but they must have existed in writing by 200 B.C.E. or shortly thereafter. For as we shall see, the story of the fallen angels, as found in chapters 6-11, was used in another document which we can date definitely during the Maccabean revolt, between 168 and 165. By that time the tale was well known and accepted without question.

The Noah-sections are not a unit. The fragments just cited do not agree with the consecutive narrative we quoted first; and even that contains some inconsistencies. But all these items are different versions of a story that is basically one. Sometimes the arch-villain is Semjaza, and the sin consists chiefly in marrying mortal women and begetting monsters. Elsewhere the worst criminal is Azazel, and emphasis is laid on the crime of revealing various secrets to mankind. But the divergences should not be exaggerated.[11]

There is also a combination of geographical backgrounds. Most of the associations are with northern Palestine. Mount Hermon was a holy site of the Canaanites and Phoenicians; vast temple ruins are still to be found on its slopes. The hot springs mentioned in one of the fragments are no doubt the famous hot springs of Tiberias. All this fits with what has been said about the North Semitic origins of this mythology.

Other references point to southern Palestine. The name Azazel is quite familiar. The ancient Atonement-Day ritual (Lev. 16) included the sending of a scapegoat "to Azazel, to the wilderness." Jewish tradition has generally considered Azazel to be the name of a place near Jerusalem; but very probably Azazel was originally a demon who inhabited the wilderness of Judah, and the scapegoat was an offering to him. The Mishnah reports that the scapegoat was thrown over a cliff at a place called Bet Hadudo. This has been plausibly identified with the Dudael where, according to our story, the wicked angels are imprisoned.[12] Thus northern and southern traditions have been intertwined.

Despite variations in detail, all these stories have a single outlook. They seek to account for evil, specifically for moral evil, through the fall of the angels. The sin of the former Watchers had a threefold aspect.

First, for angels to enter into marriage and sexual union was a defilement of their pure essence.[13] This alone proves sufficiently that our story took form in Israel. The heathen gods all had consorts, mortal or immortal; Judaism, however, exalted God above all physical needs and desires and sensed that He is pure spirit long before the Greek philosophers had defined spirit. Jews—and only Jews—would have expected that the attendants of the spiritual God should be likewise elevated above earthly necessities and impulses.

Second, the issue of these unions was evil. Here and elsewhere, the children of the mixed marriages are identified with the *Nefilim* (from *nafal*, "to fall"), though the text of Genesis does not seem to intend this. The story of the misdeeds of the giants seems intended to account for the moral anarchy that preceded and caused the Flood.

The same intent is implied in the third aspect of the sin—the arts which the rebel angels taught their wives. These forbidden matters included the arts of female adornment and makeup, which stimulate lewdness; the arts of war, especially the manufacture of weapons; and the various forms of magic. But we also meet the suggestion that the angels sinned not merely by teaching immoral practices, but above all by revealing secrets of the natural universe, which God had not intended man to know. Especially odd is the notion that the art of writing is undesirable; authentic Jewish tradition regarded writing as a divine creation given to man as a great blessing.[14] Here we have the same sort of thinking that appears in the story of the Tree of Knowledge and the Greek myth of Prometheus.

Quite possibly there was some Hellenistic influence on this and other versions of our myth. There must have been constant interchange of folk-beliefs and ideas in ancient as in modern times. Persian and Babylonian influences, though more problematical, cannot be ruled out.[15] But we can be quite sure that the chief sources of the myth are Canaanite, and that its present form is distinctively Jewish. For it was called forth by the tension between the existence of vast and seemingly triumphant evil in the world and the Jewish belief in one righteous God.

CHAPTER FOUR

The Ethiopic Enoch *(Continued)*

Somewhat later than the chapters just considered—according to Dr. Charles—are those which now follow immediately the first account of the fallen angels. Here we find the ancient seer Enoch in direct contact with the rebellious spirits. He has already ceased to be a mortal, and appears in his character of heavenly scribe.

These chapters are somewhat muddled and, instead of following them in their present disorder, it will be easier to summarize the new ideas that appear in them.

First, Enoch's association with the reprobate angels. He is summoned by the loyal Watchers to rebuke the fallen members of their order, who shall never know peace and forgiveness and shall witness the slaughter of their children. Enoch tells Azazel of the sentence imposed on him for teaching men unrighteousness. But the other fallen angels beg him to draw up a petition for their pardon and present it before the heavenly Throne. To this he accedes and, going to a place near Dan and Hermon (again the North Palestinian locale), he reads the petition aloud till he falls asleep. In a vision Enoch beholds the heavenly assize and is given the verdict. On awakening he transmits the decision to the fallen Watchers, who receive it with faces covered.

Their plea is utterly rejected. They shall never return to heaven. After beholding the massacre of their children, they shall be fettered to the earth as long as the world lasts. "You should intercede for men," Enoch must tell them, "not men for you." The nature of their sin is made clear: they, who should have been holy and spiritual, had defiled themselves by lusting for flesh and blood. "You were formerly spiritual, living the eternal life and immortal for all the generations of the world; and therefore I have not appointed wives for you." Moreover, they had committed a great wrong in revealing heavenly mysteries, for through these secrets men and women do much evil. Yet these secrets are trivial—for the truly important arcana had not been revealed even to the angels.[1]

This episode serves to underscore the greatness of their crime, which can never be expiated. At the same time it reveals the high rank to which Enoch had attained. Though his pleading was unsuccessful, he at least undertook it—whereas we read in an earlier fragment that even Michael, the greatest of the archangels, dared not intercede for his fallen colleagues.[2] Enoch has already become a favorite in the celestial halls: we shall see him attaining even greater honors later on.

A second and very important element in this section is the account of how evil spirits came into the world. Everyone believed in the reality of demons: but what was their origin? Above all, how did they originate in the world created by a good God? Our chapters explain that these dark powers are the result of the miscegenation of angels and mortals; but the details are contradictory. One passage states that the giants became evil spirits; another, that the fallen angels became evil spirits, leading men astray to sacrifice to demons, while the women they married became sirens. But the usual view is that when the giants were slaughtered, in accordance with the punishment decreed for them, the evil spirits emerged from their bodies. In any event, the demons, once they made their appearance, remain at large until the final judgment. "They take no food, but nevertheless hunger and thirst and cause offences." [3]

This story not only accounts for the existence of evil spirits, but makes more logical the belief that evil in the world is due to the fall of the angels. For the giants were murdered, the sinful angels imprisoned and mankind wiped out by the Flood. How then could the old sin have had an enduring effect? The answer is now given that the fall of the angels led to the generation of demons, who could not be drowned by the Flood and who transmitted to subsequent ages the baneful influence of their sires.

A third new item is a brief story telling how Enoch journeyed through the remote parts of the universe. In a spot which is neither heaven above nor firm earth beneath, he beheld seven great stars like burning mountains. His angel-guide explained to him that these stars were being punished for failing to rise at their appointed time. Their punishment was to last ten thousand years.[4]

This really has nothing to do with our theme. We note it only because from time to time, in ancient and medieval thought, angels and stars have been closely identified. Several scholars have suggested that the myth of the fallen angels was inspired by the phenomenon of shooting stars.[5] This may be true of the pagan sources of our myth—not the myth itself. But in the present section, wicked stars and wicked angels are not the same. The punishment of the stars is appropriate to them; it will last a long time, but not forever.

CHAPTER FIVE

The Ethiopic Enoch *(Concluded)*

N ow we come to a kind of vision, or apocalypse, quite common in the Outside Books. In it an ancient seer beholds the panorama of world history, from Creation to the coming of the Messiah. This final redemption is to be preceded by a period of great suffering. Such revelations were written to give hope and courage to the people in times of persecution. Their basic message is: Stand fast a little longer, then goodness will triumph. We can fix the date of such writings with some assurance: the point at which the review of history issues into predictions of trouble followed by the appearance of the Messiah is the point of time when the author was actually writing. Thus the vision in I Enoch 85-90 was composed during the years when the pious patriots of Judea were fighting for religious liberty against the tyranny of the Syrian, Antiochus IV. The persecution began in 168 B.C.E., and our work must have been disseminated not long thereafter.[1]

As frequently in such writings, the story of mankind is presented in cryptic form—and the symbolism here is particularly grotesque. We read that a star (Semjaza or Azazel) fell from heaven, and began to pasture among the oxen (mankind). Then a number of stars fell, were transformed into bulls, and began to cover the cows (the angels married mortal women), who in turn brought forth elephants, camels, and asses (the giants). As a result, the oxen became restless and began to bite and gore, but themselves fell prey to the wild beasts. The archangels now appear in the guise of men, and one of them stations the seer on a point of vantage where he can see what is to follow. An archangel seizes the first of the fallen stars, binds it and casts it into a horrible abyss. A second gives a sword to the elephants, camels and asses, which thereupon slay one another. A third stones the other fallen stars, binds them hand and foot and casts them into the gulf.[2]

The course of biblical history is then outlined by means of similar imagery, Israel being symbolized by sheep. Nothing new is added to the biblical story till we reach the period of the later kings. Now we read that God, the "Lord of the Sheep," becomes so disgusted with the sinfulness of his flock that He will no longer care for them Himself. He summons seventy shepherds to guard the sheep and directs them to destroy a specified and limited number of them. These shepherds are to serve singly, each in turn. But the Lord of the Sheep knows in advance that the shepherds are not trustworthy: they will surely kill more of the sheep than they were bidden. So He appoints "another" to record their actions, but not to interfere with them.

These shepherds take an active part in the destruction of the Temple and the slaughter of Israel. Thereafter, too, they kill the sheep wantonly and irresponsibly. The recorder renders a report of their wicked deeds on three occasions.[3]

The account of the Maccabean revolt leads to a description of the final struggle between good and evil. In this the shepherds apparently fight on the side of the wild beasts. The wicked powers are defeated and the last judgment follows. The rebel stars, beginning with the first to fall, appear in fetters before the heavenly court. They are convicted and thrust into the flaming abyss. Then the seventy shepherds are similarly judged and similarly punished. Evil having been exterminated, the eternal reign of goodness will begin.[4]

Who are the seventy shepherds? Various explanations have been proposed, but only one seems possible. They are the angelic patrons, the *sarim*, of the nations of mankind which, according to an ancient Jewish tradition, number seventy. We have already seen this notion of national guardian angels in the Book of Daniel, which was written during the same time as the document we are examining.[5]

Why is Israel so bitterly persecuted? In the first instance, because Israel sinned, depriving themselves of God's direct protection. He is not unable to help them, nor indifferent to their plight. But he has handed them over for punishment to the heavenly representatives of the heathen world. The latter have abused their authority; instead of chastising Israel, they have sought to annihilate them. The prophets had said the same thing about the heathen nations: "I was but a little displeased, and they helped for evil" (Zech. 1.15).

This section of Enoch sets forth a doctrine found nowhere else. Other writers held that each nation has its *sar*, the patron of Israel being Michael; or else that Israel is under the direct guidance of God, while other nations have angelic guardians. Here, however, we read that God was Israel's shepherd till the last years of the Kingdom of Judah; then in disgust He turned them over, not to their own guardian, but to the *sarim* of the Gentiles. The "other" who is to record the acts of the shepherds has been generally identified as Michael. But he plays only the role of observer and scribe, not (as elsewhere) that of Israel's militant champion.

In stating that the seventy shepherds ruled over Israel, our writer hardly meant that each of the seventy nations of mankind had literally ruled—or would rule—over Palestine. Most likely his intent was merely that all the heathen and their heavenly representatives were involved in the guilt of oppressing Israel.

Both in their sin and in their punishment, the shepherds are clearly distinguished from the fallen angels. The myth we met in the older sections of I Enoch is fully adopted; the importance attached to it is indicated by the fact that it is the only addition to the Bible story included in the vision till we come to the account of the shepherds. The fallen angels brought sin into the world; the seventy shepherds harried Israel. The two concepts meet, but do not fuse.

The later sections of Enoch—composed, according to Dr. Charles, in the first pre-Christian century—make little reference to the fallen angels. This fact is of great importance, for the content of the later chapters provides ample opportunity for such allusions. But they occur rarely.[6] In several places the Flood is explained as the punishment for human sin, and the angels are not mentioned at all.[7]

Those who wrote of fallen angels in the Book of Enoch were not playing with a folk tale. They were wrestling with a central problem of religion. To them, the realm of evil is summed up in the rebel angels and their progeny: the giants and the evil spirits. The Devil in the conventional sense does not appear in this work.[8] Semjaza and Azazel are the arch-sinners.

The belief that evil came into the world when the angels took mortal wives, taught them forbidden arts and engendered monsters and demons—all this was in its heyday before the Maccabean revolt. Never thereafter do we meet the story in such full detail and with such stress on its importance. In the later strata of I Enoch, as in other Jewish writings of the same time, the belief in fallen angels no longer holds a central place. But though its influence declined, the belief persisted.

CHAPTER SIX

Jubilees, Testaments, Zadokite Work

We come now to three writings, each unlike the others, yet all three somehow related.

The Book of Jubilees, which we possess in a secondary Ethiopic translation, retells the Bible story from Creation to the giving of the Torah, with many changes and embellishments. These reflect the peculiar religious ideas of the author, especially his distinctive calendar system. The date of Jubilees is much debated.[1]

The Testaments of the Twelve Patriarchs are a series of booklets purporting to come from the twelve sons of Jacob. Each is pictured on his deathbed. He gathers his children about him, reviews his own life and finds in it the illustration of some virtue to be adopted or some vice to be avoided. His discourse ends with a vision of the distant future. The Testaments are extant in Greek and were formerly regarded as a Christian work; but it is now agreed that the original text was in Hebrew and was composed in the latter part of the second pre-Christian century. There are many parallels and similarities between Jubilees and the Testaments; but we are not sure which author borrowed from which, or whether both drew on a common source.[2]

Among the treasures brought to light from the attic of the old synagogue in Cairo were two Hebrew manuscripts, both incomplete, which Dr. Solomon Schechter published as *Fragments of a Zadokite Work*. They contain the history and constitution of a Jewish sect which left Jerusalem to settle in the neighborhood of Damascus. The Zadokite Work refers to Jubilees by name, and seems to have borrowed some details from it. But the date of the Zadokite writing is also in dispute.[3]

Several distinguished scholars have dated both the Zadokite document and the Book of Jubilees in the period of the Maccabean kings, that is, in the same period as the Testaments. The present inquiry appears to corroborate this view: for the three works are much alike in dealing with fallen angels and with powers of evil in general, and the views they contain point to a time somewhat later than that of the oldest sections of I Enoch.

The Book of Jubilees does not introduce any demonic power into the Eden story: the serpent is just a snake. But it speaks of the Watchers who descended to earth in the days of Jared. This descent was not (as in Enoch) due to rebelliousness; nothing is said of an oath to persist in sin, or of a deliberate attempt to corrupt mankind by revealing forbidden knowledge. On the contrary, the angels came down "to instruct the children of men, and that they should do judgment and uprightness in the earth."

But despite their good intentions the angels fell from grace. They began to wed the daughters of men and were defiled. Witness against them was borne by Enoch, of whom we read that he associated with angels, acted as heavenly scribe and priest and wrote a book full of great wisdom. His warnings were ineffective: as punishment for taking human wives and begetting the giants, the angels were shorn of their power and placed in solitary confinement underground. But first they had to look on while their children slew one another.[4]

Elsewhere we read that Kainam the son of Arpachsad discovered an inscription, which he sinfully copied. It contained the teaching of the Watchers whereby they used to interpret the signs of the heavenly bodies. Though he wrote the information down, Kainam kept silent about it for fear of Noah's anger.[5] This is the only reference our work makes to the other sin of the angels, the revelation of celestial arcana; and this too was apparently more a sin of carelessness than of deliberate malice.

The author of Jubilees was familiar with the main outlines of the story found in Enoch; but he toned it down, and did not lay such emphasis upon it. For he found the source of evil chiefly in another place. Wickedness is now personified in a single sinister being.[6]

Sometimes this being is called *Beliar*. This is the Greek equivalent of the biblical Belial, more correctly Beliaal. But what a change of meaning has occurred! Belial is a compound Hebrew word meaning "without value." *B'ne Belial* (literally "sons of Belial") means simply "worthless fellows." Jubilees also uses the expression in the same sense to characterize those who neglect the rite of circumcision (15.33). But when Moses prays that the spirit of Beliar may not rule over Israel, "to accuse them to Thee, and to ensnare them from all the paths of righteousness" (1.20), a satanic figure is in the author's mind.

Usually, however, the Father of Evil is called *Mastema*—enmity. This too is a biblical word, which does not appear as a proper name except in Jubilees and the Zadokite Work. We hear of Mastema first in connection with demons, after the Flood. The passage speaks of the evil spirits as children of the fallen Watchers, and probably reflects the view we found in I Enoch that the demons issued from the corpses of the giants. Some time after the Flood had ended, the sons of Noah complained to their father that evil spirits were leading their families astray. Noah prayed that the demons should be imprisoned; and God had already instructed the angels to carry out this petition, when Mastema, the chief of the evil spirits, made a desperate appeal. "Lord, Creator," he pleaded, "let some of them remain before me, and let them hearken to my voice and to all that I shall say unto them; for if some of them are not left to me, I shall not be able to execute the power of my will on the sons of men; for these are for corruption and leading astray before my judgment; for great is the wickedness of the sons of men." God thereupon permitted one tenth of the number of the demons to remain at large in Mastema's service; the rest were confined under the earth. As added protection against the demons, Noah was instructed in medicine.[7]

Mastema's origin is obscure. He does not seem, like his followers, to have emerged from the body of a fallen giant. Though chief of the evil spirits, he appears to be different in essence. He needs them for *his* purposes. Arguing that they should not be imprisoned, he has apparently no fear that he will be fettered along with them.

In the passage just cited, and in several others, Mastema is subservient to God. His task is to tempt men to sin; if they succumb, he accuses them before God's Throne. Nor does he initiate the process of sin. Men must take the first step in doing evil: only then can Prince Mastema and his evil spirits lead them on to greater wrongdoing (11.1-5). This is in accord with the biblical view that Satan serves the divine economy. Men achieve true righteousness only if they are tempted and resist the temptation. But this outlook is not consistently sustained: sometimes Mastema seems to delight in malicious trouble-making.

In the days of Abraham, for example, Mastema sent clouds of ravens who ate up the seed sown in the fields and reduced men to near starvation. But when Abraham was old enough to understand the matter, he commanded the ravens to return whence they came; and they obeyed at once. Next year he introduced a sort of seed-drill, which protected the grain against further depredation (11.11 ff.).

The command to sacrifice Isaac was suggested to God by Mastema, as a test of Abraham's fidelity. Therefore the angel who called to Abraham to spare the boy stood beside Prince Mastema, now utterly ashamed. Despite his own steadfastness, Abraham prayed for deliverance from the evil spirits who sway men's hearts.[8] And in blessing his grandson Jacob, he voiced the assurance: "The spirits of Mastema shall not rule over thee or over thy seed, to turn thee from the Lord" (19.28).

Mastema made desperate efforts to prevent the deliverance of Israel from Egypt. The Bible (Ex. 4.24 ff.) tells that on his way from Midian to Egypt, Moses was attacked by God for failing to circumcise his son, and was saved only by the prompt action of his wife Zipporah. As Jubilees retells the story, it was Mastema who tried to kill Moses—as a measure of defence for the Egyptians—and the Angel of the Presence who thwarted his design. The Egyptian sorcerers performed their marvels with Mastema's help; but the angels would let them do only destructive wonders, not miracles of healing. The angels also kept Mastema in bonds for four days at the time of the Exodus, that he might not accuse Israel to God nor prevent them from borrowing treasure from the Egyptians. As soon as he was released, he returned to his shameless purposes. He hardened Pharaoh's heart and incited him to follow the departing Israelites. Here his malice overreached itself and the Egyptian hosts were destroyed at the Red Sea (ch. 48). Yet the forces that slew the first-born of Egypt on Passover Eve are also called the powers of Mastema![9]

Plainly, the Book of Jubilees does not give a consistent picture of this being. Sometimes he works for God as tempter, accuser and executioner—the traditional role of Satan. Sometimes he is evil incarnate, rejoicing in destruction, hating Israel. We shall find similar ambiguity in other writings. Highly important is the idea first suggested in this work, that evil spirits are an organized army, operating under a single leader.[10]

There is just one reference in Jubilees to the doctrine of national guardian angels. God, we read, "chose Israel to be His people, and He sanctified it and gathered it from amongst all the children of men; for there are many nations and many peoples, and all are His, and over all hath He placed spirits in authority to lead them astray from Him." [11]

The Zadokite Work usually calls the evil principle Belial; this figure too appears in a double light. Sometimes he acts as the agent of divine punishment, working under God's direction, or at least by His permission.[12] But sometimes he appears as a rebel. He inspired the Egyptian sorcerers, Jochaneh and his brother, to oppose Aaron and Moses. Any person who is ruled by the spirits of Belial, and speaks rebellion, is to be condemned as a necromancer and wizard. When a penitent sinner makes good his vow to improve, the angel of Mastema departs from him.[13] This document refers once to the fallen Watchers.[14]

In the Testaments of the Twelve Patriarchs the sinful angels are mentioned only twice. One reference is a passing mention of the Watchers who "changed the order of their nature" (Naphtali 3.5). The other deserves more extensive notice.

It is part of Reuben's bitter attack on womankind. They are constantly seeking to ensnare men. "Thus they allured the Watchers before the Flood, for as these continually beheld them, they lusted after them and conceived the act in their mind; for they changed themselves unto the shape of men and appeared to them when they were with their husbands; and the women, lusting in their minds after their forms, gave birth to giants, for the Watchers appeared to them as reaching up to heaven" (Reuben 5).

This writer departs radically from the traditional legend. He denies that there were actual unions between angels and mortals. Ordinarily angels do not have human form; the mere presence of the Watchers in mortal guise, and the passion mutually roused in them and in the women, caused the latter to conceive giants. But the real fathers of the giants were human. Apparently these notions were inserted into the text by a scribe who objected to the idea that angels can enter into the sex relation. But he solved no problem; the angels as he pictured them are lustful, even though they do not—perhaps cannot—act upon their desires.[15]

The passage is more curious than important. The main author of the Testaments has his own definite notion of the source of evil. It is due, not to fallen angels, but to the Devil—sometimes called Satan, more frequently Beliar. How and why Beliar came into existence is not explained; but he is consistently pictured as God's opponent.

This author is a thoroughgoing dualist. He does not seem aware of the problem which the existence of a Devil poses for Jewish monotheism: certainly he makes no attempt to meet it.

Of the frequent references to Beliar, we shall cite only a few which display this dualism most clearly. Fornication separates man from God and brings him near to Beliar (Simeon 5.3). Levi summons his children (19.1) to choose between the Law of the Lord and the works of Beliar. When the soul is continually disturbed, the Lord departs from it and Beliar rules over it. Naphtali contrasts (2.6, 3.1) the Law and will of God with the purposes of Beliar. When Israel leaves Egypt, Joseph prophesies (20.2), they will be with God in light; Beliar will remain in darkness with the Egyptians.

Hosts of evil spirits are associated with Beliar. Of their origin, too, nothing is said. Sometimes the language suggests that these spirits are no more than figures of speech, embodiments of the several vices.[16] But often they are real demons.[17]

The Messianic Age will mark the end of these dark powers. (We shall meet this idea frequently.) Levi beholds in heaven (3.3) the angels who are to punish the spirits of deceit and Beliar. In another prophecy he declares that the Messiah will bind Beliar and give to his children the power to trample the evil spirits (18.12).[18]

The Testaments speak twice of Israel's guardian angel.[19] He is not given a name, but no doubt the author is thinking of Michael. This guardian angel protects Israel against Satan, not against the angelic patrons of the heathen. The latter are not mentioned at all in the Testaments.

CHAPTER SEVEN

The Slavonic Enoch

In Jewish literature of the first pre-Christian century, the story of the fallen angels is mentioned only in passing or not at all. The one exception to this statement is, significantly, an Enoch-book. This book (called II Enoch, or The Book of the Secrets of Enoch) is quite different from the old Enoch book we have already examined. I Enoch is a compilation of the most heterogeneous materials; the present writing, which is extant only in a Slavonic version, is a fairly well-ordered composition by a single author. (But sometimes, like the other apocryphal writers, he borrows material from different sources and does not iron out the discrepancies.) In subject matter the two works are quite unlike. I Enoch deals largely with the future judgment and the coming of the Messiah; II Enoch tells of heavenly mysteries, the divine throne, the angelic hosts; it also contains a notable section on moral and pious conduct. The later work reveals considerable advance in the glorification, the all-but-deification of Enoch. Even before he is taken finally from human associations, he is transformed into an angel of cosmic importance.*

The book relates how Enoch, before his translation, was taken for a tour of the seven heavens. In the second of these spheres he beheld an unearthly darkness. Here prisoners were hanging fettered, under guard, awaiting the boundless judgment. They had rebelled against God, disregarded His commandments, and followed their own impulses. They besought Enoch to pray on their behalf; modestly he replied: "Who am I, a mortal man, that I should pray for angels? who knoweth whither I go or what will befall me? or who will pray for me?" [1]

In the sequel, we learn that Enoch did accede to their request, though his prayer was unsuccessful; for so he reports to the Watchers whom he visited in the fifth heaven. The accounts of this episode, however, are much confused. What follows here is a radical attempt to restore what the book may have contained originally at this point. The chief argument for our reconstruction is that it makes reasonably good sense—admittedly a dubious criterion when working in apocalyptic literature. The casual reader will surely content himself with this conjecture. Whoever wants scholarly exactness may turn to the notes, where full details are given; and, if he gets confused, it will only serve him right! [2]

This then is what we think the book originally told: In the fifth heaven, Enoch beheld countless soldiers, called Watchers, of human appearance but gigantic size. They were morose and silent; in this firmament there was no angelic worship. Enoch's guides explained: these are the Watchers, from whose ranks come the angels that rebelled against God, who went down to earth, violated their oaths on Mount Hermon, took human wives, begot monsters, befouled the earth. Those in the fifth heaven know of the severe judgment that God has imposed upon their brothers; therefore they are sad and have no heart to sing God's praises.

* On the date of II Enoch, see the additional note, p. 289.

Enoch now addressed the Watchers. He told them he had seen the torture of their brethren in the second heaven and had interceded for them; but God had condemned them to be under the earth (!) until heaven and earth should cease. Enoch urged his hearers to wait no longer to join in the angelic worship of God, lest they provoke Him further. Thereupon the Watchers formed four ranks and broke into a touching song.

But II Enoch has another account of the birth of evil, which runs as follows: Arriving at the divine throne, Enoch learned from God many of the mysteries of Creation. The angels were brought into being on the second day and were assigned to various orders in which they were to remain permanently. But one "from out the order of angels, having turned away with the order that was under him, conceived an impossible thought, to place his throne higher than the clouds above the earth, that he might become equal in rank to My power. And I threw him out from the height with his angels, and he was flying in the air continuously above the bottomless." [8]

A little later the same subject is resumed. The text is full of difficulties, but it seems to mean: The fallen angel, previously called Satanel, now Satan, heard of God's plan to create the earth and set man upon it as master. In his jealousy, Satan determined to spoil God's plan by leading Adam into sin. But, though Satan had lost his bright angelic character, he had not become completely amoral: he still understood the distinction between right and wrong and was aware of his own sinfulness. He led Eve astray and, through her, Adam. When the infernal plan succeeded, God cursed—not His creatures as such, but—evil and ignorance. [4]

Yet our author declares that the root of human sin is not in Satan, but essentially in man's ignorance of his own nature. [5] In another impressive passage, God affirms His absolute unity and sovereignty, denying that there is any power that resists Him or refuses Him subjection. [6]

It would be an error of method to try to reduce to a system the demonology of II Enoch. [7] Our author has drawn on contradictory sources. He tells of the revolt of Satan, motivated by power; this passage is undoubtedly inspired by Isaiah 14.12-15. Either the author or a later scribe has loosely connected this myth with that of the Watchers who fell through their lust for women.

Again the rebel angels are imprisoned in the second heaven (as the text stands, some are also detained in the fifth), but elsewhere they are said to be confined under the earth. And after devoting much space to these angelic-demonic matters, the author derives sin from the limitations of man's own nature. Plainly, he too felt the difficulties of a dualistic outlook, from which, however, he could not free himself.

CHAPTER EIGHT

The Adam Books

Though the story of the lustful angels faded from Jewish literature before the Christian era, it lingered—as we shall see—in the minds of the people. Meantime, writers continued to discourse about the Devil, by one name or another. Among the works which display this dualistic outlook, few are more interesting than a group of writings about Adam and Eve. We possess several such documents in Greek, Latin, Slavonic and other translations, which seem to go back to one Hebrew original composed before the fall of the Second Temple. In reading these texts, one cannot escape the feeling that they had acquired a certain Christian coloration. The following account is a combination of the different versions: the sources are indicated in the notes.[1]

Expelled from Eden, Adam and Eve resolved to do penance for their sin. Eve's act of expiation was to stand for thirty-seven days in the waters of the Tigris River. After eighteen days Satan appeared in the guise of a radiant angel and assured her that she had tortured herself long enough; but Adam returned in the nick of time and unmasked him.[2]

Eve cried out against Satan: Why are you our enemy? Did we take away your glory? Yes, answered Satan to her great surprise, it is all your fault. Formerly I was one of the greatest of the angels. When Adam was created, the decree went forth that we must all worship him. Michael obeyed at once and summoned me to do likewise. But in my pride I refused to worship a young and inferior being, and the angels subordinate to me followed my

example. Michael threatened me with God's anger; but I replied:
If He be wroth with me, "I will set my seat above the stars of
the heaven, and will be like the highest" (Is. 14.14). The boast
proved empty: God hurled Satan and his angels down to earth
in perpetual banishment. Grief over his fall and envy of Adam
and Eve led Satan to encompass their ruin.[3]

After learning the reason for Satan's hatred, Adam prayed:
"Banish this Adversary far from me, who seeketh to destroy my
soul; and give me his glory, which he himself hath lost." Satan
vanished, and the pair resumed their penance.

This story, like that in II Enoch, clearly represents Satan as
a fallen angel, drawing for proof on Isaiah 14. Here too his fault
was that of pride; but we read for the first time that his specific
sin was the refusal to worship Adam. This notion does not appear in standard Jewish literature, but in the Koran it becomes
the accepted explanation for the fall of "Iblis." [4]

The fall of man is related by Eve in later chapters. She had
been assigned to guard the western and southern sides of Paradise. The Devil went to the sector defended by Adam, where the
male creatures were, and suborned the serpent: "Be my vessel,
and I will speak through thy mouth words to deceive him." [5] The
serpent, then, is the tool of Satan; but this conception is not
carried through consistently. In telling of the temptation of Eve,
Satan and the serpent are confused. In one strand of the narrative, the Adversary remains outside the wall of Paradise, while
the temptation is accomplished by the snake; in another version
Satan persuades Eve to admit him to the garden.[6] After eating of
the forbidden fruit, Eve swore to give some to Adam; thereupon
"he" (Satan or the serpent?) poured upon the fruit the poison
of his wickedness, which is lust, "the root and beginning of every
sin." [7] When I urged Adam to eat, Eve confesses, the Devil spoke
through my mouth.[8]

But in God's judgment of the sinful pair, Satan is not mentioned. Eve ascribed her downfall to the serpent, who was punished as a serpent—not as Satan incarnate. Yet in denying Adam
permission to eat of the tree of life, God told him: "Thou hast
the war which the Adversary hath put into thee." [9]

Here, then, as in II Enoch, the fall of man is connected with
the hatred of Satan; but some uncertainty remains as to whether

Satan and the serpent are identical, or whether the snake is the agent of Satan. This uncertainty recurs in other writings.

This author, however, succeeded in reconciling his dualistic notions with monotheism by making Satan an angel whom God created good and who fell through the exercise of pride. Thus he escaped the embarrassment which we shall find in some other dualistic writings.

Noteworthy is the belief that Adam is to inherit the glory originally possessed by Satan. This thought recurs when the soul of Adam appears after death before the throne of God. "If thou hadst kept My commandment," he is told, "there would now be no rejoicing among those who are bringing thee down to this place (the infernal lake). Yet I tell thee that I will turn their joy to grief, and thy grief will I turn to joy, and I will transform thee to thy former glory, and set thee on the throne of thy deceiver. But he shall be cast into this place to see thee sitting above him; then shall he be condemned, and they that heard him, and he shall be grieved sore when he seeth thee sitting on his honorable throne." [10]

CHAPTER NINE

The Testament of Job

The biblical Book of Job, one of the grandest creations of the human spirit, is devoted chiefly to a dialogue, profound and passionate, on the question: why do the righteous suffer and the wicked prosper? As introduction to the dialogue, we read the story of the blameless Job who was subjected to a series of tragic and undeserved calamities. These trials were imposed by God at the suggestion of the Satan, who appears at the divine court among the "sons of God." He is not a rebel, but a servant. His task is to go up and down the earth, observing and reporting on the sins of mankind. The Satan (that is, the Adversary) doubts whether Job's piety would outlast his prosperity; and God therefore gives him permission to afflict Job. Significantly, the Satan appears only in the prologue of the book; and Job thinks of his suffering as decreed directly by God.

Far different from this masterpiece of religious thought and literary expression is a booklet in Greek (which came to light in the last century) called the Testament of Job. The author has attempted to retell the Job story with many modifications and embellishments; and he has shown himself a bungler both as story-teller and as theologian. Unlike the works we have been examining thus far, his book does not seem to have any specific ethical or religious aim.[1] It seems to be a sample of a new literary genre, which requires a bit of explanation.

Around the figures and incidents of the Hebrew Bible, there grew up a body of legends and interpretations which were transmitted by word of mouth from one generation to the next, always with new additions. This legendary lore, created by the folk imagination, came at a later time to be called *aggada* or *haggadah* —which we translate very roughly as "something told." These popular traditions were (at a time which is difficult to fix exactly) taken over by the preachers of the synagogue. Utilizing the aggada for the inculcation of ethical and religious ideals, they modified some of the traditional material radically. Some legends they suppressed altogether. At the same time, they greatly amplified the aggadic lore by their own creative efforts. This vast body of aggada, at once popular and learned, forms a considerable part of the Talmud and is the chief constituent of the midrashim— sources which we shall explore later.

Now the apocryphal and apocalyptic writers also utilized the aggadic traditions. Many incidents and ideas found in Enoch and Jubilees recur in Hellenistic and rabbinic literature, which indicates that the various writers drew on a stock of common traditional materials. But the works we have studied thus far were composed to advance rather clearly defined aims. The author of Jubilees retold the Bible story in order to emphasize his peculiar religio-legal doctrines and his calendar system. The Testaments inculcate certain moral virtues and also support the claim of the Maccabean rulers to spiritual leadership. The various apocalypses were intended to sustain the shattered morale of the people during periods of persecution. The use of aggadic materials in such books is generally incidental. The chief exception is the appearance in I Enoch of the story of the fallen angels, itself a sample of popular aggada.

But just about the beginning of the Christian era, we find a number of instances where writers utilize aggada neither as simple folklore nor for homiletic or propagandistic purposes, but as grist for their literary mills. They combine traditional stories with narratives of their own creation, and deck out the whole in pretentious form, even adding poetic embellishments.[2] Of such efforts, the Testament of Job is a rather grotesque sample. Our interest is in its treatment of the figure of Satan.

Job, so the book tells us, was a man of truly pious nature who worshipped a certain idol. He came to doubt that it was divine; at last he learned in a vision that the idol was not God, but "the power of Satan, after whom the nature of man strays." Job offered to destroy the idol; whereupon his angelic visitor warned him of dire consequences should he dare to do so. Satan would in such case rise against him, destroy his wealth, kill his children, crush him with disease. But if Job remained steadfast, he would survive all; and at the resurrection he would wake to receive a great reward, as the victorious wrestler receives the palm (2.1-4.11).

God knows, then, in advance that Satan will attack Job. Why does He not intervene, since the attack is not—as in the biblical book—a test of Job's sincerity? To this, and to other questions we shall ask, the Testament gives no answer.

Job destroyed the idol. Satan, seeking revenge, appeared at Job's door in the guise of a beggar asking for a piece of bread from Job's own hand. Apparently he could harm the saint only if he met him face to face (why?). But Job had anticipated the stratagem (how?) and sent him only a meager ration by the hand of a servant, with the message: Henceforth you shall not eat my bread, for I am become a stranger to you (5.2-7.11).[3]

Furious, Satan appeared before God and received permission to appropriate Job's wealth. (Why did God permit this?) But he could not exercise his right for seven years (why?), during which Job performed marvels of charity. Thereafter, Satan destroyed all Job's possessions. Disguised as a Persian ruler, he incited the people of Uz to rebel against Job, their king. When the people hesitated to revolt for fear of Job's sons, Satan killed the young princes.

Job accepted his bereavement with resignation. Satan, realizing that he could not drive Job to sin by the measures he had taken, returned to God for permission to afflict Job with a loathesome disease (Ch. 8-20). (But previously his aim had been revenge, not temptation!)

Banished to the ash-heap outside the city, the leprous Job was supported by the menial labor of his wife. After eleven years, her scanty wages were reduced; and to buy three loaves, she had to cut off and sell her hair. Satan, of course, was the baker who drove the hard bargain. She returned to Job in utter despair and urged him to curse God and die. But he comforted her with promises of great reward and warned her that the demon was following her to confound them both (ch. 21-26).

Satan appeared and Job challenged him to open battle. But Satan knows when he is beaten. He replied: "See, O Job, I am turned back before thee, though thou art flesh and I am spirit; thou art smitten with plagues, but I am in great confusion. Thou art like a wrestler who wrestles with another. The first throws the second; he who has the upper hand closes the mouth of the defeated and fills it with sand, and breaks all his bones. Yet he bears all this with fortitude and does not give in, till the victor cries out in consternation. So art thou, O Job! Lo, thou art down, and smitten with plagues; yet thou hast striven with me in all that I have wrestled with thee, and hast also prevailed" (27.1-5).

So Satan left Job alone "for three years" (27.6)—and indeed is mentioned only once more in the Testament. But despite the withdrawal of Satan, Job was as sick and poor as ever. His three friends and Elihu arrived, and a discussion ensued. This strangely muddled section is devoted largely to an inquiry into Job's sanity! The colloquy is interrupted by a touching scene in which Job's wife dies, after beholding her children in heaven (ch. 28-40).

After the discussion had continued for twenty-seven days, Elihu broke into it. He resented the attitude of the three friends who showed some sympathy with Job's claim of righteousness. At first Elihu too had lamented Job's misfortune; but his confident expectation of a throne in the sky roused Elihu's wrath.

Elihu spoke "in the spirit of Satan" (ch. 41). When God appeared in the storm, He showed Job that not a man, but a beast, had spoken through Elihu's mouth. The four kings were rebuked: but while the three friends obtained pardon through the sacrifices Job offered in their behalf, Elihu remained unforgiven. Eliphaz sang a most extraordinary song, rejoicing in his own salvation, and condemning Elihu in the most savage and vehement terms (ch. 42-43).

The healing of Job was accomplished by heavenly girdles which God gave him when He appeared in the storm. Job gave these girdles to his daughters before his death, and then was taken into heaven in a divine chariot (ch. 47).

The confusion and uncertainty of the author as to the character of Satan is manifest. Satan is the spirit of idolatry and malice. God foresees that he will take vengeance on Job, yet cannot or will not prevent him. Still, Satan cannot attack Job without God's permission. Certain quasi-magical procedures are important to the success of his plans. His intention is not only revenge, but also to drive Job to rebel against God. Yet he is not altogether bad: he admires Job for resisting him successfully. He is the cause of Job's sufferings; but his defeat does not terminate them. Only God, in whom Job sees the source both of pain and relief, can cure him. These inconsistencies are due only in part to the incompetence of the writer: far abler men than he struggled unsuccessfully to reconcile belief in a full-blown power of evil with Jewish monotheism.

Brief mention will suffice for other Palestinian writings which antedate the fall of Jerusalem in 70 C.E. The Assumption of Moses (of which only a fragment in Latin survives) promises that in the Messianic age "Satan shall be no more, and sorrow shall depart with him." The section of the book now lost may have contained an old legend—which we can piece together from Christian sources—that Satan fought with Michael for the body of Moses.[4]

The Ascension of Isaiah, an early Christian apocryphon, begins with an account of Isaiah's martyrdom which is doubtless of Jewish origin.[5] Before King Hezekiah died, Isaiah informed him that his son Menasseh would be led astray by Samael Malchira, and would serve Belial. Nor could Hezekiah prevent the catastrophe: the counsel of Samael had already been consummated.[6] The prophecy was tragically fulfilled. Samael dwelt in Menasseh, who served Satan, his angels and his powers. And he served Beliar, "for the angel of Lawlessness, who is the ruler of this world, is Beliar, whose name is Matanbuchus."[7]

We meet here for the first time the name Samael ("poison of God"). It is variously applied in later writings to Satan, to the angel of death, and to the guardian angel of Rome.[8] No single conception is identified with the name. Malchira means "king (or angel) of evil." Matanbuchus is a riddle still unsolved. In this story Beliar, Satan, and Samael are most likely *not* separate beings, but only different names for the Devil. It is a distinctively Christian usage to call the Devil "the ruler of this world." [9]

Our survey of this literature would be incomplete if we did not record that many of the "outside books" are completely silent on our theme. The pre-Maccabean Book of Tobit speaks of Asmodeus; but he is a commonplace demon who can be put to flight by foul-smelling smoke. He has no cosmic significance. The Wisdom of Ben Sira, also early, never mentions demons; and the single reference to angels declares that God has appointed rulers over the heathen, but reserved Israel as His own portion.[10] The Books of the Maccabees, Judith, and the Testament of Abraham contain nothing for our purpose.[11] More surprising, the strongly Pharisaic Psalms of Solomon do not once mention either angels or evil spirits. In short, the dualistic concepts we have been studying, and the myths in which these concepts were embodied, were never accepted by all the Jewish teachers. And many important thinkers had discarded them before the rise of Christianity.[12]

CHAPTER TEN

Esdras, Baruch, Pseudo-Philo.

The fall of the Jewish state, the destruction of Jerusalem, and the burning of the Temple were an overwhelming tragedy for all Jewry, and especially for the Jews of Palestine. More than ever were they conscious of the reality and pervasiveness of evil. Shortly after the debacle, two great apocalypses were written which struggle with the problem of divine justice as passionately and poignantly as does the Book of Job. One is the Apocalypse of Ezra (IV Esdras), which has come down to us in Latin; the other is the Apocalypse of Baruch, which survives in Syriac. They manifest a spiritual level higher than anything else in apocalyptic literature, and contain many parallels to the rabbinic aggada.

In their effort to solve the problem of evil, these writings make no use of dualistic myths concerning fallen angels, evil spirits, or devils. The Ezra apocalypse does not even hint at the existence of such dark beings. It finds the source of evil in the sin of Adam, whose misdeed occasioned the downfall of all his posterity (7.116-118). The author here reveals a measure of spiritual kinship with his older contemporary, the apostle Paul.

The Baruch apocalypse also traces the beginning of evil to Adam's sin, which brought untimely death, disease, grief and pain into the world. "Sheol kept demanding that it should be renewed in blood, and the begetting of children was brought about, and the passion of parents produced, and the greatness of humanity was humiliated, and goodness languished" (56.5, 6). And he adds: "the darkness of darkness was produced. For he (man) became a danger to his own soul: even to the angels he became a danger. For, moreover, at that time when he was created, they enjoyed liberty. And some of them descended and mingled with women. And then those who did so were tormented in chains. But the rest of the multitude of the angels, of which there is no number, refrained themselves. And those who dwelt on the earth perished together with them through the waters of the deluge (*ibid.*, vv. 9-15).

Here the story of the fallen angels recurs for a moment; but in how changed a setting! The tale is substantially the same. The author can summarize it as something familiar to his readers. But its meaning is completely reversed. The fall of the angels is not the source of evil or the cause of human sin; instead, it is the sinfulness of mankind that caused the fall of certain angels. The episode reveals the measure of human corruption, not its origin.[1]

But our seer will not go as far as the author of IV Esdras in making Adam the cause of human depravity. Sin indeed began with Adam and brought suffering and death into the world. But Adam's sin did not corrupt human nature at the root, as IV Esdras implies and as is taught explicitly in the Christian doctrine of original sin. For in a prayer of Baruch we read: "Though Adam first sinned and brought untimely death upon all, yet of those who were born from him each one of them has prepared for his own soul torment to come, and again each one of them has chosen for himself glories to come . . . Adam is therefore not the cause, save only of his own soul, but each of us has been the Adam of his own soul" (54.15, 19).

Dating from the same period as these two great apocalypses is a book now called *The Biblical Antiquities*. It has had a strange history. The Latin text was published in 1527 as a work of Philo, the Jewish philosopher of Alexandria, whose genuine writings we shall examine shortly. Azariah dei Rossi, the great Jewish historian of the Renaissance, knew the volume and pointed out some of its many parallels to rabbinic literature. Then, somehow, the book was forgotten by scholars; and only in recent years has it received scientific treatment. Meantime some selections from the work turned up in a medieval Hebrew manuscript called *The Chronicles of Jerahmeel*. It was natural for Dr. Gaster, who published this manuscript, to see in these selections part of the lost Hebrew original of Pseudo-Philo. But it has been shown that *Jerahmeel* (or one of his sources) merely translated from the Latin text.[2] The book is a Palestinian chronicle which relates the Bible story from Creation to the death of Saul with many aggadic elaborations.

Though written after the fall of the Temple, in the same epoch as the Baruch and Ezra apocalypses, it has little of their deep and gloomy earnestness. Our author sought only to tell an interesting story, utilizing both traditional aggada and embellishments of his own. But he resembles the two apocalyptic authors in his close affinity to the rabbinic tradition and in the slight attention he gives to demonic powers. As his English translator remarks: "Esdras never mentions them, Baruch very seldom, Philo rather oftener, but not often, and always vaguely."[3]

Pseudo-Philo tells the story of the sons of God and the daughters of men in briefest summary, without interpretation and without mention of the giants (3.1, 2). Though ordinarily he delights in expanding and ornamenting the biblical narrative, he apparently wants to dispose of this matter as quickly as he can. And in his entire version of the Pentateuchal story we find nothing for our purpose.[4]

In his paraphrase of Judges, he is a little more venturesome. He represents Ehud (Judges 3.12 ff.) as a Midianite wizard who lured Israel by the practice of sorcery, "commanding the angels that were set over sorceries because for a long time he did sacrifice to them. For this was formerly in the power of the angels, and was performed by the angels before they were judged, and they would have destroyed the unmeasurable world; and because they transgressed, it came to pass that the angels had no longer the power. For when they were judged, then the power was not committed unto the rest; and by these signs do they work who minister unto men in sorceries until the unmeasurable age shall come. And God, willing to try Israel, whether they were yet in iniquity, suffered the angels, and their work had good success." [5]

This tale seems to be the author's own invention: Jewish tradition would hardly have blackened the name of Ehud, a national hero. It should be noted that God tolerated the sin of the angels only to test Israel; further, that magical power was withdrawn even from the loyal angels once this power had been abused.

Our text mentions the Watchers occasionally—here they seem to be guardian angels.[6] The Adversary appears just once, in amicable conversation with God.[7] There are a few allusions to evil spirits. The tribe of Issachar sought oracles from the evil spirits of the idols.[8] Eli feared that the call to Samuel might have come from an evil spirit. He then ruled: "If one call unto another twice in the night or at noonday, they shall know that it is an evil spirit. But if he call a third time, they shall know that it is an angel." [9]

The Bible tells that when Saul was troubled by an evil spirit, he found relief in David's music. Pseudo-Philo supplies the song with which David drove away the evil spirit. It refers to the first steps of Creation and suggests that spirits were brought forth on the second day. They were born of "a resounding echo in the abyss. But one to be born to David's loins will rebuke them." [10]

These casual references, scattered through a rather bulky volume, show how little importance the writer assigned to demonic forces. In this respect, as in many others, he kept close to the central Jewish tradition.

CHAPTER ELEVEN

The Apocalypse of Abraham

The last of the Outside Books we must consider, though extraordinarily interesting, has been somewhat neglected by scholars.[1] It is the Apocalypse of Abraham, preserved in a Slavonic translation which contains many unintelligible passages and several additions by Christian scribes. The original was composed in Palestine after the destruction of the Temple. Unlike the Baruch and Ezra apocalypses, which date from about the same time, it presents an extreme dualistic doctrine.

The first part of the book tells how Abraham came to believe in one God and sought to spread monotheism. This story, much like those told by the rabbis, is rationalistic in tone.[2] A similar rationalistic monism appears sometimes in the second part, the apocalypse proper; but more often we find in this section a mood of mystery and mysticism, an intense consciousness of a realm of evil, and a dualistic doctrine that reminds us of the trend called Gnosticism—a movement we shall consider a little later. The philosophic and mystical elements are so interwoven that we can be sure the book comes from a single author who drew on a variety of sources.

Abraham, the apocalypse relates, ascended to heaven on the back of a pigeon, accompanied by the great angel Jaoel.[3] As they flew upward, an unclean bird appeared and urged Abraham to return to earth, lest the heavenly beings destroy him. The unclean bird, the angel explains, is ungodliness, that is, Azazel. And Jaoel cries out: "Disgrace upon thee, Azazel! For Abraham's lot is in heaven, but thine upon the earth. Because thou hast chosen and loved this for the dwelling-place of thine uncleanness, therefore the eternal mighty Lord made thee a dweller upon the earth, and through thee every spirit of lies, and through thee wrath and trials for the generations of ungodly men; for God the eternal mighty One hath not permitted that the bodies of the righteous shall be in thy hand, in order that thereby the life of the righteous and the destruction of the unclean may be assured." And Jaoel warns him to depart from Abraham, who is his enemy, and whom he will not be able to overcome. "For behold, the vesture which in heaven was formerly thine hath been set aside for him, and the mortality which was his hath been transferred to thee (ch. XIII).[4]

Now the angel commands Abraham, the chosen of God, to rebuke the evil being, "who hath scattered over the earth the secrets of heaven and hath rebelled against the Mighty One. Say to him: Be thou the burning coal of the furnace of the earth; go, Azazel, into the inaccessible parts of the earth." But after he has uttered this exorcism, Abraham is to have no further words with Azazel; for God has given him power over those who answer him (ch. XIV).

The myth of the fallen angels seems to be echoed here, not only in the name Azazel, but in the charge of revealing heavenly secrets and in the banishment of Azazel to a fiery netherworld. But basically this Azazel is a malignant Satan, not (like his namesake in I Enoch) an amorous angel. His character, and his place in the divine economy, become clearer as the apocalypse proceeds.

Abraham comes before the divine throne and receives revelations of the future (ch. XVIII ff.). The angels now fade from the picture and we have a direct colloquy between God and Abraham, though the discussion is sometimes hard to follow. God promises Abraham a numberless posterity, "a nation and a people, set apart for Me in My heritage with Azazel." This is dualism with a vengeance—God appears to divide the world with the Prince of Evil! The author seems horrified by his own bold thought; for Abraham recalls Azazel's taunts, and asks: "How then, while he is not now before Thee, hast Thou constituted Thyself with him?" (ch. XX).

No clear answer is given, and Abraham's attention is directed to a vision of the earth, the netherworld, Leviathan, and Paradise. He beholds (on earth?) a multitude of human figures, half on the right side, half on the left. God explains that the lot of men is predestined. Those on the left are assigned, "some for judgment and restoration, and others for vengeance and destruction at the end of the world. But these which are at the right side of the picture, they are the people set apart for Me of the people with Azazel." They are, in short, the posterity of Abraham, whom God will call "My people" (ch. XXI-XXII).

Next the seer beholds the fall of Adam and Eve. The forbidden fruit resembles a bunch of grapes.[5] The serpent has human hands and feet, and bears six wings on each shoulder. But it is not clear whether he is identical with Azazel, or is only the agent of the Devil.[6] Again Abraham asks why God has given such destructive power to the forces of evil, and receives the reply: "They who will to do evil—and how much I hated it!—over them I gave him power, and to be beloved by them." But Abraham persists: Why did God create man with the will to do evil? (ch. XXIII).

To this clear and desperate question, a muddled reply is given. Canon Box restates it thus: "God allows men to desire evil (with its inevitable punishment later) because of the treatment meted out by the nations to the chosen seed."[7] But this is no answer at all; and it may be that the text, here and elsewhere, has been mutilated.

The vision is resumed. Again Abraham sees Adam and Eve with "the cunning Adversary, and Cain who acted lawlessly through the Adversary, and the slaughtered Abel, and the destruction brought and caused upon him through the lawless one" (ch. XXIV). This, it seems, is the only place in the book where Satan is called by his usual title; and it is the first instance where Satan is said to have incited the murder of Abel. Further visions of sin and of the Temple are shown to Abraham; but he is still wrestling with the basic problem, and again asks: Why does God permit sin? This time God answers that both Abraham and his father Terah had free will. "As the counsel of thy father is in him, and as thy counsel is in thee, so also is the counsel of My will in Me, ready for the coming days" (ch. XXVI).

And it is of the coming days that the rest of the book tells, of the destruction of the Temple, of ultimate redemption, of the final judgment upon the wicked.[8] During the final visions—which become more and more obscure until the abrupt end of the text—Abraham is again on earth. He hears of plagues prepared for the heathen and of the coming of the Messiah. As for the wicked, "I have prepared them to be food for the fire of Hades, and for ceaseless flight to and fro in the air of the underworld beneath the earth." Those who followed idols and their murders shall "putrefy in the body of the vile worm Azazel, and be burnt with

the fire of Azazel's tongue, for I hoped that they v.
Me, and not have loved and praised the strange gc
have adhered to him to whom they were not allotted, bu.
they have forsaken the mighty Lord" (ch. XXX-XXXI).

The original conclusion of the apocalypse seems to be lost; a.
it is probable that the author was not as confused as the present
state of the text indicates. His answer to the problem of evil may
have been something like this: God permitted evil to exist that
man might reveal himself in his true colors and stand or fall by
his own efforts. The resultant evil is to be overcome by Israel, the
seed of Abraham, by voluntary consecration of themselves to the
service of God. Such a solution may well have been mutilated
by the Christian adapters of the apocalypse.

But even in its present state, the book shows this writer struggling manfully—if not successfully—with his difficulty. To him,
wickedness is so real and so enormous he cannot but believe that
there is a cosmic power of evil at work. He struggles to integrate
this conviction with his Jewish faith. At one moment he affirms a
completely deterministic order; at another he argues for free will,
and presumably finds in this, rather than in Azazel's rebellion,
the root of human sin. Sometimes Azazel appears to be coordi-
nate with God in the rule of the universe; elsewhere he works
evil only by God's sufferance.

The problem is stated over and over with powerful force; the
solutions are confused and obscure. We can understand why the
main body of Jewish teachers turned away from this type of
thinking altogether.

PART THREE

Crossroads

CHAPTER TWELVE

Hellenistic Writings

The long array of books we have examined were all, or nearly all, written in Palestine, in Hebrew or the related Aramaic language, and for Jewish readers. But during the same years, Jews in Egypt and elsewhere were producing a voluminous literature in Greek, the international language of the time. This literature reflects the cosmopolitan Hellenistic culture; it is addressed to non-Jews as well as Jews, sometimes primarily to Gentiles. The Hellenistic-Jewish writings provide a few items for our study, though their chief value lies in other directions.

The oldest of these documents is the Greek translation of the Bible, the SEPTUAGINT, produced in Alexandria some centuries before the common era. In this rendering, the Hebrew *satan* is regularly translated *diabolos,* which in Greek means, not only accuser, but false accuser, slanderer—a connotation absent from the original Hebrew word. From this Greek term our word "devil" and all its cognates are derived.

The Septuagint rendering of Genesis 6 is not the same in all manuscripts. In some, *bene haElohim* is translated "sons of God," in other texts the reading is "angels of God." Both readings are quite old. The tale of the fallen angels was no doubt known to the Jews of Alexandria.[1]

FLAVIUS JOSEPHUS, a Palestinian by birth, had a varied, colorful, cosmopolitan, and somewhat shady career. His writings constitute in part an apology for his own conduct; but in large measure they are intended to give the Roman-Hellenistic world more knowledge of the Jews and Judaism, and that in the most favorable and sympathetic terms.

In his massive *Antiquities of the Jews* Josephus tells briefly of the many angels who consorted with women, and begot sons who were beguiled to wickedness by their own strength. "For the tradition is that these men did what resembled the acts of those men the Grecians call giants." Josephus adds that Noah remonstrated with the sons of the angels for their villainy, and they became so angry that he fled with his family to another land: a story found nowhere else.[2] From this passage we learn merely that Josephus knew the old tale, and that he did not attach great importance to it. He relates it as an evidence of the moral degeneracy of mankind, not as a cause of the corruption. Perhaps he included it because of the parallel to the Greek myth of the Titans; for Josephus loved to suggest resemblances between Greek and Jewish ideas.

This mild and superficial rationalist makes small mention of evil powers. In the account of Saul's melancholia he speaks of evil spirits;[3] and he knows of Solomon's skill in casting out demons. The contemporaries of Josephus had apparently inherited this art; for he relates in some detail the methods of a Jew named Eleazar who exorcised in the presence of Vespasian and his army. A ring containing a root, whose virtues Solomon first discovered, was the instrument employed. Reciting Solomonic incantations, the exorcist applied the ring to the nostrils of the possessed victim and the demon was drawn forth. The patient fell unconscious.

Eleazar adjured the demon never to return; and to prove that he had really been expelled, he was required to upset a bowl of water placed some distance away.[4]

In his history of *The Jewish War*, Josephus had already told at length of the root *baaras* which has the power of driving out evil spirits. These latter, he declares, are spirits of the wicked dead which enter men and kill them unless help is given.[5] This notion is borrowed from Hellenistic folklore. Authentic Jewish sources often speak of demons, and occasionally of ghosts; but never identify the two.[6]

Josephus was much concerned with "public relations." His older contemporary, PHILO of Alexandria, had loftier aims, in consonance with his earnest and deeply religious nature. Philo was convinced that the entire Scripture, especially the Torah, is an allegory of spiritual truths; and he tirelessly searched the holy books to discover their profounder meaning.

A brief but beautiful treatise, *Concerning the Giants*, is devoted to the interpretation of Genesis 6. Philo, as usual, bases his exposition on the Greek translation of the Bible; and his copy of the text contained the rendering "angels of God" only. Had he found the phrase "sons of God" in his text, he most certainly would have been inspired to comment on it.

Philo denies that the passage is a myth. We have no reason, he holds, to deny the existence of creatures who live in the air.[7] Some of these beings keep themselves perfectly pure of earthiness; others sully themselves with material desires. "Souls and demons and angels are but different names for the same one object." Knowledge of this fact will keep us free from superstitious dread of the demons. For just as the words "soul" and (in Greek) "demon" are applied both to good and evil beings, so too the title "angel" is given both to the spirits who have kept themselves free of physical desire and to those who succumb to its lures. Of such our passage speaks who, instead of courting the daughters of right reason, woo pleasure.[8]

And again, says Philo, the mention of the giants is not a myth. It is to teach us that some men are earth-born (*gegenes*, a word-play on *gigas*, giant), while others are heaven-born, and the highest are God-born.[9]

Why is Philo so insistent that Genesis 6 does not contain a

myth? Obviously because a mythological interpretation of the story was current. But even as allegory, the popular tale is objectionable to him. Philo has a special reason for this.

Following his master, Plato, Philo is a philosophical dualist. Matter and spirit are sharply sundered entities, radically opposed to each other. Matter is evil, mind good. Or, matter is unreal, spirit is real. Philo can therefore not conceive of beings both immaterial and wicked: the angels can become evil only by descent into material forms. Thus the angels could not have desired mortal women until they had first committed the cardinal sin of donning materiality. This is not very different from the descent of the human soul into the body, which Plato had described as a sort of "fall"; and Philo echoes the idea in this very treatise.[10]

But this philosophical dualism has little connection with the dualistic mythology we are examining. For Philo, the fallen angels are not rebels against God, nor the source of human corruption.

Yet the Hellenistic world did know a cycle of dualistic myths which bear the general label "Gnostic." We shall say something of these in our next chapter.

CHAPTER THIRTEEN

Where the Ways Divide

Standing at the crossroads, we glance backward, then look ahead. We have seen many variations of the myth of the rebel angels. We have recognized in this myth the attempt of certain Jewish teachers to solve the riddle of human suffering and moral evil. The long drawn out tragedy of Palestinian Jewry—above all, the terrible fate that overtook the most pious and loyal—made this no mere academic problem. Faith was threatened: without faith a people cannot endure. We who in our generation have witnessed an unparalleled outburst of savage cruelty can understand how these ancient Jews reacted; mere human selfishness has seemed inadequate to explain the bestiality of the Nazis. The workers of iniquity appear to be driven by a demonic force that exults in malice and glories in destruction. It is not surprising that some of our forebears concluded that human wickedness is inspired and directed by mighty angels who have rebelled against God.

The astounding thing is that, after some centuries of experimentation with this idea, the authoritative teachers of Judaism dropped it altogether. But the nascent Christian faith adopted and extended the dualistic viewpoint of the apocalyptic writers. The main line of Jewish thought returned to an uncompromising monotheism in which there was no room for satanic rebels. This is, indeed, a notable parting of the ways.

It is no wonder that a conservative like Ben Sira, who kept close to the biblical viewpoint and whose own life was sheltered and tranquil, should have disregarded the myth of the fallen angels. But those who were more receptive to new religious influences, and who lived through the mounting horrors of Roman oppression and the fall of the Temple, also rejected this myth. What was their reason?

Did they object to the story because it drew on foreign sources? Probably not. For the Pharisees adopted the belief in resurrection and made it a cardinal principle of faith, though it was borrowed from the Persian religion. This they did despite their difficulty in finding Scriptural support for the resurrection-doctrine, whereas in the case of the fallen angels they had to explain away biblical passages that seem to teach the idea!

Nor did the Synagogue reject this belief because the Christian Church adopted it. Representative Jewish writers, some of them unmistakably Pharisaic, had dropped the notion of rebel angels well before the Christian era. Witness the Psalms of Solomon, the later strata of I Enoch, and the Testament of Abraham. On this point the Ezra apocalypse is particularly instructive. Composed toward the end of the first Christian century, it contains speculations about original sin much like those of Paul. Yet despite this spiritual kinship to Christian thought, it never mentions Satan or the fallen angels.

The fact is: all such beliefs are inconsistent with an effective monotheism. Not logically, it is true. Christian theologians were to meet the requirements of theoretical monotheism by the doctrine that God created all angels good, but endowed them with free will. When they rebelled against Him, neither His omnipotence nor His goodness were impaired. But no matter how subtly one may elaborate this theory, it still leaves some Satan or Azazel in active opposition to God. Maybe it is only by divine tolerance, even by divine intent, that the demon retains his power. Maybe God utilizes the Devil's evil purposes in order to work ultimate good. Maybe God can destroy him at any time, and will do so some day. But for the moment he remains an active and determined enemy of God and man. The average person looks on the Prince of Evil with a fear that amounts almost to reverence. To escape the Devil may become a more pressing concern than to serve God.

The leaders of Judaism through many centuries displayed comparative indifference toward the demands of systematic theology and philosophy, together with a sensitive regard for the influence of beliefs and observances on the religious life of the common man. Questions of formal consistency rarely troubled them; they judged doctrines and practices by their practical results. Christianity could integrate the concept of Satan into its philosophy; but it could not always protect its adherents from over-anxiety about the Devil. It was evidently because they sensed the religious danger of the belief in fallen angels that the Jewish leaders sought to suppress it.

It is often said that Judaism is an amythical religion. Our study shows that the statement is substantially correct, yet in need of qualification. From time to time, Judaism displays a reversion to myth. Nor is this merely a symptom of decline and decadence, of infidelity to that clear, prophetic, ethical rationalism which is the classic expression of Jewish faith. Rationalism tends to become shallow; ethicism may become insipid. "There are more things in heaven and earth, Horatio, than are dreamed of in your philosophy." A rationalism worn thin must be corrected by a new vision of the profundities of existence. This new vision is likely to take a mythical form. Then the Jewish community, profoundly shaken by the experience, comes to realize that however deep the mystery may be, no myth can explain it: and the mighty simplicities of monotheism, revitalized and deepened, are restored to their place.[1]

The belief in angels, though well established in Jewish tradition, was itself a source of difficulty for many Jewish thinkers.* They were bound to object to a tale of angels who were capable

* The author hopes to discuss this subject fully at a later time.

of earthly amours. But in the long run, the belief in any sort of Devil (whether we trace his fall from a heavenly estate or, with the author of the "Testaments," merely assume his existence) is just as mythological. The essence of myth is not colorful narrative, but the idea that God has a history. If God has an opponent whom He will one day destroy, He has a history indeed; and it was precisely this that Judaism could not accept.

In both the Bible and the Talmud—the Jewish writings that precede and follow the Outside Books—Satan is a familiar character. But he is not a Devil in the Christian sense. He works under God's direction and with His consent. At times he begins to show some diabolic malice; but the Jewish teachers are not caught off guard. It must have been to counteract the danger here involved that they told many tales—to which we shall come presently—in which Satan appears in a sympathetic light, as one who does God's dirty work faithfully and gets precious little credit for his trouble.

We have already noted that the story of the angels who married mortal women is associated with the figure of Enoch, and that the rejection of the story seems to go hand in hand with a de-emphasis on Enoch's greatness. To understand this matter more fully, we must make a side trip before setting forward from the crossroads.

In the early centuries of the Christian era, and no doubt for some time previously, there was a tendency, centered in Egypt, which is known as GNOSTICISM. It was not a unified movement; there were many Gnostic sects which differed widely in doctrine and practice despite a certain family resemblance. Those about which we know most were Christian heretics; our information about them comes almost entirely from the Church Fathers who vehemently attacked them. The subject of Gnosticism has had great fascination for scholars, because it provides such rich opportunities for theory and hypothesis. It is usually said that there were pagan and Jewish, as well as Christian, Gnostics.

Gnosticism drew on ancient Babylonian, Persian and Egyptian myth; upon biblical lore and Jewish piety; and upon Greek philosophy. The Christian Gnostics, of whom we learn from Irenaeus and other Fathers of the Church, taught an extreme and thoroughgoing dualism. They found an irreconcilable conflict between matter and spirit, the consequence of which was often a

rigid asceticism. They also drew a distinction between the true
God, who is transcendant, unknowable and all good, and the
Demiurge or Creator, the God of this world, who is not good
at all. To this they added the belief not only in fallen angels, but
in fallen souls. The descent of spirits into matter was a cosmic
catastrophe. Only selected individuals (*pneumatic* persons, in the
Gnostic jargon) can find the way back to redemption, which is
that of mystic ascent and union with the good God. To this end
the soul must not alone employ the means of religious purification—fasting, prayer and contemplation—but also magical formulae and incantations to vanquish the evil spirits that would
prevent the return of the spirit to God.[2]

The records of Jewish Gnosticism, *so called,* are such visionary
documents as the Slavonic Enoch and the Apocalypse of Abraham, a few mystical fragments preserved in the Talmud, and
some more extensive mystical writings of the post-talmudic
period, which we shall examine later. These writings do have certain affinities with Gnostic teaching. When, for instance, the
Apocalypse of Abraham speaks of the good souls aligned on the
right of God and the evil souls on His left, it is employing a
conventional Gnostic metaphor. The theme of the talmudic and
post-talmudic mysticism is the ascent of the soul from level to
level until it arrives at the throne—or, to use a more familiar
symbol, the chariot—of God.

But the essential features of Gnosticism are missing from these
works. Judaism tolerated only a moderate ascetic practice. Celibacy was condemned. The Jewish teachers refused to brand the
body and all its works as completely evil. Nor would they admit
that the souls have fallen away from God by entering the body.
The ascent to the heavenly chariot is not a quest of redemption
from evil: it is a blessed pilgrimage.[3]

Nor do the Jewish Gnostics admit the doctrine of a Demiurge.
Judaism teaches that the creation of the world was a manifestation of God's love, not a rebellion against Him. A faint echo of
the Demiurge idea is found in the notion of an archangel who
bears God's name within him, and who is vouchsafed all but
divine honors. Sometimes he is called *Sar haOlam* (the Prince
of the World) or *Sar haPanim* (the Prince of God's Presence).
It is he who in the Apocalypse of Abraham and certain other
works is called Jahoel (Jaoel); in the Talmud and elsewhere he

bears the cryptic name of Metatron. But at the most, he is only an important angel.[4]

Now in late Jewish writings, Metatron is identified with the translated Enoch!

Two conceptions seem to have merged here. The older accounts of Enoch do not represent him as the *Sar haPanim;* the earlier accounts of Jahoel-Metatron say nothing of his earthly origin. But the increasing glorification of Enoch may be readily traced in the two pre-Christian books that bear his name. His identification with the archangel—in a post-talmudic Hebrew Book of Enoch—is foreshadowed plainly in the Slavonic Enoch-book.[5]

Now we understand why this hero was dropped from the catalogue of ancient Jewish worthies. It was not because of anti-Christian sentiment which saw a damaging parallel between the translation of Enoch and that of Jesus; for the rabbis did not minimize the translation of Elijah, which is an even closer parallel. Equally mistaken is the notion that the later Jewish teachers, in their nationalistic narrowness, cared only for Abraham and his seed and disregarded the glory of pre-Abrahamite saints. For the Jewish mystics of the post-talmudic era glorified the heavenly Enoch more than ever, and even called him "the lesser Yahweh." Moreover, Enoch's importance is deprecated in early universalistic writings, such as the Wisdom of Solomon and the discourses of Philo.[6] The reason can only have been that the Jewish teachers objected to the eccentric and dangerous doctrine that had grown up around the figure of Enoch.

This low opinion of Enoch helped to discredit the ideas found in the Enoch books, just as the objectionable ideas found there, such as the myth of the fallen angels, helped to bring the hero Enoch into disrepute. The Church, on the other hand, which retained the belief in wicked angels, kept Enoch in its list of Old Testament saints. There was no danger that he would take on cosmic attributes—they were reserved for the Incarnate Word. The translation of Enoch, like that of Elijah, was hailed as a prototype of the ascension of the risen Savior.

For the rest, we need not concern ourselves with the bizarre forms which the Gnostics gave to the dualistic myth. These heresies were far too extreme for the Church to accept. But the Jewish teachers could not tolerate even the controlled dualism of Catholic Christianity. The roads branch here to right and left.

PART FOUR
The Early Christian Church

CHAPTER FOURTEEN

The New Testament

We have dealt up to this point with writings which, with a few exceptions, have had little direct influence on world culture. Many of them were long unknown even to the learned. We come now to literature which has profoundly affected the life and thought of mankind—the Christian Scriptures. The New Testament authors transmitted to their vast audience many of the ideas that we have discovered in the Jewish Outside Books—books with which the early Christian thinkers were well acquainted. Certain trends, notably the trend toward a mythological dualism, which appear sporadically and tentatively in the pre-Christian literature of Israel, recur in more developed and systematic form in the New Testament literature.

The composition of the New Testament began in a sense when

the followers of Jesus collected and transmitted their recollections of his deeds and words. But the documents we now possess were written over a period of about a century, beginning some twenty years after his death. The New Testament authors included men of Jewish and of Gentile birth; some hailed from Palestine, some from other lands. In background and education, in personal temperament and religious concepts, in their interpretation of the personality and career of Jesus, they differed considerably. All the more striking, then, is their agreement on the doctrine that there is an organized force of evil in the spiritual world. Though the story of the angels who succumbed to the charms of mortal women was known to them, they made little use of it. But the consciousness of the Devil, as a rebel against God and man's chief enemy, is almost everywhere present. Through the New Testament this consciousness has penetrated deeply into the soul of the Western World.

We begin with the Apocalypse of John, which is placed last in the order of the New Testament books. In date, however, the Apocalypse comes midway in New Testament literature—it was composed probably about the year 100. It is a convenient starting point for us because it resembles the Jewish apocalypses we have been studying. Some scholars have even thought it an originally Jewish work, adapted for Christian use by a few additions and changes.[1] More probably, the author was a Jewish Christian who was thoroughly at home in the ideas and imagery of Jewish apocalyptic. We need not doubt that what little he tells us about himself is true. (Incidentally, he was not the same John who wrote the Fourth Gospel and the Johannine Epistles.) He gives little attention to the pageant of world history, which so fascinated the authors of Daniel and I Enoch. Nor does he speculate on God's justice, like the seers who assumed the names of Baruch and Ezra. John starts directly with the crisis of his own time. But what distinguishes him most from his Jewish predecessors is a dualism more extreme than anything we have yet encountered.

He proceeds for nearly a dozen chapters without significant reference to the demonic world.[2] The famous "four horsemen"—pestilence, war, famine, and death—who are followed by Hades (6.1 ff.), the angels who blow destructive blasts on their trumpets (8.6 ff.), and Appolyon, the angel of the abyss, who rules over the locusts (9.11) are all instruments of God's righteous anger. But presently we begin to hear about the Devil.

He appears first as a beast, rising out of the abyss to make war on the witnesses of God (11.7). Then he is depicted as a Dragon with seven heads, each bearing a diadem, and ten horns; his tail casts a third of the stars down to earth. He is waiting to devour, as soon as it shall be born, the child of a woman in travail. The child is the Messiah, the woman probably represents Israel. But the Dragon is foiled: as soon as the child is born, it is caught up to the throne of God, while the woman takes refuge in the wilderness (12.1 ff.).

Next we read of war in heaven. Michael and his angels engage the hosts led by Satan and completely defeat them. "So the huge dragon was thrown down—that old serpent called the Devil and Satan, the seducer of the whole world—thrown down to earth, and his angels thrown down along with him" (12.7-9). This fall, we must understand, did not occur in the long ago, but at the very moment when John beheld it in his vision. A heavenly voice announces that Satan, who had been accusing "our brothers"— the Christians—night and day before God, has been expelled. These accusations had been apparently directed against the Christian souls that were already in heaven; for the voice continues: "Rejoice for this, O heavens, and ye that dwell in them! But woe to the earth and the sea! The devil has descended to you in fierce anger, knowing that his time is short" (12.10-12).

So the Devil in the form of the Dragon resumes his attack on the woman who bore the man child; by a series of miracles she escapes. Enraged, the Dragon wars on the rest of her offspring, "on those who keep God's commandments and hold the testimony of Jesus" (12.13-17).

Now we read of another beast, *the* Beast, who derives his power from the Dragon (ch. 13).[3] Many details are obscure, but the general meaning is plain. Satan, beaten in heaven, seeks to accomplish his designs on earth; therefore he stirs up the Roman government to persecute the Christians. The Beast is the Antichrist, the evil counterpart of the Christ or Messiah. The Antichrist is the human representative of Satan, as the Messiah is the earthly agent of God. This idea was complicated by popular belief—held by pagans as well as Christians—that the Emperor Nero would return to life for one last fling of supreme wickedness before the final judgment. The Antichrist has the characteristics of Nero, as exaggerated by popular hatred. The idea of the Antichrist has its first clear expression in one of Paul's letters and is repeatedly stressed in Revelation by the symbolism of the Beast.[4] The "mark of the Beast" is placed on those Christians who escape persecution by worshipping the Emperor's image (13.15 ff.).

After many vicissitudes, the seer beholds the Messiah mounted on a white horse, a sharp sword issuing from his lips. He engages the Beast and the kings of the earth and defeats them. The Beast and the "false prophet" are flung alive into a lake of burning brimstone; the rest are slain by the sword of the Messiah's mouth (19.11-21).

But the struggle against evil is not yet over. An angel descends from heaven, bearing a heavy chain and the key of the abyss. This angel—not the Messiah!—imprisons the Dragon, "that old serpent, who is the devil and Satan," in the abyss. For a thousand years the Messiah reigns, the martyrs who refused to worship the Beast are happy, and the nations are secure from the seductions of the serpent. But after the millennium, Satan will have to be released for a little while. He will rouse the nations, even Gog and Magog, to attack the saints and the beloved city. Then fire will descend and consume them; the Devil will be cast into the brimstone lake, where the Beast and the false prophet are, to suffer eternal torture. Evil will cease to exist: only goodness will endure (ch. 20).

The picture of Satan in the Apocalypse is quite clear. He is the power of unmixed and ruthless wickedness. His aim is not to test the saints, but to destroy them. Yet he appears to have certain limited rights.[5] He was allowed to reside in heaven and lodge accusations against the martyrs, until the good angels flung him out. At the end of the Messiah's thousand-year reign, he *has to be* released for his final effort at rebellion. The Messiah, be it noted, prevails only over the Devil's earthly representative, the Antichrist. It is an angel who binds Satan in the abyss: his final destruction is by the direct intervention of God.

We turn back now to the earliest written documents of the Christian Church—the letters addressed to various communities by Paul, the apostle to the Gentiles. Thirteen letters make up the present collection; but scholars disagree as to how many are really the work of Paul. For our purpose, this critical question is not important. The keen awareness of a demonic world runs through the entire Pauline literature.

This is the more surprising because Paul's theology did not require the existence of a personal Devil. The source of evil, he held, was Adam's sin. The author of IV Esdras, whose views were somewhat similar, never mentions Satan. Paul's belief in evil powers was not a logical consequence of his system, but the reflection of his own inner experience. For this reason, his convictions on the subject appear to have fluctuated in intensity. The consciousness of the demonic is much more strongly marked in some letters than in others.[6] Paul, physically frail and emotionally violent, was subject to many changes of mood.

But these variations did not affect the substance of the belief. Satan was a very real being, with whom Paul had to reckon. It was Satan who kept him from going to Thessalonica (I Thess. 2.18); his physical infirmity was "a messenger of Satan" (II Cor. 12.7). Those whose vile conduct required their expulsion from the Church were formally consigned to Satan, but with hope of their ultimate redemption (I Cor. 5.5; cf. I Tim. 1.20).

Temptation by the Devil leads to sin—to sexual misconduct, and to false doctrine and unbelief (I Cor. 7.5; I Tim. 5.15; I. Thess. 3.5; II Tim. 2.26). Religious leaders are especially exposed to his attacks, through the conceit their high office may engender and through the embarrassment which slander may cause them (I Tim. 3.6). In a situation where open conflict threatened, Paul counseled tolerance "lest Satan should take advantage of our position—for well I know his manoeuvres!" (II Cor. 2.11; cf. Eph. 4.27).

The second letter to Corinth manifests a particularly vivid consciousness of Satan. He is the god of this world, who blinds the eyes of believers. There can be no harmony between Christ and Belial. Satan masquerades as an angel of light; no wonder that his followers represent themselves as ministers of righteousness! (II Cor. 4.3, 6.15, 11.14 f.).

Elsewhere Satan is called "the Power of Darkness" (Col. 1.13) and "the Prince of the Air—the spirit which is at present active within those sons of disobedience" (Eph. 2.2). In an early letter to Thessalonica, Paul speaks of the "lawless one" whose rebellious activity must take place before the return of the Messiah. The lawless one is certainly the Antichrist, for "his arrival is due to Satan's activity." The basic conception is like that found somewhat later in Revelation, though the details are different—possibly Paul expected Caligula, who was not yet Emperor, to reveal himself as Antichrist when he ascended the throne.[7] To this subject Paul does not return: his chief interest is the redemption of individuals rather than the approaching world judgment. But he is sure that at the end God will crush Satan under the feet of the faithful.[8]

Paul speaks several times about "the elemental spirits of the world" and about angelic "hosts, principalities, and powers." Sometimes he represents them as subordinate beings, whose authority has ceased with the advent of Christ (Gal. 4.1-9). But elsewhere he suggests an opposition between Christ and these inferior beings. The Colossians are warned against theosophic speculations "corresponding to the elemental spirits of the world and not to Christ." For when the Savior wiped out the tale of mankind's previous sins, "he cut away the angelic Rulers and Powers from us, exposing them to all the world and triumphing over them in the cross" (Col. 2.8 ff.). The antagonism is still more explicit in the first letter to Corinth. "Our wisdom," says Paul, "is not the wisdom of this world, or of the dethroned powers who rule this world . . . none of the powers of this world understands it; if they had, they would never have crucified the Lord of glory" (I Cor. 2.6-8; cf. 15.24 ff.).[8a]

Most dramatic of all is a famous passage in Ephesians which, though probably not by Paul, is not untrue to his spirit. The author has announced the superiority of Jesus to the angels and has foretold that the latter will learn certain items of divine wisdom from the Church.[9] Then comes the stirring cry: "Put on God's armor, so as to be able to stand against the stratagems of the devil. For we have to struggle not with blood and flesh, but with the angelic rulers, the angelic authorities, the potentates of the dark present, the spirit forces of evil in the heavenly sphere. So take God's armor, that you may be able to make a stand upon the evil day, and hold your ground by overcoming all the foe . . . above all, take faith as your shield, to enable you to quench the fire-tipped darts of the evil one" (Eph. 6.11 ff.). There is no more eloquent expression of both the beauty and the terror of the Christian outlook than this.

From Paul's mystical rhapsodies over a Christ perceived only by the eye of the spirit, we pass to the life story and sayings of a concrete, visible Jesus who lived as a man among men. The Gospels of Matthew, Mark and Luke are commonly called the SYNOPTIC GOSPELS because of their many similarities. It is generally agreed that Mark is the oldest, as it is the briefest, of the three. Most of Mark's gospel was incorporated into the accounts of Matthew and Luke, along with materials derived from other sources. We shall start with the reports of Mark, with parallels from the other gospels, then present the items peculiar to Matthew and Luke.

The Synoptic Writings manifest a strong dualism in a form appropriate to their graphic and popular character. Evil appears as a personal, tangible Satan who directs an army of wicked spirits. These demons are everywhere; demonic possession is a frequent cause of disease, especially of madness. One of the chief tasks of Jesus, as Mark narrates his career, was to expel these unclean spirits.[10]

Now the existence of demons and the phenomena of possession and exorcism were commonplaces of ancient life. But the Gospel adds two new and significant features. First, Jesus does not expel the evil spirits by the usual magical or pseudo-medical hocus-pocus. He simply orders the demons to depart, and they must yield to his superior strength. Second, they are not a casual element in creation. They are an organized body, operating under the generalship of Satan-Beelzebul.

The scribes of Jerusalem try to belittle Jesus' achievements, and even to make them appear sinister, by declaring that Beelzebul is the familiar of Jesus and that by the prince of demons he casts out demons. Jesus retorts: "How can Satan cast out Satan? A house divided against itself cannot stand; if Satan has risen against himself and is divided, he must come to an end. You cannot plunder a strong man's house unless you first tie up the strong man." [11]

The demons, then, are subordinate to Satan. When they yield to Jesus, they are surrendering to a stronger opponent, not to a superior officer. By exorcising demons, Jesus is raiding enemy territory.

When the disciples of Jesus go forth, the casting out of demons is one of their chief duties.[12] After the resurrection, Jesus again assures his followers that they will expel demons in his name.[13] Particularly interesting is the story of a spirit which the disciples could not exorcise. Jesus drove it forth, and explained to his crestfallen pupils that "this kind" can be expelled only by fasting and prayer. So Mark tells the story; but Matthew ascribes the failure of the disciples to lack of faith.[14]

In recent years, a hitherto lost passage came to light which belongs to the conclusion of Mark's Gospel. In this section, the disciples say to the risen Jesus: "This age of lawlessness and unbelief lies under the sway of Satan, who will not allow what lies under the unclean spirits to understand the truth and power of God." To this excuse for their own shortcomings, Jesus answers: "The term of years for Satan's power has now expired; but other terrors are at hand." [15]

We pass on to the other Synoptic Gospels by way of the temptation in the wilderness, which Mark relates with utmost brevity. He tells us no more than that Jesus was carried by the spirit into the desert that he might be tempted by Satan, that he was in the company of wild beasts, and that angels ministered to him. As to the nature of the temptation Mark says nothing, but his successors inform us more fully. The temptation had three parts. Jesus was hungry; the tempter urged him to transform some of the stones into bread. Then Satan conveyed Jesus to a pinnacle of the Temple and invited him to throw himself down. (Apparently Satan wanted Jesus to work miracles for his own selfish interest; or perhaps to test God, thereby manifesting imperfect faith.) Finally the Devil offered all the kingdoms of earth to Jesus, if the latter would worship him. To this Jesus replied: "Begone, Satan! It is written: 'You must worship the Lord your God, and serve Him alone.'" [16]

Note that Jesus rejects the offer because the condition is wicked; but he does not question Satan's ability to make the offer good. To the gospel writers, as to Paul, Satan was the ruler of this world.

Matthew has a number of references to the Devil and his evil hordes which are not found in Mark. Some persons, for example, supposed that John the Baptist had a devil, because his mien was sad.[17] At the end of days, God will say to the wicked: "Begone from Me, accursed ones, to the eternal fire which has been prepared for the devil and his angels." [18]

In one of his discourses, Jesus suggests that those who backslide from his teaching will descend to a more degraded level than they occupied before his coming. He illustrates his thought thus: "When an unclean spirit leaves a man, it roams through dry places in search of ease, and it finds none. Then it says: I will go back to the house I left, and when it comes, it finds the house vacant, clean, and all in order. Then off it goes to fetch seven other spirits worse than itself; they go in and dwell there, and the last state of that man is worse than the first." [19] Though this is just a parable, it was plainly intended as a realistic account of demonic behavior.

Some important passages are peculiar to Luke. When the disciples returned from their first missionary efforts, they reported: "Lord, the very demons obey us in your name." "Yes," replied Jesus, "I watched Satan fall from heaven like a flash of lightning. I have indeed given you the power of treading on serpents and scorpions and of trampling down the power of the enemy; nothing shall injure you. Only rejoice not because the spirits obey you; rejoice because your names are enrolled in heaven." [20] Here too the evil spirits are part of Satan's army: their defeat goes hand in hand with his downfall.

Luke is the first evangelist to state that Satan entered Judas Iscariot and so caused him to betray Jesus—a thought further developed in the Gospel of John.[21] At the last supper, Jesus explained to Peter: "Satan has claimed the right to sift you all like wheat, but I have prayed that your faith may not fail." Again we see Satan endowed with certain rights; as ruler of this world, he can test the disciples, and even God apparently cannot deny him the opportunity.[22]

As a sequel to his gospel, Luke composed the Acts of the Apostles. Here we see notions of the Devil and his demons much like those already encountered. Exorcism is frequently mentioned. Especially striking is the tale of certain Jewish exorcists who tried to drive away evil spirits "in the name of Jesus, whom Paul preaches." The spirit replied: "Jesus I know, and Paul I

know, but you—who are you?" And the possessed man attacked
the would be exorcisers, wounded them and chased them off.[28]

When Paul called Elymas the sorcerer, "you son of the devil,"
the context suggests that he was using more than a conventional
term of abuse (13.10). Elsewhere Paul declares to Agrippa that
on the road to Damascus he had received a commission to rescue
both Jews and Gentiles "from the power of Satan, to God" (26.18).

THE GENERAL EPISTLES also provide a modicum of evidence. The
little homily which bears the name of Jude (about the beginning
of the second century) refers plainly to the legend of the fallen
angels. To illustrate the certainty of divine retribution, Jude declares: "The angels who abandoned their own domain, instead
of preserving their proper rank, are reserved by Him within the
nether gloom in chains eternal, for the gloom of the great day." [24]
This tallies with the account in I Enoch, a book which Jude cites
by name. He also mentions the legend that Satan and Michael
fought for possession of the body of Moses.[25] Jude's reference to
the fallen angels is echoed by a still later writer, whose work was
mistakenly ascribed to the apostle Peter (II Peter 2.4, 10).

Altogether different from these writings is the tone of the
Epistle to the Hebrews, which is closer to the allegorical style
of Philo. But this document also declares that Jesus died to "crush
him who wields the power of death—that is to say, the devil;"
(2.14) and the author includes Enoch in his catalogue of spiritual
heroes.[26]

The author of I Peter warns his readers: "Your enemy the devil
prowls like a roaring lion, looking out for someone to devour;"
and he adds, "Resist him, keep your foothold in the faith" (I
Peter 5.8). More difficult is a passage which in its original form
may have spoken about Enoch and his dealings with the fallen
angels. But if the name of Enoch was ever in the text, it has disappeared from our manuscripts, which appear to make Jesus the
one who preached to the fallen spirits. Out of this single reference developed the legend of the "harrowing of hell"—that is,
that between his death and resurrection, Jesus released all those
who had been imprisoned in hell up to his time—a legend which
we shall meet again, and which has made some impress on literature and art.[27]

Even the Letter of James, despite its simple ethical tone and its marked affinity to Jewish thought, shows the same preoccupation with the demonic world. "You believe in one God," says the sage. "Well and good. So do the devils, and they shudder" (2.19). That is to say, correct belief, unless complemented by righteous action, can only cause misery. And again James says: "Resist the devil, and he will fly from you" (4.7). Any one such passage might be taken as figurative; but the sum of all the items requires us to interpret them literally and realistically.

The Gospel and Epistles of John possess a doctrine and style all their own. In them Jesus is not the vivid and dramatic personality of the Synoptic Gospels. Instead he is presented as the incarnate Logos, "the word of God" that has taken on the garment of flesh. Instead of homely sayings and parables concerned with the day to day experience of common men, the Jesus of the Fourth Gospel delivers abstract and symbolic discourses. Characteristic of this gospel also is its depiction of a basic and bitter antagonism between Jesus and the Jews. This Johannine literature is generally regarded as the latest stratum of the New Testament.[28]

John is not interested in demons, and his spiritualized Jesus performs no exorcisms.[29] Indeed, angels are rarely mentioned in the Fourth Gospel, not at all in the Epistles of John.

But the Devil appears in concrete form. Jesus says bluntly to his Jewish antagonists: "You belong to your father, the devil, and you want to do what your father desires; he was a slayer of men from the very beginning, and he has no place in the truth because there is no truth in him, for he is a liar and the father of lies" (8.44). Satan suggests the betrayal to Judas; and at the last supper, as Judas receives a piece of bread from the hand of Jesus, Satan enters the body of the disciple and drives him on to treason.[30]

John, like Paul, recognizes Satan as the ruler of this world. "Now is this world to be judged," says Jesus shortly after his entry into Jerusalem; "now shall the prince of this world be expelled" (12.31). At the last supper he announces: "The prince of this world is coming. He has no hold on me; his coming will only serve to let the world see that I love the Father" (14.30-1).[31] Before his death he prays for his disciples, "not that Thou wilt take them out of the world, but that Thou wilt keep them from the evil one" (17.15).

The same outlook pervades the First Epistle of John. "We know," this writing states, "that we belong to God, and that the whole world lies in the power of the evil one" (5.19). And again, "He who commits sin belongs to the devil, for the devil is a sinner from the very beginning. This is why the son of God appeared, to destroy the deeds of the devil" (3.8). Such clear cut statements require us to take the other references to the Devil—they are frequent in this treatise—literally. Though ethical in emphasis, these utterances are not mere rhetoric. But I John uses the word Antichrist as a figure of speech, to designate those who teach false doctrine.[32]

Our survey of New Testament literature has revealed in every important document, transcending all differences of doctrine, the common element of a deeply marked dualism. It is derived no doubt from Jewish apocalyptic, but is more extreme. It recognizes a cosmic evil embodied in Satan, his angels, and his host of demons and unclean spirits. These powers are diametrically opposed to God and His servants. Sometimes Satan seems to have a place in the celestial economy, or to possess certain temporary rights which even God cannot deny him. This lower world is his domain, over which he shall rule till his overthrow in the end of days.

The names given to the Devil in Jewish literature reappear in the New Testament: Belial, the Accuser (this is the meaning of *Satan* and *Diabolos*). But he is also known by titles which are foreign to the Jewish writings: Beelzebul, the enemy, the evil one, the prince of this world, the prince of the air.[33] These are precisely the names which indicate that Satan occupies a separate sphere of his own, apart from and opposed to God and the good —a concept which was utterly repudiated by the leaders of Judaism.

CHAPTER FIFTEEN

The Church Fathers

Some of the early Christian writings were accepted as authoritative; others were excluded from the New Testament as apocryphal. A few, like the Shepherd of Hermas, once regarded by some Christians as Scripture, are now classified among the "Apostolic Fathers." The oldest documents in this group belong to the same age as the latest writings in the New Testament. But soon we encounter a new type of Christian literature, discursive, often argumentative, basing its authority on the events and documents of an earlier day.

The term "Church Fathers" is somewhat vague. It includes the leaders and teachers of the Church from the apostolic period to some date in the Middle Ages. The age of the Fathers is sometimes thought to end with Gregory the Great (Pope from 590 to 604), but the patristic library edited by Migne includes many later authors.

The literary output of the Fathers is voluminous and diversified —including works in Greek, Latin and Syriac. Aside from the official pronouncements of Church Councils, we have treatises on theology, histories, sermons, liturgies, hymns, letters, biblical commentaries and other forms. Every conceivable subject is somehow touched upon; but the prevailing interest is doctrinal. The Fathers were deeply concerned with defining the teachings of the Christian faith and with defending it against pagans, Jews and Manicheans, and against heretics within the Church.

One is not surprised to find a pronounced dualism in the thought of the Church Fathers. For their basic source, the New Testament, is pervaded by this spirit. Few of the personalities we shall meet, diverse as they were in background and temperament, failed to devote much attention to Satan, his past history and present enterprises, to evil angels and wicked spirits. These matters, derived from Jewish apocalyptic and elaborated in the Christian Scriptures, were developed still further by the scholars of the Church. To present this subject fully would require a massive volume—we shall touch upon a few of its main features.

THE INTERPRETATION OF GENESIS VI. The early Christians seem to have known the tale of the angels who consorted with the daughters of men, as told in the Book of Enoch. But aside from two New Testament references already quoted,[1] the matter is not discussed till we come to Justin Martyr, in the middle of the second century. Justin, a Palestinian of non-Jewish origin, composed an *Apology for the Christians,* addressed to the Emperor Antoninus Pius, and a *Dialogue with Trypho, a Jew.*

Justin ascribes all evil to the demons, of whose reality he is intensely conscious. In the *Apology* he insists repeatedly that the persecution of the Christians is due to baseless slanders—slanders invented and spread by demons.[2] These demons are the offspring of angels, to whom God had committed the care of mankind, but who transgressed by succumbing to love of women. (Sometimes Justin confuses the wicked angels and their demon children.) [3]

The so-called gods of the heathen, declares Justin, are none other than these demons, who have imposed their false divinity on men, partly by deceit, partly by terror.[4] This is something new. It has some precedents in Hellenistic thought, but none whatever in Judaism. The rabbinic teachers did not doubt the existence of evil spirits; but they *never* identified them with pagan gods. The latter, Judaism always held, have absolutely no existence. Justin's view, however, was widely adopted by Christian thinkers.

And he used it cannily. For, says Justin, the evil spirits, having set themselves up as deities, made advance preparations to prevent their overthrow by Christianity. They devised myths (like that of Dionysus) to suggest "that the things which are said with regard to Christ were mere marvellous tales, like the things which were said by the poets." They also invented rituals similar to those of the Church, to discredit the latter.[5]

In the *Dialogue with Trypho* Justin makes more frequent mention of Satan than he does in the *Apology;* but the fallen angels are not overlooked. In arguing with Trypho, Justin stresses the free will of the angels, who are therefore liable to sin and subject to punishment.[6] Trypho, however, protests vehemently against the "blasphemous" assertion that the angels sinned and rebelled against God.[7] Now the *Dialogue* represents Trypho as conceding point after point, allowing arguments which no professing Jew could have admitted. It is all the more convincing that on this matter, of the sinfulness of the angels, Justin depicts his antagonist as unyielding. Clearly, this was an important issue between the mother and daughter religion.

Justin's disciples held somewhat similar views. Tatian likewise identifies the demons with the gods of Olympus; but the demons of whom he speaks seem to have originated from the fall of Satan, not of the amorous angels.[8]

Athenagoras adds several novelties to the development of our myth. He attempts to combine its two forms by making Satan, the ruler of matter, encompass the ruin of the angels by the daughters of man. (These angels had been stationed in the first, or lowest heaven: they were not so eminent as the Watchers of whom Jewish seers had spoken.) The fallen angels are not imprisoned, but roam the earth; their self-defilement prevents them from rising again to heaven.

Athenagoras distinguishes carefully between these fallen angels and the demons—the latter are the souls of the giants.[9] Tatian and Athenagoras agree that the angels have free will and can rebel if they choose.

Irenaeus was Bishop of Lyons in the third century—he is the first European we have encountered in our study. A great foe of the Gnostics, he makes several references to our myth, especially the episode in which Enoch announces the condemnation of the fallen angels.[10] He also cites an interesting epigram against a certain Gnostic who possessed:

> "Wonders of power that is utterly severed from God and
> apostate,
> Which Satan, thy true father, enables thee still to
> accomplish
> By means of Azazel, that fallen and yet mighty angel." [11]

Here again, two forms of the myth are fused.

The Fathers of the third century mention the story as something familiar and use it for moralistic purposes.[12] Most original are the explosive comments of Tertullian, an extreme misogynist even for an age that gave small honor to women.

The angels, says the African doctor, were seduced by the daughters of men.[13] But after they had already fallen, the angelic spouses taught their wives astrology, magic—and the cosmetic arts. Now why, asks Tertullian ironically, should the angels have instructed the women in self-beautification? Surely women who could charm angels without the use of makeup could please men as well! And to what greater conquests could the women have aspired? No, the angels taught their consorts these arts out of sheer malice toward God. "These are the angels whom we are destined to judge; these are the angels whom we in baptism renounce." [14] Naturally, Tertullian defends the authenticity of the Book of Enoch.[15]

This Father has the keenest awareness of demonic forces. They *must* exist because they are the objects of universal belief. Men "call on Satan, the demon chief, in their execrations, as though from some instinctive soul-knowledge of him . . . We are instructed, moreover, by our sacred books (!) how from certain angels who fell of their own free will, there sprang a more wicked demon-brood, condemned of God along with the authors of their race, and that chief demon we have referred to." [16] Satan is chief of the demons; but he has a different ancestry. Here again, the two forms of our myth come together.

A more thorough and artistic fusion appears a generation later in the *Institutes* of Lactantius, who apparently borrowed much from Athenagoras. The "Christian Cicero" states bluntly that God from the beginning gave the Devil power over the earth. But to prevent him from utterly corrupting and destroying mankind, He sent angels to protect and guide men. These angels, being endowed with free will, were themselves liable to sin; God foresaw their disobedience and warned them against transgression. But Satan, "that most deceitful ruler of earth," enticed them to sin with women. Banished from heaven, they became Satan's underlings. Their children were neither angels nor mortals and could not even be consigned to hell; they wander about the earth, doing all sorts of evil at the Devil's order. So there are two kinds of demons: the fallen angels, and their semi-human offspring. These demons, though harmless to the faithful, do great injury to the unwary. Astrology, magic and idolatry are their inventions; and they are the beings whom the Greeks and Romans worship as gods.[17]

The most extraordinary variations on our theme are found in the Clementine writings. This literature is not recognized as authoritative by the Churches, and represents something of a by-path in Christian thought. The Clementine *Homilies* and *Recognitions* constitute a sort of religious novel in which romantic incident is combined with dialogue and debate on theology. Though some scholars of the last century exaggerated their importance for Christian history, they are writings of unusual interest. They display much more sympathy toward Judaism than do most Christian documents of the period. Generally anti-Gnostic, the Clementines sometimes adopt Gnostic ideas.[18]

Among several accounts of the fall of the angels, the fullest runs thus: The angels who dwell in the lowest levels of heaven were grieved at man's ingratitude to God. They asked that they might enter man's life and, by becoming fully human, convict the sinners and bring them to punishment. This was granted. The angels transformed themselves into gold and gems, and let themselves be stolen so as to convict the covetous. They also changed themselves into beasts, birds and fish—as told by the heathen poets. Thus they accomplished their purpose; but having donned mortality, they in turn fell prey to mortal weakness and were overcome by lust.

Soon the fiery substance of the angels congealed, because of their passions, into solid flesh. Never again could they return to heaven or resume their former state. When asked by their mistresses to display their primal splendor, they could not grant the request. As a sort of compensation, they taught their ladies all the secret and forbidden arts they knew. (This is a new and unparalleled explanation!) The women bore giant young. God perceived that the earth would not suffice to sustain them, so He sent down manna for their nourishment. But the giants had an inborn hunger for blood; they began to eat human flesh and soon were devouring one another. The Flood was the inevitable outcome of this horror. After it had subsided, God established laws for the souls of the giants, which are larger in size (!) than human souls. They were forbidden to trouble any man unless he subjects himself to them by practicing idolatry, immorality, the eating of blood, or other heathenish deeds. "But those who betake themselves to My law, you not only shall not touch, but shall also do honor to, and shall flee from their presence. For whatsoever shall please them, being just, respecting you—that you shall be constrained to suffer." But those men who disobey God's law will be punished at His order, either by the demons or by some other agency.[19]

Another somewhat different account of the demons states that they are spirits who desire to enjoy the pleasures of food, drink and sex. These delights they can experience only by entering the bodies of men and using them for their own gratification.[20]

The Clementines also have much to say about Satan, but this is not connected logically with the fall of the angels. Side by side with the kind of naive, mythological supernaturalism we have illustrated, the Clementines present nuggets of philosophic thought, such as the following discussion of the origin of evil.

The inquiry: why did God create evil beings? is answered by the assertion that there is no evil in substance. God created His children with freedom of choice, and evil results only when they abuse their freedom and choose wrongly. So far we are on familiar ground. But the questioner persists: Why, if God foresaw that His creatures would make the evil choice, did He nevertheless create them? To this the reply is given: It would have been beneath God's dignity to change His good plans just because His creatures would not conform to them. Besides, their disobedience serves an ultimately good purpose. "He foresaw that there would be faults in His creatures; and the method of His justice demanded that punishment should follow faults, for the sake of amendment. It behooved therefore that there should be ministers of punishment, and yet that freedom of will should draw them into that order." [21]

Several of the fourth-century Fathers state that the angels sinned with the daughters of man. The last to do so is St. Ambrose of Milan, who commits himself on the question with some hesitancy.[22] For a reaction, which had begun at least a century before, now set in strongly.

The first Christian to challenge the traditional story seems to have been Julius Africanus, a third-century historian. He noted that in some Greek Bibles, Gen. 6.2 read "sons of God" instead of "angels of God." (None of these writers knew the Hebrew original.) Julius states as his opinion that the descendants of Seth were called sons of God because of their righteousness, while the wicked posterity of Cain were called the seed of man. He also mentions the view that the sons of God were angels who taught women astrology and magic, and by whose power the giants were conceived; but without flatly rejecting this view, he indicates his preference for the naturalistic explanation.[23]

We shall see that Jewish sources considerably earlier than Julius Africanus explained the "sons of God" as human beings; but nowhere do the rabbis suggest that evil resulted from a union between the hitherto righteous Sethites and the dissolute Cainite women. This notion seems entirely of Christian origin; perhaps it was derived from Gnostic sources. For we know of Gnostic sects who venerated Seth, and others whose patron Saint was Cain.[24]

Origen, the exponent of a highly philosophic and spiritual conception of Christianity, also had difficulty with the familiar myth. He considered Genesis 6 an allegory of the descent of souls into bodies. "Even before us," says Origen, "there was one (Philo?) who referred this narrative to the doctrine regarding souls, which became possessed with a desire for the corporeal life of man." [25]

The great Alexandrine thinker also had his doubts about the Book of Enoch. He cites it a few times in his exposition of the Christian faith; [26] but elsewhere he questions its genuineness. In his polemic against the heretic Celsus, Origen derives much amusement from a passage which Celsus had cited from Enoch without naming his source. It states that the sixty or seventy (!) angels who descended together are chained under the earth, and that hot mineral springs are due to the tears of these prisoners.[27] This is apparently the only Christian source that mentions the subterranean punishment of the angels. Most of the Fathers felt that the rebels and their demon offspring were but too dreadfully at large.

The other third-century Fathers, less philosophic than Origen, seem to have had no trouble with our story. But soon the opposition becomes vocal. The Syrian authority Ephraem declares that Genesis 6 refers to the Sethites and Cainites; the same view appears in one passage of the Clementines which may be of Syrian origin.[28] In the west, Hilary of Tours brushes away the tale of fallen angels "about which some book or other exists," as unimportant. "We need not know those things which are not contained in the book of the Law." [29]

Meantime, in Palestine, Jerome, the great Hebraist of the Church, was handling the subject most warily. Apparently he doubted the reliability of the Enoch-book, and did not like the myth of the fallen angels; but for some reason he hesitated to speak plainly.[30]

Others were more forthright. St. Caesarius of Arles insisted that angels are incorporeal, and therefore could not have mated with women. Genesis 6 tells of the union between the Sethites and Cainites. Philastrius of Brescia branded as actual heresy the opinion that the giants were born of angel fathers. Leading figures in the East likewise adopted the rationalistic view.[31]

The issue was finally decided by St. Augustine, after years of pondering. In his studies on Genesis, he states his difficulties clearly. How could angels copulate with women? Moreover, giants are sometimes born of normal human parents. It is easier to believe that men who were previously righteous fell from grace than that incorporeal angels yielded to sensual sin. Still, adds Augustine, incubi are too well attested a phenomenon to be lightly disregarded.[32]

In the *City of God* he repeats the problems in much the same terms; but now Augustine has made up his mind. Genesis 6 must refer to intermarriage between the clans of Seth and Cain. True, Scripture teaches that angels sometimes appear in visible and palpable forms. That demons can enter into sexual relations with human beings is affirmed "by such persons, and with such confidence that it were impudence to deny it." Augustine is not certain whether devils, embodied in air, can experience or impart sexual sensation. But he is now sure "that God's angels could never fall so at that time." II Peter 2.4 refers to the angels who rebelled along with Satan. Giants are still occasionally born; this is an unusual, but not a miraculous phenomenon. As for the interpretation of Genesis 6, we should bear in mind that Scripture sometimes applies the term *angel* to men. Careful reading of the passage reveals further that there had been giants on earth even before the "sons of God" took the daughters of men. Finally, Augustine denies the authenticity of the Enoch-book. Jude's testimony proves that Enoch wrote Scripture, but not that the extant work is genuine.[33]

Thereafter, the earlier view is mentioned by the Fathers only for the purpose of refuting it.[34] That the "sons of God" and the "daughters of men" were the Sethites and the Cainites respectively becomes the standard interpretation of Catholic, and later of Protestant exegetes down to the modern period.[34a]

The Fathers who accepted the myth changed its character in several respects. The fallen angels are no longer of the highest order, the Watchers, but of an inferior grade. The story is detached from its association with the landscape of Palestine. The imprisonment of the angels is disregarded, and the story is used chiefly to account for the existence and multitude of the demons. The identification of the demons with the heathen deities, a notion without precedent in Judaism, remains general among the Christian teachers.

The final rejection of the myth is an indication that Christian thought was becoming increasingly systematic. The thinkers we have been considering have not attained the philosophic discipline of the medieval scholastics. Yet Augustine is a far more philosophic mind than Tertullian. We saw that Origen, the profoundest thinker of the early Church, did not accept the story literally; and several of the more orderly writers, like Lactantius, tried to combine it with the myth of Satan. Gradually the Fathers realized that this crude tale involved serious difficulties: how could incorporeal angels enter into a carnal relationship? At the same time, they must have seen that the story was unnecessary. The origin of evil, and of evil spirits, was fully explained by the rebellion of Satan.

SATAN. That Satan is the arch rebel, the source of all wickedness, was the belief of educated theologians and simple folk alike. Thus the problem of evil found its full and often detailed solution. A doctrine so clearly suggested in the New Testament naturally found frequent expression in the writings of the Fathers from the earliest days.

Thus St. Ignatius (who carried on the mystical tradition of Paul) mentions the Devil about a dozen times in the seven brief letters that bear his name. Sometimes he uses the names Devil and Satan; but often, following Paul, Ignatius speaks of the "Prince of this world." [35]

The *Epistle of Barnabas* represents an approach to Christian theology very different from that of Ignatius, but the same consciousness of demonic forces. The "Black One," says Barnabas, now dominates the world, though soon to be destroyed. "There are two ways of teaching and power, one of light and one of darkness ... over the one are set light-bringing angels of God, but over the other angels of Satan. And the one is Lord from eternity to eternity, and the other is the ruler of the present time of iniquity." [36]

These Apostolic Fathers simply affirm the existence of Satan, seemingly as a reflection of their own inner experience. But soon the ecclesiastical writers began to speculate more broadly about Satan's character and his place in the universe. How did the power of evil originate? Why does God tolerate the Devil? What is his connection with the process of salvation—the process which, to the Fathers, was the very core of Christianity?

Justin Martyr, we have seen, refers the evils of the world to the demons who sprang from the intermarriage of mortals and angels. But he also knows a personal Devil, to whom similar misdeeds are ascribed. The Devil likewise created heathen myths and rites, similar to the history of Christ and to the sacraments, in order to confuse mankind.[37] He is the deceiving serpent—the being called the serpent by Moses, the Devil in the Books of Job and Zechariah, and Satan by Jesus is one and the same. Earlier writers had suggested this identification, but Justin makes it explicit. The serpent fell by leading Eve astray. Here Justin follows, though not exactly, the view of the Adam-books that Satan's fall occurred after the creation of man, and because of his hostility to man.[38] Tatian varies the idea somewhat: Satan, the most subtle of the angels, persuaded men to regard him as a god. Thereupon men became mortal, and "that first begotten one" became a demon.[39] The majority of Christian thinkers, however, adopted the notion we first encountered in II Enoch—that at the very beginning Satan rebelled out of sheer pride; and he attacked mankind, who were created after his downfall, out of malice and vengefulness.[40]

Athenagoras presents the doctrine in more abstract form. There are powers that rule matter, and one of these in particular is hostile to God. Not that anything is completely opposed to God, for then it could not exist at all. But the spirit which directs matter, though created by God, is opposed to the good which is God's necessary attribute. It is this "prince of matter" who causes the injustices which make us doubt God's providence.[41] In short, Athenagoras gives a quasi-Platonic form to the Christian belief that Satan has a certain claim to rulership in the present world.

In the more elaborate system of Irenaeus, Satan plays a signifi-

cant role.[42] According to Irenaeus, Adam's fall had two basic
results: it made man subject to Satan, and robbed man of immortality. Hence the salvation wrought by the sacrifice of Jesus has
two stages: it redeems man from the power of Satan, and it confers upon him divine immortality. Irenaeus finds a point to point
correspondence between the subjection of Adam by Satan and
the defeat of Satan by Jesus.

"The death of Jesus contributed to man's salvation in three
ways. It was at once the crowning act of obedience, a recapitula-
tion of Adam's fall, and the payment of a price to Satan in return
for man's release." [43] This last item is of extraordinary importance.
It goes far beyond the suggestion that Satan is the temporary
ruler of the present world. Irenaeus admits that Satan has claims
against mankind which God, through His Son, is obliged to
satisfy. One is startled to learn how much authority was accorded
this view.

The serenely philosophical Origen was among those who
adopted it. "In agreement with some of the Gnostics, Origen
maintained that God offered the devil the soul of Christ in exchange for the souls of men, and that Satan accepted the offer, not
knowing, as God did, that he would be unable to hold Christ
after he had him in his possession." It is notable that Origen included the belief in the Devil and his angels among the principles
of the Christian faith, though this doctrine is not mentioned in
the "Apostles' Creed." [44]

A more popular version of the idea is found in an apocryphal
writing, the *Gospel of Nicodemus*, which perhaps dates from the
fourth century. It elaborates the story that, between his death and
resurrection, Jesus descended to hell and released those imprisoned there. Before Jesus arrived, Satan had a long discussion with
Beelzebub, the prince of Hell. The latter wanted to abandon the
struggle with the savior, but Satan was implacable. "I tempted
him," he declares, "and stirred up my old people, the Jews, with
zeal and anger against him." And he will resist to the end. Soon
that end comes. The "King of Glory" tramples upon death, deprives Beelzebub of power, and "takes our earthly father Adam
with him to his glory." Now the defeated Beelzebub turns angrily
on the author of his misfortunes. "Why," he demands of Satan,
"didst thou venture without either reason or justice to crucify
him, and hast brought down to our regions a person innocent

and righteous, and thereby hast lost all the sinners, impious, and unrighteous persons in the whole world?" As he is speaking thus, Beelzebub is notified by the "King of Glory" that henceforth Satan shall be subject to him, in place of those Christ has redeemed.[45]

Gregory the Great worked out still more fully the myth that Satan was outwitted by God. Satan, Gregory declared, was justly in control of the human race; for being sinful, they deserved nothing better than death. But he who demands more than his due loses even that to which he is entitled! Christ put on flesh. Thinking him to be a sinful human, Satan caused his betrayal and crucifixion. But Christ was really pure and stainless, not legitimate prey for Satan. By attacking him (however mistakenly), Satan undermined his own position and lost his valid claim on the souls of mankind.[46]

That such views were maintained by Origen, one of the profoundest intellects of the Church, and by Gregory, perhaps its most influential personality, is most instructive. We see how realistically Satan was conceived, and how important was his part in the scheme of salvation. It is true that the views of the atonement held by Irenaeus, Origen and Gregory were ultimately rejected by the medieval Church. Instead, the so-called Latin doctrine of atonement, most fully elaborated by Anselm, was adopted. According to this view, the death of Jesus was a satisfaction paid to God, not a ransom paid to the Devil or a device for tricking the Devil. Yet a contemporary Protestant theologian has gone back to the old discarded views, despite their grotesque mythological expression, as the truly classical doctrine of the atonement.[47]

Those Fathers who tended to Neo-Platonic mysticism, like Clement of Alexandria and the pseudo-Dionysius, made Satan a less vivid figure. For such men, evil is not-being rather than a positive force. Even the demons, according to Dionysius, are striving for the good.[48] But the main current of Christian thought was in this matter much closer to Tertullian, for whom the Devil was a real, concrete and terrifying being, whose existence all men intuitively recognize. Augustine, despite his own inclination to Neo-Platonic thought, took the demonic powers very literally and devotes to them many chapters of his chief work, *The City of God.*[49] Augustine makes plain that the Devil rebelled out of pride, and that his fall preceded the creation of man. The plot against Adam was the effect, not the cause, of Satan's expulsion from heaven. And here, apparently for the first time, Augustine propounds a theory that was to become very popular.

This theory is that God created mankind as a sort of substitute for the servants He lost when Satan and his angels rebelled. The number of souls to be saved by God, from the beginning till the last resurrection, is equal to the number of angels that fell with Satan. This view (which makes the fallen angels much more numerous than the early Jewish sources supposed) was adopted by Gregory and by the profound Anselm.[50]

We conclude this section by noting that some tender-hearted Christians thought it possible that the Devil would ultimately be redeemed. This view has been ascribed to Origen and seems, in fact, to be a logical inference from his system; but he is said to have become angry when accused of teaching so radical a doctrine. From the fourth to the sixth centuries, there were violent quarrels over Origenism, and many errors—rightly or wrongly ascribed to Origen—were condemned. Certainly the Church never considered acceptable the notion that the Devil can be saved.[51]

THE LIMITATIONS OF CHRISTIAN DUALISM. The preceding section might have been expanded indefinitely; but there is really no need for us to pile up evidence. Despite variations on matters of detail, the Fathers all held that, in the great drama of man's salvation by Christ, an indispensable role is played by Satan. For every good drama must have a villain. In this doctrine, we have seen a genuine dualism. But, we must add, it is a dualism kept under control. The evil principle is not eternal, as is God, the Author of goodness. Satan was created, and he was created good. By abusing the gift of free will he rebelled, and thus evil was born. Satan exists now only by God's tolerance, and in the end of days he will be utterly destroyed. Thus the belief in Satan was at least formally harmonized with monotheism.

But there were Christians who proclaimed a much more thoroughgoing dualism. All such the Church branded as heretics and fought with her every resource. They are the sects we call Gnostic. Their tenets were diverse and often fantastic; but they all affirmed a radical and uncompromising opposition and conflict between matter and spirit, this world and the divine world. The Christian Gnostics saw in the visible universe the work, not of the one and eternal God, but of the Demiurge, an inferior and actually evil being. For Marcion and others, this Demiurge is the one who is called God in the Old Testament—he is the Jewish God, the God of vengeful justice, to whom are ascribed the characteristics of Satan. The God of love was formerly hidden from mortal ken; now revealed through Christ. He alone is the eternal Deity. Against such views some of the greatest personalities of the Church—Irenaeus, Tertullian, and others—insisted that the Old Testament is holy, a revelation of God the Father. There is no basic conflict between the old dispensation and the new one that has succeeded it; the God who created the world is the same who revealed Himself through Christ.

In the third century one Manes or Mani appeared in Persia and founded a new religion which under the name of Manichaeism flourished for many centuries in the West as well as the East. Basically, the faith of Mani was the old dualism of the Persian religion; with it was combined a measure of heretical Christianity, mostly of Gnostic character. For a long time this religion was a serious competitor of Catholicism; and many of the Fathers were constrained to write anti-Manichaean tracts. Augustine, who in his youth was attracted to the sect, was among the most notable of those who combated it.

Thus the Church admitted dualism only in measure and in a form that could be accommodated to monotheism. But even this limited dualism was flatly rejected by the recognized exponents of Judaism.

PART FIVE
The Rabbis

CHAPTER SIXTEEN

Talmud and Midrash

Turning from the Fathers of the Church to the Fathers of the Synagogue, we encounter an entirely different kind of literature, with entirely different problems. The Talmud comes from the same period as the writings of the Church Fathers and deals with some of the same issues. Talmudic literature, like patristic literature, is largely an exposition of authoritative Scripture. But there the resemblance ends.

The Church Fathers wanted to clarify Christian doctrine, combat heresy and construct a complete theological system. To this end they composed elaborate treatises. Almost every statement quoted in the preceding chapter can be ascribed to a known author, dated with accuracy and interpreted with confidence in the light of an extended context.

But the talmudic-midrashic literature which we are now to consider is a compilation of materials from various ages, which were transmitted by word of mouth for a long time before they were written down. The Mishnah was edited about 200 C.E., the Babylonian Talmud (*Gemara*) in the middle of the fifth century, the Midrashim later still. But these works contain some elements that go back centuries before the Christian era.

The authoritative parts of this material, those that were transmitted with the greatest care and subjected to the most critical analysis, deal with *halakah*, that is with Jewish religious law. Our concern, however, will be chiefly with *aggada*, that is (speaking loosely), with the homiletic sayings of the Jewish teachers. Such utterances were not regarded as official or binding. Inconsistencies appear frequently; and even when they are noted, the effort to reconcile them is superficial. No serious effort was made to integrate the theological opinions of the rabbis into a coherent system. The emphasis of traditional Judaism was on correct conduct rather than on doctrinal conformity.

Furthermore, the aggadic sentences are generally brief. For the sake of emphasis, the aggadists often resort to exaggerations which must not be taken literally. Many sentences are anonymous. Even when they appear in the name of a certain rabbi, we cannot tell from what period of his life they come, or what circumstances called them forth, or even whether the thought he expressed was original with him.

It is therefore unsafe to draw any conclusion about rabbinic Judaism from one or two aggadic statements. Even if they have been accurately transmitted and correctly understood, they may represent no more than the speculations of a single teacher. Only when a view is found with some frequency, and when it accords with the general spirit of rabbinic thought, dare we say that this is the opinion of "the rabbis of the Talmud."

For these reasons, we must be greatly impressed by the complete unanimity with which the rabbinic teachers rejected dualism, even the kind of modified dualism we have been studying. They must have been familiar with these notions; but they repudiated them emphatically.

THE SIN OF THE ANGELS. The Talmud *never* speaks of fallen or rebel angels. This is no accident; nor were the rabbis ignorant of the legend. They knew and suppressed it.

What, asks the Talmud, is the meaning of the name Azazel (Lev. 16.10)? It derives from the fact that the scapegoat "atones for the sins of Uzza and Azzael." [1] Who Uzza and Azzael were and what sins they had committed, we are not told. But in later Jewish literature, the leaders of the fallen angels bear these names, which indeed are but variants of the names Shemhazai and Azazel we already know so well.

Elsewhere the Gemara remarks that the giants Og and Sihon were children of Ahijah, the son of Shemhazai. [2]

From these two cryptic statements alone, we should never suspect that the Talmud was referring to fallen angels. It does not even say that these beings were angels of any sort. But the allusion must be to the familiar tale. The very terseness of the references is significant.

Who then were "the sons of God" mentioned in Genesis 6? The *Targum,* the Aramaic translation which was accepted for use in the synagogues, renders this phrase: "the sons of the nobles." This rendering of the passage is standard in Jewish tradition. Humanity before the Flood became corrupt, as the Bible fully relates. The young aristocrats of the day set the pace for immorality, making free with the "daughters of man," that is to say, with women of lower rank, taking whomever they pleased. It was entirely for human sinfulness that God sent the Flood. [3]

R. Simeon b. Johai (second century) cursed those who translated *bene haElohim* literally as "sons of God." The proper rendering, he said, was "sons of the judges," which agrees substantially with the *Targum.* We are not entirely sure who was the specific object of R. Simeon's curse; but he clearly wanted to preclude any supernatural interpretation of the passage. [4]

Two other scholars of the same period differed as to the meaning of the word *vayinahem* in Gen. 6.6. R. Judah says it means: "He regretted." God was sorry that He had made man on earth. Had He set man in heaven, he would have remained sinless, as the angels are sinless. R. Nehemiah says it means "He was comforted." God consoled Himself for man's moral failure by considering that He had made man on *earth.* Had He set him in the neighborhood of the angels, man would have roused them also to rebellion. [5] The point at issue between the two scholars is whether regret can properly be ascribed to an all-knowing God. Both agree that the angels did not rebel, whether because they were protected from contact with sinful man, or because they are naturally sinless.

The latter view is more common. We have seen how strongly Trypho objected to Justin's statement that angels could sin.[6] According to a famous legend, the angels sought to keep Moses from receiving the Torah because they wanted it for themselves. But their purpose was thwarted. The Torah is not suitable for angels, because they have no inclination to do evil.[7]

Strangely, these statements do not derive from awe of the angels. Whereas apocalyptic Judaism emphasized the importance of the angels, but held that some of them fell from grace, rabbinic Judaism rejected the myth of the rebel angels, yet belittled angels as a class. We shall elaborate this point later. Certainly the angels do not appear in a favorable light in the legend just mentioned. Selfishly, and in complete ignorance of what the Torah contains, they wish to keep it for themselves. Moses scores an easy victory over them. Their very sinlessness is represented as a sort of deficiency. Just as a child who has lost several fingers cannot learn the art of silk weaving, so the angels cannot use the Torah because they lack the sinful impulse![8] This paradox reveals a polemical intent in the story. The rabbis knew the legend of the fallen angels, and found it objectionable. But they did not directly challenge such views. In refuting the heretic, they wisely discerned, you publicize his doctrine. The rabbis therefore attacked such beliefs indirectly, as in the present instance.

ENOCH. The rabbis were not the first to reject the myth of the fallen angels. We saw the same trend in apocryphal literature. Similar was the fate of the Enoch legend. Enoch, the great hero of early apocalyptic who was to be glorified in Christian writings, has dropped out of sight in the later Jewish apocrypha. In the two Talmuds and in the tannaitic literature he is not mentioned at all.[9] In the standard Midrashim he appears only two or three times. The most notable passage reports that Enoch was not translated to heaven. He died like any other mortal. God recognized that his righteousness was not very deep-rooted. So before Enoch had a chance to sin, God took him from this world at the early age (for an antediluvian) of three hundred sixty-five.[10] It is certainly no accident that the character who in earlier writings was so glorified, and who in certain post-talmudic sources was exalted to all but divine heights, should have been, so to speak, snubbed by the rabbis.

THE FRAILTY OF ANGELS. The rabbis at times manifest a certain distaste for angels as a class, in accordance with the biblical dictum, "Behold He putteth no trust in His servants, and His angels He chargeth with folly" (Job 4.18). We touch on this subject now only to make plain that it has nothing to do with the belief in fallen or rebellious angels. God alone is perfect. Therefore the angels are bound to make mistakes.

The Talmud reports that the Angel of Death once sent his agent (evidently an angel of lower rank) to take the soul of Miriam the Hairdresser; but the emissary blundered and brought the soul of Miriam the Child's Nurse. The angels sent to deliver Lot were severely punished for revealing in advance that God planned to destroy Sodom. But they let the secret slip inadvertently; they had no intention to disobey God.[11]

According to a familiar aggada, the angels opposed the creation of man. The first company of angels whom God consulted on the subject said: "What is man, that Thou considerest him?" Whereupon God consumed them with fire. The same fate overtook a second company. When He presented His proposal to a third group, they replied: "What did it avail the former groups to speak out before Thee? The whole world is Thine; do as Thou wilt!"[12]

Behind this remarkable story are important polemical motives. The biblical phrase "Let us make man" (Gen. 1.26) had to be explained, especially as the Gnostics and Christians had eagerly seized upon it as proof that the Godhead contains several persons. Hence the rabbis picture God as consulting the angels.

But why should the angels have objected to God's purpose? There was an opinion among the Gnostics (which Philo shared, at least in part) that God did not create man, or that inferior powers had a considerable share in man's creation. The purpose of this doctrine was to clear God of responsibility for man's sinfulness. But to the rabbis, such a view was inadmissible. To emphasize that God alone is the Creator, they taught that the angels, far from participating in the creation of man, actually opposed it.[13]

In the Koran, this story recurs in combination with the other

legend, that Satan-Iblis refused to join the other angels in worshipping Adam. Such a compound is unknown in rabbinic
sources, which nowhere mention that the angels were required
to give divine honors to men. On the contrary, a story in the
Midrash seems to be directed against this apocryphal legend.
Said R. Hoshaya (third century): When Adam was created in
his primal glory, the image of God on earth, the angels confused
him with the Creator, and sought to recite "Holy, holy" before
him. God thereupon cast a deep sleep upon Adam, and the angels
realized their mistake.[14] This tale rules out the notion that the
angels had to worship Adam; it makes plain the limited knowledge of the angels and the fact that they had no share in the
making of man.

THE CHARACTER OF SATAN. Satan is a familiar character of the
aggada, and is even mentioned in a few of the prayers which
have a more official character. It is therefore most important for
us to understand how the rabbis thought of him. We begin with
certain negative facts.

*Satan is never called in rabbinic literature the Evil One, the
Enemy, Belial, Mastema, or Beelzebul*—names familiar to us from
the pseudepigrapha and the New Testament. Sometimes he is
called Samael—a name also given to the Angel of Death, with
whom Satan is often identified.[15]

*Nowhere in talmudic sources is Satan depicted as a rebel
against God. Nowhere is it even hinted that he was once an
angel of light. Nor does the aggada foretell Satan's downfall or
destruction in the future.* The classic sources do not involve Satan
in the Eden story: the serpent of Eden is a literal snake.[16]

*The Satan of the Talmud is essentially the Satan of the Hebrew
Bible. He is an agent of God.* His role is unpleasant, even un-
savory. He is spy, stoolpigeon, *agent provocateur,* prosecutor,
hangman. It appears that the economy of heaven, like that of
earth, requires the service of such characters, who are not always
animated by pure devotion to the public weal.

Satan's functions are clearly described in a tannaitic statement:
He descends to earth and leads men astray. Then he ascends and
inflames God's wrath by reporting their sins. Having received
permission, he deprives them of life.[17] He works altogether un-

der God's direction. His job is to test the genuineness of man's virtue.

In the context of this statement we have the famous saying of Resh Lakish (third century): "Satan, the evil inclination and the Angel of Death are one and the same." This highly rationalistic remark means: Satan is but the personification of sin that leads to death.[18] The Angel of Death appears many times in our sources, always as a servant of God, never as a rebel. And, as we shall see, God created the evil impulse for a useful purpose.

The propriety of Satan's intentions is further attested by a remarkable fact. The role ascribed to Satan in one version of an aggada is sometimes assigned to the angels, or to God's Attribute of Justice (*Middat haDin*), in other recensions.

Thus we read that Satan complained: At all the feasts Abraham prepared for the birth and weaning of Isaac, he set aside no animal for sacrifice to God. Thereupon God voiced His assurance that if required, Abraham would even sacrifice Isaac. But in another version of the same tale, it is the angels who make accusation against Abraham, and to whom God makes this reply.[19]

When Esau went hunting venison for Isaac, an angel released every animal he caught, thus giving Jacob time to practice his deception and secure his father's blessing. But one parallel says that God sent Satan to delay Esau.[20]

When Ahasuerus invited all his subjects to a banquet, Mordecai warned his fellow Jews not to attend, for by going they would give Satan an opportunity to accuse them. Many went to the banquet nonetheless, and straightway Satan entered God's presence and charged them with violating the dietary laws. But in some sources it is God's justice which accuses the Israelites and demands their punishment.[21]

Many other aggadot dealing with biblical characters mention Satan. Rarely does he overstep his legitimate functions; occasionally he seems more crudely malicious. We present a fair sampling of this material.

When Abraham and Isaac set out for Moriah, Satan met them on the road and tried to dissuade them from obeying the command to sacrifice Isaac. There are various accounts of the conversation that ensued. According to some versions, Isaac's assurance was a little shaken; but Abraham had the courage and determination to withstand the tempter. Arrived at the mountain, Abraham hid Isaac and built the altar with his own hands, lest "he whom God rebuke" strike Isaac with a stone and so render him unfit to be a sacrificial victim. The post-talmudic sources elaborate on these episodes and present Satan as much more diabolic.[22]

When Tamar was brought to trial for adultery, and produced the cord, signet and staff of Judah, Samael removed them; but Gabriel replaced the evidence.[23] In this talmudic story, Samael seems to have no other motive than the desire to make trouble.

Particularly important are the aggadic comments on the Book of Job, for in the opening chapters of this book Satan plays a prominent part. There were various opinions among the rabbis as to when Job lived. R. Jose (second century) held that Job was a contemporary of Moses. When Israel were awaiting deliverance from Egypt, Satan accused them of the many sins they had committed—thus delaying their release from bondage. Then God incited Satan to accuse Job, and while Satan was distracted by this new undertaking, God set Israel free. It is like the case—a later preacher adds—of a shepherd whose flock was attacked by a wolf and who sent a sturdy ram to hold off the intruder; or like the banqueter who was attacked by a vicious dog and said: Toss him a piece of meat to tear at.[24] In this story, Satan does no more than his duty in accusing Israel of real sins. He is the spirit of strict justice, and God has to circumvent his legitimate prosecution in order to redeem Israel, the objects of His special favor.

Still more sympathetic to Satan is the account of the Job story given in the Babylonian Talmud, an account which locates Job in the patriarchal period. On one of his visits to the heavenly court, Satan spoke in the highest praise of Abraham. God suggested that perhaps Job was equally righteous; but Satan insisted that Job could not be compared to Abraham until, like Abraham, he had withstood severe trials. Hence the suffering imposed on Job. How completely Satan worked under God's orders is made plain by R. Isaac: "Satan had more trouble than Job. It was as if a master should tell his slave: break the cask, but save the wine," so was God's command that Satan afflict Job, but spare his life. Another teacher says explicitly: "Satan acted from the highest motives (*leshem shammayim*). When he saw God inclined to favor Job, he said: Heaven forefend that the piety of Abraham be forgotten." And the Talmud adds, when R. Aha bar

Jacob repeated this interpretation in a sermon at Paphunia, Satan came and kissed his feet in gratitude! [25]

More truly devilish was Satan's part in the episode of the Golden Calf. The people were nervous over Moses' prolonged absence; they began to fear that he would never return. Then Satan created an illusion: the people thought they saw Moses lying dead on his bier, suspended between heaven and earth. Confused and terrified by this vision, they lapsed into idolatry.[26] But Satan's device was only a contributory factor in the sin, not an excuse for it.

When God decreed that David should suffer by falling into the hands of Yishbi, the Philistine giant, Satan lured him into enemy territory by taking the form of a deer. Later on, God decided to subject David to temptation; Satan, in the guise of a bird, broke the lattice that concealed Bathsheba. In both these legends, Satan is under direct instructions from above.[27]

Some of the references to Satan are little more than rhetoric. He who takes to himself a woman captured in war "brings Satan into his house." So long as Israel lives in peace among themselves, even though they worship idols, God (if one dare say so!) will not let Satan touch them. Rabbi Judah the Prince warned his sons not to get in the way of an ox as he emerges from a swamp, for "Satan dances between his horns"—that is, he is likely to be vicious.[28]

One who performs certain ritual laws meticulously will be protected (for the time being) from the accusations of Satan. What this means is clear from the plaint of R. Zeira: "I fulfilled these laws, yet I was caught in a royal labor-draft and forced to carry myrtle branches to the palace." [29] Ceremonial ordinances for which no rational explanation can be given—the dietary laws, for example—are described as "those against which Satan and the Gentiles can argue." (In a parallel, the evil inclination is mentioned instead of Satan.) [30]

"R. Isaac declared: Wherever you find idleness, Satan leaps forth. R. Helbo said: Wherever you find tranquility, Satan accuses. Said R. Levi: Wherever you find carousing, 'the chief robber' cavorts." But parallels to this passage—some early—merely state that ease and idleness lead men to sin.[31] A somewhat different Midrash declares that when the pious are vouchsafed a little peace and quiet, Satan at once makes trouble. Since they are to enjoy the unspeakable bliss of the future world, he argues it is only right that they should endure trials in this life.[32]

A traveler should always seek the company of the righteous, for ministering angels travel with them, whereas "angels of Satan" go along with the wicked.[33] Mar Samuel would not ride on a ferry unless there was also a heathen passenger; for he said: "Satan does not have power over two nations at the same time." [34]

In some at least of the passages just cited, Satan is no more than a figure of speech. But ofttimes the reference is to a very realistic "accuser." The evening benediction *Hashkivenu* ("Cause us to lie down in peace") contains a petition that God "break Satan," or, according to another version, "remove Satan from before us and from behind us." The full text of the prayer, including this passage, first appears in the prayerbook of R. Amram Gaon, a teacher of the ninth century. But the prayer is mentioned in the Mishnah and cited in the Palestinian Talmud; and the reference to Satan may well have been in the original text.[35] For Rabbi, the editor of the Mishnah, included in the grace after meals a special benediction for a guest, containing the words: "Let not Satan rule over the work of his hands, nor over the work of our hands." [36]

Palestinian sources frequently state that "Satan accuses in the hour of peril." That is, when one is in physical danger (traveling, for example), Satan at once reminds God of that person's sins, seizing the occasion to prosecute when the means of punishment are ready to hand. The implication is that one should both abstain from sin and avoid unnecessary hazards.[37] And when the rabbis said "One should not open his mouth to Satan" [38]—that is, one should not utter an ill-omened suggestion—they probably had in mind a very vivid Satan, waiting to pounce on any incautious utterance that might enable him to claim a victim.

A very ancient belief, which goes back at least to the days of the prophet Zechariah, held that Satan was present in the Holy of Holies on the Day of Atonement to deliver his accusations and to prevent the High Priest from making expiation for the sins of Israel.[39] The Pharisaic-Rabbinic teachers sought to suppress this notion and the superstitious customs associated with it; but a number of allusions to it have survived in talmudic literature. The most explicit is the following: At the dedication of the tabernacle, Moses said to Aaron: "Aaron my brother, though the All-

Present has agreed to forgive thy sins, thou needest still to put something into Satan's mouth. Send a present before thee ere thou comest into the sanctuary, lest he accuse thee when thou enterest the sanctuary." [40]

The late Dr. Jacob Z. Lauterbach, in one of his most brilliant essays, assembled and explained these stray references to the activity of Satan on Yom Kippur. The ancient ritual of the Day, Dr. Lauterbach said, sought to negate Satan's hostile efforts in three ways. The Azazel-sacrifice was to appease him. The smoke of the incense was to drive him away, for demons find smoke offensive. And the white robes of the High Priest, so different from his usual elaborate garb, were a disguise. White garments are the characteristic attire of an angel; and it was thought that Satan might not recognize the High Priest among all the white-clad beings.[41] These notions, it should be remembered, were ancient and traditional; the rabbis tried to suppress them, but were not entirely successful.

Even after the Temple fell, the people remembered that Satan is particularly energetic at the High Holy Day season. The blowing of the shofar, according to one opinion, is designed to confound Satan.[42] The Babylonian Talmud states that Yom Kippur is the only day of the year when Satan is powerless to accuse Israel; but other opinions seem to have been current.[43]

A very late Midrash, not entirely typical of the rabbinic outlook, gives this graphic account: "On Yom Kippur, Satan comes to accuse Israel and enumerates their iniquities. He says: Master of the World! There are adulterers among the Gentiles, but also among Israel; there are thieves among the Gentiles, but also among Israel. The Holy One (blessed be He!) enumerates Israel's merits. The merits and the iniquities are placed in the opposite pans of the scales and are found to balance each other. So Satan goes to bring more iniquities, that he may put them in the pan of iniquities and tip the scales in that direction. But while Satan is searching for more sins, the Holy One (blessed be He!) removes iniquities from the pan and hides them under His royal robe." [44] Thus the merits of Israel are made to outweigh their faults; God's love for His people protects them from the relentless severity of the accuser.

Diverting and instructive are the tales of encounters between Satan and the talmudic rabbis. R. Meir was contemptuous of sinners until one day Satan appeared on the opposite bank of a river in the guise of a voluptuous woman. Inflamed with sudden and unconquerable passion, Meir tried to reach the charmer by means of a rope suspended across the stream. When he was half way over, Satan released him from the spell, adding: "Did they not proclaim in heaven: 'Have a care for Meir and his learning,' your blood would not be worth twopence." [45] Here Satan plays the role of moralist, instructing the unsympathetic in tolerance for the sinful.

A less famous scholar, a Babylonian named Pelimo, used to ward off temptation by exclaiming daily: "An arrow in Satan's eye!" Once, on an Atonement evening, Satan appeared in the semblance of a beggar and by hook or crook got himself a place at Pelimo's table. His repulsive manners brought upon him a rebuke from his host, whereat the "beggar" collapsed, apparently dead. Immediately an outcry spread through the town that Pelimo had committed murder, and to escape arrest he had to hide in a privy. Then Satan came to him with respectful greeting, revealed his identity, and asked: "Why do you always curse me so?" "How then," Pelimo replied, "should I have spoken to drive you away?" To which the Accuser replied with dignity: "You might have said, May the Merciful One rebuke Satan!" [46]

Satan is not always so good-natured. He stirs up quarrels among men and keeps them bitter. When R. Meir once settled a long drawn out feud, Satan was heard to say: Alas, Meir has driven me from my house! [47]

The Satan of the Talmud is essentially different from the Satan of the apocalyptic Judaism and of Christianity. The Persian concept of Ahriman, the principle of cosmic evil, deeply colored the picture of Satan in these literatures. It is not surprising that occasionally the Satan of the rabbis displays some malicious trait. Far more important is the material, for which there is no parallel in the older Jewish or the later Christian writings, in which Satan is depicted as a sort of genial practical joker, or as the mouthpiece of God's justice, or as a faithful but somewhat narrow-minded agent of the heavenly authority. Because God's love is boundless, He sometimes circumvents Satan's purposes. For Satan has a certain amount of ill will toward men, especially toward Israel; he delights in getting convictions, like an over-zealous district attorney. But he is in no sense a rebel; he works on God's side.

THE EVIL INCLINATION. The rabbis operate constantly with the notion that man has two natures or inclinations within him, one good, one evil. The task of morality is to control the evil nature by exercising the good nature. There are a few remarkable passages in which the evil inclination, the *yezer ha-ra*, sometimes identified with Satan, takes on a separate personality.

Especially striking is the legend that the "impulse to idolatry" was delivered into the hands of the Men of the Great Synagogue after the return from Babylon. It appeared to them in the form of a fiery lion emerging from the ruins of the Holy of Holies. They caught the beast and plucked out some of its hair; whereupon it roared so violently that they were afraid "Heaven might show mercy to it." God's pity, it appears, might extend even to the spirit of idolatry. So they shut the creature up in a receptacle of lead, which muffles sound. Having achieved this success, they sought control over the spirit of physical passion, and this too was delivered into their power, but we are not told in what form. They did not dare to destroy it; for it warned them that to do so would be to destroy the world. In perplexity, they imprisoned the monster for three days, by which time "a fresh egg could not be obtained for an invalid in all the land of Israel." And so they were constrained to let the sexual impulse roam at large, first however reducing its ferocity by daubing its eyes.[48]

This amazing legend accords with the prevailing rabbinic doctrine concerning the evil *yezer*. It too is God's work. He created the evil inclination and provided the Torah as an antidote thereto. He made us subject to temptation, that by vanquishing it we might attain greater reward. "God saw all that He had made, and, behold, it was very good" (Gen. 1.31). "Good" refers to the good impulse, "very good" refers to the evil inclination. "Thou shalt love the Lord thy God with all thy heart" means: thou shalt serve Him with both good and evil natures.[49]

We must remember such statements when we consider other passages which invest the evil *yezer* with a certain demonic quality. R. Amram Hisda, a Babylonian savant, once overcame a severe sexual temptation. Then, by means of an oath, he forced his evil *yezer* to depart from him, and something that looked like a column of flame emerged from his body. "Thou," he averred, "art fire, I am but flesh; yet have I prevailed over thee."[50]

An earlier tradition foretells that God will slaughter the evil inclination in the future, a statement that reminds us of those apocalyptic passages which prophesy the ultimate extinction of the Devil and his works. But it is doubtful if there is a real parallel. The point of our statement is rather in the ethical reflection that follows: "To the righteous, the evil *yezer* will appear as huge as a mountain; to the wicked it will seem thin as a hair. The righteous will marvel that they could overcome so great a power; the wicked will be amazed that they succumbed to so slight a force." [51]

Another old statement (based on Joel 2.20) declares that in the future the evil inclination will be banished from human habitations, for it caused the destruction of both Temples and of the scholars who abode in them. Moreover, it prefers to victimize Israel rather than the Gentiles. Resh Lakish (he who rationalistically identified Satan, the evil *yezer* and the Angel of Death) once said that man's evil impulse seeks to slay him every day, and that man is saved only by divine grace. R. Jonathan remarked that the *yezer* tempts man in this world and testifies against him in the next. [52]

But the weight of rabbinic teaching compels us to explain such utterances as mere dramatic expressions of the dangers of temptation. The imagery may be a survival of old dualistic notions; it could hardly have been meant literally. The world remains a moral unity.

THE SERPENT. The dualistic writers, we have seen, introduced Satan into the Eden-story. Some identified him with the serpent, while others held that the serpent was suborned by the Devil to bring ruin on Adam and Eve. [53] Such notions are not found in the talmudic sources. The latter picture the serpent as endowed with many superior qualities before his fall—with upright stature, speech and wisdom; still he was a beast, not a demon. [54]

But one interesting exception is to be noted. R. Johanan, the greatest teacher of third-century Palestine, declared: "When the serpent assaulted Eve, he cast filth into her. This filth was removed from Israel after they stood at Mount Sinai; but since the idolaters were not present at Mount Sinai, their filth has not been purged." [55]

Old oriental folklore held that serpents have a passionate desire for women; and this belief is certainly in the background of R. Johanan's extraordinary statement.[56] But much more is involved. "The filth of the serpent" is not a mere physical defilement, but a spiritual contamination which was transmitted to all Eve's descendants. This contamination can be neutralized only by the power of the Torah. R. Johanan was experimenting with a theory of original sin, to which he joined the notion that the primal serpent was diabolic, a source of moral defilement.

But this little flyer in experimental theology had no immediate influence. R. Johanan's statement is not quoted in any Palestinian source; and even the Babylonian authorities who preserved it were dubious about its implications. R. Aha b. Raba asked R. Ashe (the dominant figure in Babylonian Jewry at the close of the talmudic period): What about converts? Are we to say that they are still filthy, since neither they nor their ancestors stood at Sinai? R. Ashe replied: Though they were not present, their destiny (*mazzal*) was there, as it is written (Deut. 29.14), "with him that standeth here with us this day before the Lord our God, and also with him that is not here with us this day." [57] It is hard to make clear sense of this statement, yet its intent is plain. R. Ashe would not admit that proselytes to Judaism are tainted by inherited sinfulness. No far-reaching conclusions for "rabbinic theology" can be drawn from R. Johanan's unique remark.

THE DEMONS. The existence of demons is taken for granted throughout rabbinic literature. The sources often speak of "evil spirits," more commonly of *mazzikin* ("injurers") or *shedim* (a biblical term borrowed from Assyrian). The scholars shared with the unlearned the belief that there are such beings. Even the authoritative religious law, the *halakah,* takes cognizance of them.

Although the Mishnah never mentions angels, it speaks of demons twice. An aggadic passage states that the *mazzikin* were created on Sabbath eve, at dusk, among a number of other extraordinary phenomena.[58] More significant is the purely legal remark that one may extinguish a lamp on the Sabbath out of fear of an evil spirit, or of certain more tangible dangers.[59]

The Mishnah provides elsewhere that if a man falls into a deep pit from which he cannot for the moment be extricated, and if he calls out to those nearby that they should give his wife a bill of divorce, his instructions are to be obeyed. But the Amora, R. Johanan, would limit this rule (and a similar one mentioned in the context) by the requirement that the bystander must be able to see at least the outline (*bubiyah*) of a human figure in the pit. Otherwise we might be deceived by a malicious demon mimicking human speech. R. Hanina held that this restriction applies only to the country, for demons do not lurk in pits near centers of population; R. Abin, however, believed that they may be found also in city neighborhoods.[60]

These serious legal discussions show how deeply the belief in demons penetrated rabbinic thought. References in aggadic literature are very numerous, but we need not examine them all. They list the names and characteristics of the various spirits, or describe the specific means of defense against each. A general survey and a few illustrations will suffice.

1. The number of the demons is vast, their power to do harm great.[61] But they are not an organized body under the leadership of the Prince of Darkness, any more than wild animals are organized to harm mankind. Ashmedai is mentioned as the king of the demons, but nowhere do we find him actually ruling. His one important appearance is in the legend of his dealings with Solomon. There he is pictured as a rather genial sort, of great might and crude good nature, inclined to drink and to lust, but by no means vicious.[62] *Nowhere does the Talmud speak of Satan as the leader of the evil spirits.*

2. The demonology of the Talmud is largely incapsulated in an area of superstition. Discussions on this topic are kept separate from those which deal with the sublime religious and ethical truths of Judaism. The two elements are not integrated; for this could only result in the defilement of religion. The Babylonian Gemara devotes considerable space to demons, and to the techniques by which we may see them and protect ourselves against them.[63] These sections operate almost entirely with magical procedures and words; little or no effort is made to give the procedures a Jewish religious character. It is often said that piety protects man against evil spirits, and that God's blessing especially avails against them; but we are not advised to pray for protection from the demons, nor do the daily prayers contain such petitions.[64]

Demonic possession is rarely mentioned; exorcism appears only in a few cases and seems to have had no religious significance. The fullest discussion is a story concerning R. Johanan b. Zakkai (before 70 c.e.) and a Gentile who complained that the law of the red heifer (Num. 19) smacks of witchcraft. R. Johanan replied with a question: How is the demon *tezazit* (epilepsy) exorcised? The Gentile answered: Herb roots are brought and caused to smoke under the patient. He is then sprinkled with water, and the demon flees. The law of the red heifer, retorted the rabbi, is similar. Contact with a corpse causes an unclean spirit to enter a person; sprinkling with water containing the ashes of the red heifer drives the bad spirit away.

After the Gentile disputant left, the pupils of R. Johanan dismissed the explanation he had given as mere "stubble," and demanded the true meaning of the law of the red heifer. He replied: "The dead do not defile, nor do the waters purify. The entire ceremony is the decree of the Most High King." [65] Should we then conclude that R. Johanan and his school did not believe in the theory of demons and of exorcism? This would be going too far. But in the next century, R. Jose—who held rationalistic views on many subjects—declared that one should not murmur a charm against *shedim* even on weekdays, still less on the Sabbath.[66]

3. Though the rabbis attached no special religious importance to demons, though they did not make exorcism a concern of faith or a duty of religious leaders, though they left demons for the most part in the limbo of superstition where they properly belonged, they still had to make some place for these beings in their scheme of the world. And first they had to answer the question: Whence did the demons come?

According to many apocalypses, the demons issued from the bodies of the giants whom the wicked angels had engendered with the daughters of men. *This opinion never appears in talmudic sources.* Instead, the demons are said to have been directly created by God. We have already noted the view that they were among the unclassifiable beings formed at dusk on the eve of the first Sabbath.

This notion was elaborated by Rabbi Judah the Prince. The demons are not complete. God created their souls late on Friday afternoon, and Sabbath came on before He could create their bodies. Therefore He left them unfinished, as an example to

Israel that they should stop work promptly upon the approach of Sabbath.[67]

This opinion, however, was not generally accepted. An anonymous teaching of comparatively early date enumerates three resemblances between angels and demons: they have wings, can move from one end of the earth to the other, and know the future. But in three respects the demons are like men: They require food and drink, reproduce their kind, and die.[68] The common opinion, then, was that the demons do have bodies.

Since they have a sexual nature like that of humans, it is not surprising that intercourse between demons and humans should sometimes occur. Jewish lore knows the incubus and succubus; [69] but since the Jews condemned celibacy as sinful and usually married young, they were not terrorized by these demon consorts as were the ascetics of the Church. In the standard rabbinic sources, such miscegenation is mentioned only in the case of Adam and Eve who, during the period when they were separated from one another, mated each with spirits of the opposite sex. Demon offspring resulted from these unions.[70] The reader may recall in this connection the familiar legend of Lilith, the demon who was Adam's consort before Eve was created; but this tale is of much later origin.[71]

The demons are always dangerous and often malicious. There are two types of protection against them, as there are against disease and other physical dangers. First, one takes specific measures in accordance with the nature of the menace. Demons are more likely to attack a solitary person than a company of two or three; therefore one should not go out alone at night or sleep in a deserted house. Special precautions must be taken in a privy, for filth attracts evil spirits.[72] The magical sentences which repel demons are roughly comparable to medical prescriptions which cure disease.

Second, learning and piety are a prophylactic against demons, as against all other ills. The saintly Hanina b. Dosa was immune to the bite of a deadly reptile, and equally immune to injury from the demon queen Agrat bat Mahlat.[73] Modesty in the privy is a protection against snakes, scorpions and demons.[74] God's blessing above everything else protects us from the evil spirits.[75] But there is no specific religious procedure to defeat them.

4. The demons, though far from good, are not utterly evil. Cer-

tainly they are not rebels against God. They have their kindlier moments. An old Midrash compares the temperament of house spirits and field spirits: "Some say house spirits are friendly, because they grow up in our company; some say they are dangerous, because they know our weaknesses. Some say field spirits are unfriendly, because they do not grow up with us; others say they are harmless, because they do not know our weaknesses." [76]

When Noah became the partner of the demon Shamdan in planting a vineyard, the latter warned him: Be careful not to enter my portion of the vineyard; if you enter, I will hurt you.[77] This suggests that his intentions are basically not unfriendly.

Not a few of the talmudic sages had encounters with demons. Agrat bat Mahlat met Hanina ben Dosa and told him that she would have injured him had "Heaven" not warned her to leave him alone. Hanina replied: If I am of such great account in heaven, I forbid you to enter inhabited places! But Agrat pleaded so pitifully that Hanina allowed her to be at liberty on Wednesday and Saturday nights. Centuries later, Abaye had a similar encounter with her and tried to banish her altogether. But the Talmud sadly notes that his efforts were not entirely successful, and the demons are still especially active on these two nights of the week.[78]

R. Jannai and R. Jonathan were once walking in a forest and met a demon, who saluted them with: "Peace, lads!" R. Joseph and R. Papa were friendly with a demon named Joseph, who gave them information about his tribe.[79]

The Midrash tells of a friendly spirit which inhabited a spring. Then a vicious spirit tried to usurp his place, and the old inhabitant invoked human aid. Under his direction, the dangerous interloper was killed, to the benefit both of the gentle spirit and of its human friends.[80]

Once R. Simeon b. Johai was sent to Rome to secure the abrogation of some anti-Jewish decrees. In this mission he was helped by a demon named Ben Temalyon. While R. Simeon was on his way, this creature hastened on ahead and took possession of the daughter of Caesar. All efforts to exorcise the demon were futile; but when R. Simeon arrived and summoned the demon to depart from the maiden, he was obeyed at once. In gratitude, Caesar annulled the hateful decree. R. Simeon, however, was not entirely pleased at the kind of help he had received. "An angel," he complained, "appeared twice to my ancestor's slave-woman (Hagar), but not even once to me!" [81]

5. The classic sources never predict that demons will be destroyed in the future. For, as one ancient source remarks, God's glory will be enhanced by rendering the *mazzikin* harmless more than if He exterminated them. In the same way, noxious plants, ferocious beasts, poisonous reptiles—all of which, like the demons, God created for His own good purposes—will no longer be baneful in the days of the Messiah. [82]

THE PRINCES OF THE GENTILES. We come back now to an idea that we met much earlier in our inquiry. It is that the patron angels of the great world-powers are responsible for the sufferings of Israel. God, indeed, had instructed these angels to punish his sinful people, but they far exceeded their orders. With savage glee they incited their peoples to persecute Israel, while they pitted their might against Israel's angelic defenders. When, therefore, God judges the nations, He will also punish their guardian angels.

We found this conception in the earliest apocalypses. [83] Thereafter it disappears. Some of the later apocalyptic authors were preoccupied with the belief in a cosmic Satan; others dispensed altogether with a superhuman origin of sin. Christian thought held that both individuals and nations have guardian angels, but knew nothing of a conflict among them. The highly developed concept of Satan left no room in Christianity for any other independent source of evil; nor was there reason for the Church to retain a notion that was rooted in Jewish national consciousness. But the rabbinic teachers, who so completely rejected a cosmic dualism, admitted the belief in hostile angels, patrons of the nations that oppressed Israel. This squared with their opinion that angels in general are far from perfect.

We meet this view first in an old Midrash to Exodus. Before God drowned the Egyptians at the Red Sea, He cast their heavenly prince into the waters; and as soon as Israel beheld the downfall of this angel, they began to sing God's praises. "And also in the future, the Holy One (blessed be He!) will punish the Gentiles only after He has first punished their guardian angels." This statement is supported by three significant proof texts. The first is "The Lord will punish the host of the high heaven on high, and the kings of earth upon the earth" (Isaiah 24.21), which the rabbis understood quite literally. The second is Isaiah 14.12: "How art thou fallen from heaven, O day-star, son of the morning! How art thou cast down to the ground, that didst cast lots over the nations!" This verse, we have seen, was held by Christians to describe the fall of Satan; perhaps·the rabbis introduced it here to preclude such a dangerous interpretation. As they understood it, the first sentence refers to the discomfiture of Babylon's heavenly champion, the second to the downfall of Nebuchadnezzar. In a similar way they understood the third proof text: "My sword hath drunk its fill in heaven; behold, it shall come down upon Edom" (Isaiah 34.5).[84]

The later Midrashim repeat this aggada and elaborate upon it. For instance: God cast down the patron angels of Sihon and Og, the Amorite kings, before Israel attacked the earthly rulers. It is like the case, said R. Abba b. Kahana, of a king who captured and bound the foe of his son, and said to the boy: Now do to him as you please! [85]

On the basis of Ezekiel 10, the Babylonian scholars constructed an elaborate legend. When the First Temple was about to fall, God determined to destroy Israel by fire and so notified Michael, their guardian angel. Michael begged God to be content with the righteous minority, but God decreed that even they must perish in the general conflagration. Gabriel was ordered to take coals from under the divine chariot, wherewith to destroy Israel. But instead, he asked the cherub to hand him the coals; in the interim they cooled slightly, and so Israel escaped complete annihilation. Gabriel, however, fell into disgrace for not obeying exactly. Either he should have continued to beg God for mercy on His people, leaving the coals alone, or he should have taken them as he was commanded. So Gabriel was exiled from the divine presence and had to remain "outside the heavenly curtain"; Dobiel, the guardian angel of Persia, was put in his place, which he occupied for twenty-one days. During this period, great territories were added to the Persian empire. Dobiel further obtained decrees that all Israel, even scholars, should pay a poll tax to the Persian government. When these decrees were about to be sealed, Gabriel called from outside the curtain, reminding God of Daniel's righteousness. He was now readmitted to the heavenly throne-room and at once sought to snatch the unfavorable decrees from Dobiel; but the latter quickly swallowed them. Some say the decrees had not yet been sealed; others say they were already sealed, but were smudged and blotted when Dobiel swallowed them. Either opinion will explain why not all the Jews of Persia have to pay the poll tax. But later on, in the days of Antiochus, the guardian angel of Greece attacked Israel; and that time Gabriel's best efforts on behalf of the people proved ineffectual.[86]

In this legend, as in the Book of Daniel, both Michael and Gabriel appear as Israel's champions. This is not unusual, though most frequently it is Michael who has the distinction. There is also another view, which appears from time to time, that Israel is under the direct guidance of God alone, and that only the Gentiles are ruled by guardian angels.[87]

The belief in these national angels sometimes appears without the implication that the latter are hostile to the Jewish people. Among the many interpretations of Jacob's dream is one (ascribed to R. Meir) in which the angels are the patrons of Babylonia, Media, Greece and Rome. Each ascends the ladder, to symbolize the rise of his people, and then descends to typify their downfall.[88] Again we read that at the final judgment, the guardian angels of the Gentiles will argue that Israelites have been just as sinful as the rest—why then should Israel be saved, while the Gentiles descend into hell? [89] God's rejoinder does not concern us here; we note only that the guardian angels proceed in a legitimate fashion, much as Satan acts the role of accuser.

But generally these angels are regarded as malicious. When Abraham bound his son to sacrifice him (so a Palestinian preacher declares), God in recompense bound the guardian angels of the Gentiles on high. But when in the days of Jeremiah, Israel cast off all restraints, God loosed the bonds of the angels, and the downfall of Judah followed.[90]

There are many opinions as to the identity of the mysterious being with whom Jacob wrestled at the ford of the Jabbok. According to R. Hama bar R. Hanina, Jacob was attacked by the guardian angel of Edom (Rome). This is like the case of a king who had a vicious dog and a tame lion. He encouraged his son to fight with the lion; then if the dog ever wanted to attack the boy, the king could say: The lion could not overcome him, how then can you withstand my son? Even so, if the Gentiles attack

Israel, God will say to them: Your heavenly chief could not prevail against Israel, still less can you! [91]

Resh Lakish declared that in the future the guardian angel of Rome will seek sanctuary from the punishment he deserves by fleeing to Bozrah. But he will make a threefold error. The city of refuge is not Bozrah, but Bezer; one cannot obtain asylum from the consequences of a deliberate crime, but only of unintentional homicide; and the cities of refuge are a protection only to men, but not to angels. And so the angel of Rome will suffer his just doom.[92]

CHAPTER SEVENTEEN

Interlude: The Legend in Islam

The compilation of the Talmud did not close an epoch in the development of Jewish thought. A vast body of material which had circulated orally or in private notebooks was now safely preserved in writing; but the content of the living tradition was not exhausted even by these voluminous works. The scholars continued to study the same subjects in much the same spirit as previously.

The great Midrashim, collections of sermonic material, were edited in Palestine in the centuries following the completion of the Talmuds. These works contain the teachings and reflect the conditions of the talmudic period, not of the age in which they were compiled. Some Midrashim are quite late: Exodus Rabba, for example, is dated by Zunz in the eleventh or twelfth century. Yet in substance and tone it does not differ much from earlier collections: it can be used as a source for "talmudic" Judaism.

But in the post-talmudic centuries other Jewish writings appeared (some in midrashic form) which reveal new trends of thought and reflect the influences of their own time. Among these influences, the rise of Islam was certainly one of the most important.

The decisive events of Mohammed's career occurred between 622 and 632 c.e. At his death (in 632) he was master of Arabia;

less than twenty years later, his successors had conquered Syria, Palestine and Persia. Thus the chief centers of Jewish life passed under Moslem rule.

The new prophet derived his doctrine largely from Judaism, with some additions from Christianity. The Koran, which he promulgated as the ultimate revelation of God, is full of bits of biblical-aggadic lore, which Mohammed had picked up from Jewish and Christian acquaintances. Sometimes he gave the old stories a new twist, either because he had not understood, or because his own taste prompted him to change, what he had heard. Many of his followers likewise borrowed Jewish aggadic traditions, which they handled with much originality. In late Hebrew writings, old Jewish legends sometimes crop up in their Islamic form; and our literature even contains some stories of purely Mohammedan origin.

The Arab writings not infrequently mention fallen angels; and the legends appear with certain novel features. Some of these appear also in the later Jewish books. Did the Jewish writers depart from their own traditions to copy the Islamic sources? There is some reason, we shall see, to doubt this. But we are handicapped in drawing definite conclusions because few of the Jewish documents can be accurately dated. We cannot even divide them with certainty into pre-Mohammedan and post-Mohammedan works. Besides, we may find in a single writing some elements that certainly and others that possibly reflect Islamic influence, while other new trends almost surely are the product of internal development. The only practical procedure therefore is to present in this interlude some salient items from Moslem literature, and then to treat the "new" aggada in a separate chapter.

IBLIS. The angels—so the rabbis declared—opposed the creation of man and resented the favor God showed him. Adam, however, displayed his superior qualities by naming the animals, a feat the angels could not equal.[1] Mohammed borrowed this legend and combined it with the apocryphal story that Satan fell because in his pride he refused to worship Adam. This combination occurs repeatedly in the Koran; in the fullest version, Iblis explains why he will not worship the man: "I am better than he; Thou hast created me of fire, while him Thou hast created of dust." Thereupon God banishes Iblis for his arrogance; but the Devil is reprieved long enough to lead Adam and Eve astray, and he still tempts mankind to sin.[2]

Probably, Mohammed drew here on Christian as well as on Jewish lore: the Adam-books, the chief written source for these tales, were preserved by the Church. So likewise the name Iblis, derived from *Diabolos,* suggests Christian influence; for Arabic has an exact cognate, *Shaitan,* to the Hebrew *Satan.* In the Jewish-Christian sources of the legend, Satan was a great angel before his fall. The Koran, however, states that "he was of the *jinn,* so he transgressed" (18.50). This accords with another statement that God created the *jinni* of fire (15.27; 55.15). The *jinni* are demons, like the *shedim* of whom we learned from the rabbis.

One might ask: if Iblis was only a jinn, of a subordinate and spiritually inferior caste, why was it so important that he worship Adam, and why was his disobedience so severely punished? But we should not expect logical consistency from the unlearned prophet of Arabia. He took the existence of the Devil and of demons for granted; yet his uncompromising doctrinaire monotheism left no room for dualistic conceptions. He did not worry over the question why Allah, the all-powerful and all-merciful, should have created evil and malicious beings and tolerated their plots against mankind; here, as in other matters, he left serious theological difficulties to his more reflective successors. A dim recognition of the problem appears in the statement that the Devil "has no authority over those who believe and rely on their Lord. His authority is only over those who befriend him, and those who set up gods with him" (16.99, 100). This is fair enough, if you don't scrutinize it too carefully. Mohammed combined the superstitions of his own people, the bits of Jewish and Christian lore he had acquired and his own unbudging monotheism; and he remained comfortably unaware of the contradictions involved.

HARUT AND MARUT. The Koran does not speak explicitly about fallen angels, but one brief and obscure passage requires our attention. In the old rendering, by Sale, it runs: "They (presumably the Jews) followed the device which the devils devised against the kingdom of Solomon; and Solomon was not an unbeliever; but the devils believed not, they taught men sorcery, and that which was sent down to the two angels at Babel, Harut and Marut; yet those two taught no man until they had said:

Verily we are a temptation, therefore be not an unbeliever. So men learned from those two a charm by which they might cause division between a man and his wife; but they hurt none thereby, unless by God's permission, and they learned that which would hurt them and not profit them" (2.102 f.).[3]

Here once more we find angels teaching men witchcraft—not however in rebellion against God, but to test the fidelity of mankind. The text does not indicate that the angels had fallen previously or that they fell after the events described; they bear names we have not met before, names of Persian origin.[4] Whether the brevity and vagueness of the allusion is intentional or not is hard to determine. But it is certain that the successors of Mohammed based on this passage a fuller story about the fallen angels, which they told in many varied forms.

Before turning to the later literature, we should note two facts. The defense of Solomon in this Koran passage is in line with Moslem tradition, which glorified Solomon as the magnificent monarch—whereas Jewish aggada stresses the apostasy of Solomon's later years, and regards him as a sad example of the demoralizing effects of wealth and power.[5] Second, Mohammed refers several times with respect and approval to Enoch, whom he calls Idris, the instructor (9.56, 21.85). The same attitude toward Enoch appears in later Moslem writers.

The story of Harut and Marut engaged the attention of the commentators on the Koran. Tabari (839-923) was especially interested in the subject and in his commentary gives no less than ten versions of the tale, most of which have a strong family resemblance.[6] Without listing every variation, we shall present the distinctive features of the legend as it appears in these sources.

Only two angels fall from grace. In most of the versions, their descent is not made on their own initiative. The angels as a group deplore the sinfulness of mankind and dismiss the excuse God offers—men are subject to error and to desire—as insufficient. Challenged then by God to prove that they can do better, they select Harut and Marut as their representatives. The latter go down to earth to act as judges, at a place named Babil—sometimes identified as Babylon in Iraq, sometimes as a place in northern Persia. Several versions state that the angels return nightly to heaven, by the use of a holy name.

The fall of the angels occurs when a beautiful woman appears before them in a lawsuit. They seek to enjoy her favors; according to one version, she insists that they first reveal to her the divine name, and then by its use she evades them, flies up to heaven and is transformed into a star. Most of the accounts, however, accuse the angels of more serious crimes. They had been warned in advance not to admit the existence of other gods, to murder, or to drink intoxicants. But it is precisely these crimes which the charmer demands as the price of her complaisance. After fruitless attempts to resist temptation, they finally agree to drink wine—as the least of the sins demanded—and the lady yields to them. Later they murder a passerby who has observed their crime.

Their paramour ascends on high by the use of the heavenly name. They, however, find themselves earthbound. They seek intercessors—sometimes angelic, sometimes human—but God will not forgive them. The utmost concession is that they may choose between punishment in this world and in the next. They decide to suffer in this world and are fettered in Babylon. Only one source cited by Tabari reports that they have continued in their imprisonment to teach men magic.

The lady who tempts the angels is called variously Zuhra, Beduht, and Anahid. These last two are names of Persian goddesses.[7] In most accounts, she is no more than a beautiful woman; but in some this is only an appearance. One version (not in Tabari, but derived from a commentary printed with his) states that Zuhra was a star who descended in the form of a woman, while the angel set over this star took the shape of an idol which Harut and Marut were required to worship.

Among the versions quoted by Tabari, that ascribed to Mujahid is particularly interesting. The angels marveled at the wickedness of mankind, since they possess "the Prophets and the Books and the Signs." Thereupon God had them choose representatives to demonstrate the moral superiority of angels. Harut and Marut, having been charged with the laws they must obey, acted as just judges, returning each night to heaven. Now Zuhra appeared as a beautiful woman, whose lawsuit they decided against her. Afterwards, they admitted to each other that they were smitten by her charms; so they invited her to return and reversed their decision. (Another account details their discussion of the matter. They are quite aware that their deed will deserve punishment, but decide to sin and "hope in the mercy of God.") Zuhra gives herself to them, but there is no actual physical contact. "They uncovered their shame in her presence; but their lusts were only in their soul; and they were not like men in their desires or in the enjoyment of love." [8] Then Zuhra flew away to her former abode. At evening the wings of Harut and Marut would no longer bear them up to heaven.[9] They besought a man to pray on their behalf, and he replied: How can dwellers on earth pray for denizens of heaven? [10] But when they assured him that God looked on him with favor, he complied with their wish; and, in response, he received the message that they might choose between punishment now or in the hereafter.

Still further variations appear in later Moslem sources. One declares that the two angels are punished by being suspended head downward in a well in Babylon, a punishment that will continue till the resurrection. They teach men magic; but no one sees them unless he goes to the spot to learn their evil lore. In other books, we learn of *three* angels who descended on earth; one, however, realized his susceptibility to female charms and returned to heaven without undergoing the test.[11]

These stories have persisted in living Moslem tradition; and various forms have been found in recent centuries among the inhabitants of Persia and Algeria and among the Moriscos of Spain.[12] The Moslems of India also know the tale; a modern version tells that Zuhra had a companion, Mushtari, who played a similar role and was also transformed into a star. This name is also originally that of a Persian deity.[13]

Without laboring every detail, we may note the chief novelties in the Moslem version of our myth. Perhaps the most obvious is the reduction in the number of the sinful angels. In the old Jewish versions, they amounted to a few hundred and were led either by Satan, or by Shemhazai and Azazel. In Christian belief, the number who fell with Satan swells enormously, till the view develops that the total sum of souls to be saved by the Church throughout history will equal that of the fallen angels. But in the Mohammedan account only Harut and Marut sin. We shall see, however, that this change had probably been made by Jewish aggadists prior to the rise of Islam.

Instead of the "daughters of man" whom the fallen angels

marry, the Moslem story knows usually of but a single charmer, who lures the angels to spiritual ruin, while she is translated to the skies. This last is a familiar mythological motif; moreover, the names given to the lady are those of goddesses, associated particularly with the planet Venus. In some versions, she is a heavenly being who takes earthly form just long enough to tempt the angels. This, as well as the names Harut and Marut, represents a borrowing from Persian—perhaps ultimately from Babylonian—lore.

Other new elements are the inclusion of drunkenness among the sins of the angels—reflecting Mohammed's ban on intoxicants—the choice given to the angels as to when they shall be punished, and the notion that they continue to instruct men in sorcery.

Many of these new variations recur in later Jewish sources. In Islam, however, the belief in fallen angels, though persistent, was not very important. Some Mohammedans, both in medieval and modern times, have rejected the whole tale and explained that Harut and Marut were human beings.[14] The belief in Iblis and his fall, clearly stated in the Koran, could not be so readily dismissed; but it never had anything like the importance which the same doctrine had in Christian theology.

CHAPTER EIGHTEEN

New Paths: The Visionaries

For centuries after the Talmud was completed, world Jewry had its spiritual center in the academies of Babylonia. The presidents of these academies, from the sixth century onward, bore the title of Gaon, "Excellency." The period up to about 1000 is known in Jewish history as the Gaonic period.

The writings we shall now consider come from the age of the Gaonim (for convenience we shall include a few later works), but little of this literature is by the Gaonim themselves. Those dignitaries devoted themselves chiefly to exposition of the law as laid down in the authoritative Babylonian Talmud. A few—

notably Saadia, Sherira and Hai—pioneered in biblical and talmudic philology, and in history, literature and philosophy. But
the books we are to examine emanate from circles somewhat removed from these sober legalists, circles with a tinge of hetero-
doxy.

The Gaonic period, like the centuries just before the Christian
era, witnessed great intellectual and religious ferment. The Karaite author, Al-Kirkisani (tenth century), enumerates no less than
seventeen Jewish sects, most of which still existed in his own day.
The rise of Islam with its different contending parties no doubt
stimulated sectarian trends in Jewry.

The parallel with the pre-Christian age is surprisingly com-
plete. The Rabbanites headed by the Gaonim correspond to the
Pharisees and represent the main body of Jewish thought. The
Karaites, who rejected popular tradition and interpreted the bib-
lical text with strictest literalness, remind us of the Sadducees.
The pre-Christian Essenes have their counterpart in the later
"Mourners of Zion" and the mystical "Chariot Travelers"—dev-
otees of an ascetic, other-worldly piety.

The parallel extends also to Jewish literature in the pre-Christian and the post-talmudic ages, especially the literature which
came from circles not quite sectarian, but slightly off the beaten
track of orthodoxy. In both periods this literature took three distinctive forms:

First, apocalypses: visions of the end of days, the Messiah, the
final judgment and the resurrection.

Second, mystical books, quasi-Gnostic in tone, about the divine
Chariot-Throne, the angels and the ascent into the presence of
God.

Third, unorthodox aggada-books. Jubilees is a good instance
from earlier times; in the Gaonic period, the Chapters of Rabbi
Eliezer are the outstanding example.

These resemblances are neither formal nor accidental. There
is a true inner relation between the Old Testament pseudepigrapha and what we may venture to call the talmudic pseudepigrapha. It was not a matter of direct literary borrowing; few of
the old apocrypha were in Jewish hands during the Gaonic
period. But there was a continuous living tradition of mystical
and messianic doctrine.

The rabbis rejected the Outside Books for various reasons.

They considered certain ideas in these works objectionable, other ideas dangerous. Thus the talmudic writings are in substantial agreement with the apocalypses in their expectations of the future; but in the rabbinic books these topics are given but limited space. Some of the scholars, moreover, voice stern warnings against excessive preoccupation with the mystery of the end of days. They wished not to combat, but to "de-emphasize" the apocalyptic teachings.

Similarly, the Talmud makes no attack, open or implied, on the mystical doctrines. Some of the greatest of the rabbis were adepts of mystic lore. But they insisted that it remain esoteric, that only a few choice disciples might be initiated into the doctrine by brief hints which they must follow up for themselves. To publish the intimate secrets of divinity, they held, was a kind of sacrilege, and actually dangerous.

But there were other notions which the rabbis sought to suppress entirely. The belief in fallen angels was only one of these. They also rejected an old legend of the bloody wars which the sons of Jacob waged with the Canaanites, and some picaresque tales about the youth of Moses which probably originated in Egypt. These stories were not in consonance with rabbinic ideals and were therefore omitted from the talmudic writings.

But the "conspiracy of silence" was not wholly successful. Some of the rabbis themselves cultivated mysticism as a secret doctrine. Outside the official circles, many beliefs and traditions were quietly kept alive. After the close of the Talmud, conditions changed, vigilance relaxed and the suspected doctrines came from underground.

I. APOCALYPSES

The earliest apocalypse to which we can assign a definite date is now part of a larger midrashic work, the Pesikta Rabbati. The apocalyptic section was almost certainly written within a few years after Mohammed's death in 632.[1] It presents a unique conception of a Messiah who at Creation undertook to suffer for the sins of Israel, that his people might ultimately be redeemed—a conception obviously borrowed from Christianity. Satan, we read, asked God about the light which was streaming forth from beneath the Throne of Glory. God replied: This is he who is to drive you back and humiliate you. Satan begged to see the Messiah, and his request was granted; but at once he reeled back exclaiming: Surely this is the Messiah who will cast me and all the princes of the heathen into Gehenna.[2] Satan's humility before God is an inheritance from Jewish tradition; but the notion that he will be cast into Gehenna, and by the Messiah at that, is a further borrowing from Christian thought which had little or no influence on later Judaism. The combination of Satan and the guardian angels of the Gentiles is common in post-classical aggada.[3]

This document makes a passing reference to the fallen angels. When the Messiah appears, sinful Israel will seek to justify themselves before God. They will say: "Master of the World! Thou didst plant a heart of stone within us, and it led us astray. If Azza and Azzael, whose bodies were of fire, sinned when they descended to earth, how much more natural was it for us to do so!"[4] Obviously the story was well known to the Jews of that day, and in the later form according to which there were only two sinful angels. *The reduction of the number of rebels to two occurred before Islamic versions could have influenced Jewish tradition.*

The other post-talmudic apocalypses are independent works, mostly brief and of slight literary merit. In purpose and technique they are very like the older visions. Their authorship is ascribed to earlier worthies, sometimes to biblical characters, sometimes to talmudic heroes. They seem to date from about 750 onward, and some are as late as the Crusades.[5]

A distinct family resemblance runs through these writings. They lack the rich variety of mythological elements which we found in pre-Christian apocalyptic. The chief interest is centered on the time and circumstances of the messianic advent. But new and startling is the picture—we can hardly say, doctrine—of the Antichrist. This creature, Satan's earthly representative, though foreshadowed in older Jewish writings, first appears distinctly— as we have seen—in Christian literature. In Jewish books, aside from a few brief allusions we shall note later, he is mentioned only in the medieval apocalypses.

Thus the *Book of Elijah* foretells that the last king of Persia will wage several campaigns against Rome and will overcome three mighty men who emerge from the sea to meet him. Then another king, the basest of all, the son of the slavewoman, Gigith, will come up from the sea and spread terror over the world. This king will be "long faced, with a raised area (*gabhut*) between his eyes, very tall, the palms of his hands high (?), and his shoulders thin." He will persecute Israel, but the faithful will be able to repent.

Later in the same work we read: "A king shall come up from the sea, and ravage and shake the world; and he shall go up against the mount of beautiful holiness and burn it. Cursed among women be she who bore him!" [6] Apparently this is the same king previously mentioned. He is not a sea monster, for he has a base-born mother. His role in the cosmic drama is obscure; the entire *Book of Elijah* is fragmentary and cryptic.

The other writings in this group all tell of a horrible being called Armilus. What seems to be the oldest source (*The Midrash of the Ten Kings*) predicts: As the end of days approaches, Satan will descend and go to Rome where he will have sexual contact with a statue of a woman. The statue will conceive and bear Armilus, who will reign forty days. "He will make evil decrees against Israel, so that righteous men cease and thieves multiply." If Israel are meritorious, the Messiah son of Joseph will appear in upper Galilee, go to Jerusalem, rebuild the Temple and restore the sacrificial worship. He will be killed by Gog and Magog, the leaders of the last rebellion of the heathen; and only later will the Messiah of the house of David appear.[7]

The Messiah son of Joseph derives from early rabbinic thought. He is not exactly a false Messiah, but a sort of premature forerunner of the Messiah and will come to grief before the advent of the genuine Davidic redeemer. Gog and Magog (Ezekiel 38 and 39) are associated also in the Talmud with the death of Messiah ben Joseph.[8]

The Gaonic apocalypses usually state that he will meet his death at the hands of Armilus. Thus we read in *The Secrets of R. Simeon ben Johai*, a work slightly later than the *Ten Kings*, that the wicked king Armilus will appear, slay the Messiah ben Joseph and himself die by the breath of the mouth of Messiah ben David. Armilus is described as "bald, his eyes are small, a mark of leprosy is on his brow." His right ear is stopped and his left is open —if a man comes to say anything good, Armilus turns his deaf right ear to him; but when anything evil is to be said, he hears it with his good left ear. He is "the son of Satan and the stone." [9]

A very similar description in the *Midrash Vayosha* adds one more unprepossessing detail: His right arm measures only a hand-breadth, while his left arm is two and a half cubits long.[10]

In the *Prayer of Rabbi Simeon ben Johai*, however, wicked heathen (not Satan) have intercourse with the statue. Nine months later it bursts open and Armilus emerges. He claims to be the god and messiah of Edom and is hailed as such by all the heathen. Then he demands that Messiah ben Joseph acknowledge him as god and savior. The Jews bravely refuse him homage and are massacred by Armilus. After many disasters, Michael blows his horn, God manifests His presence and the Davidic Messiah appears. But in this vision, he does not destroy Armilus. God says to him "Sit down at My right hand" (Ps. 110.1), and the Messiah has only to look on while God destroys the wicked.[11]

This material is repeated in the *Wars of the King Messiah* where, however, the appearance of Armilus is due to God's intervention. He Himself preserves the seed of the rascals who embrace the statue and causes Armilus to be born.[12]

There are two brief references to Armilus in the Targumim—probably very late insertions. R. Saadia Gaon, in his great work on Jewish philosophy and theology, mentions Armilus as the slayer of the Messiah ben Joseph, but omits all reference to his supernatural origin. He holds, moreover, that the prophecies of the messianic terrors are conditional and will be fulfilled only if Israel fails to repent before the appointed time.[13]

One might have thought that recognition by Saadia, the great legalist and rationalist, would have conferred respectability on Armilus; but in fact he never acquired a secure position even in Jewish folklore, still less in Jewish theology. Scholars are still uncertain whether his name is derived from Ahriman, the evil deity of Persia, or from Romulus the founder of Rome. The legend of his birth resembles a medieval legend about Virgil. The statement that Armilus will try to force the Jews to recognize him as god and messiah suggests that he was regarded as a personification of Roman Christianity.[14]

If we were to consider this irrational legend in a logical fashion (which would be an illogical procedure!), we should have to say that it implies a thoroughgoing dualism. It is therefore interesting to note that in some sources, the part of Satan in begetting the Antichrist is eliminated; and in at least one version God Himself produces the creature—no doubt as a final trial of the righteous.

In short, dualistic elements appear only here and there in medieval Jewish apocalyptic. A number of works from the same period give rather extended accounts of paradise and hell. In none of them is anything said about Satan and the satanic; the punishment of sinners is entrusted to destructive angels.[15]

But in one interesting vision Satan has a part. Israel, we read, will come to Jerusalem under the leadership of the Messiah and will claim the Temple; this claim will be contested by the King of the Arabs. He will suggest that each side bring a sacrifice, and the Temple shall belong to those whose offering is accepted. But alas! Israel's sacrifice will be rejected, for Satan will prefer charges against them; yet God will receive favorably the gift of the sons of Kedar.[16] This document no doubt expresses the disappointment among Jewish visionaries when the wars between Christianity and Islam resulted in the appropriation of the holy sites by the Moslems, and not—as had been hoped—in their restoration to Israel.

II. MYSTICAL WRITINGS

The Jewish mystics of the Gaonic period were the heirs of a tradition already very old. Its antecedents are recorded in such writings as II Enoch and the Apocalypse of Abraham; and the tradition was continued by at least some of the talmudic rabbis. But the latter permitted speculation on the divine chariot and the cultivation of mystical ecstasy only within a small closed group. In the post-talmudic period this reticence largely vanished and the divine mysteries were made available in writing.

One of the most extensive of these mystical records is the Hebrew Book of Enoch (III Enoch). It is a compilation of diverse documents, probably put together in the early Gaonic period.[17]

Only the opening chapters constitute the Book of Enoch. In this writing, the glorification of the ancient worthy is carried to incredible extremes. In the Ethiopic Enoch, as we saw, Enoch was a great seer whom the fallen angels chose as their advocate. In the Slavonic Enoch-book, he was transformed into an angel even before he was finally taken from earth. But according to the Hebrew account, Enoch became Metatron, the greatest of all angels. He was given dominion and power over all the heavenly hosts, loaded with honors and called by God "the lesser YHWH." [18] This is close to blasphemy, since YHWH is the "explicit" name of God, a name too sacred for human utterance.

The Babylonian Gemara refers a number of times to Metatron, the great angel, "whose name is the same as his Master's." [19] But there is no hint in the Talmud that Metatron was formerly Enoch. This notion must have been developing during talmudic times; and we can readily understand why the rabbis said so little about Enoch, and that little derogatory.

Enoch, however, did not get all this prestige without opposition. When God proposed to make him the celestial majordomo, three angels objected: their dignity would be compromised were they subordinate to a former mortal. These angels were named Uzza, Azza, and Azzael: familiar names indeed! But in this document they are not rebels: they are respectable, if class-conscious, members of the heavenly household. God replies to them by insisting that Enoch-Metatron is his favorite. He calls him *naar*, lad, as a term of affection, because he is younger than the primeval angels; but he is not inferior to them. [20]

Inserted into this account is one that contradicts it. The generation of Enosh (four generations, by the way, before Enoch) were a wicked lot. They caused the sun, moon and stars to descend from the sky in order to make them objects of worship. The feat was done by witchcraft, which the evil generation learned from Uzza, Azza and Azziel. [21] Here the rebel angels play their conventional role. The two stories cannot be reconciled and have no connection.

Another insertion is the story, taken from the Talmud, that Metatron unwittingly caused the ruin of Elisha ben Abuya, the famous apostate. For Elisha confused Metatron with his Master and thus was led to heresy and blasphemy. Thereupon Metatron was subjected to flogging with lashes of fire. This legend was added, according to Odeberg, by a scribe who wished to limit in some measure the supernatural glamour of the translated Enoch. [22]

All the angels fear Enoch-Metatron, even Samael, the chief of the accusers (*mastinim*), the greatest of the guardian angels of the nations. [23] In a later section of the work, Samael is specifically identified as the heavenly representative of Rome, as Dobiel is the prince of Persia. Each day Satan (here not identical with Samael) confers with the guardian angels of the Gentiles, and together they draw up memoranda of Israel's sinfulness. Satan gives the accusations to the seraphim for transmission to God, that Israel may be exterminated. But the angels know God does not wish His people destroyed; so they burn the indictments. That is why they are called seraphim, burners! [24]

It can be seen that the outlook of the Hebrew Enoch (and the same applies to the other mystical writings of the period) is essentially monistic. That is why it appears inaccurate to speak of Jewish Gnosticism. The ultimate connection of this mysticism with Gnostic trends is undeniable; but the radical dualism of the Gnostic sects is so transformed as to be hardly even vestigial. Enoch-Metatron is no demiurge: he is just a much decorated servant. Satan and the guardian angels of the heathen world confine their activity to making charges against Israel, which is their legitimate province.

There is a whole series of writings which describe the mystical progress of the soul through the different chambers (*hekalot*) of heaven until it finally arrives at the divine throne. Much of this material is still buried in manuscript, and what is available has not been adequately edited. For the present, we limit ourselves to the work called *Hekalot Rabbati* (The Larger Treatise on the Chambers). According to Prof. Gerhard Scholem, the outstanding authority on Jewish mysticism, this work was completed in the sixth century, but some of its components are earlier.[25]

The spirit of the entire booklet is monistic. The mystical pilgrim knows only the Most High God and the innumerable angels who surround His Throne and who have no function except to increase God's glory. Dr. Scholem has pointed out that the demons who lurk in the way of the Gnostic to destroy him, and who must be overcome by pronouncing magical charms, are transformed in the *Hekalot* into mere gatekeepers appointed by God to keep out the unworthy.[26] Metatron appears but once in this work; though many names are applied to him, that of "YHWH the Lesser" is significantly missing.[27]

Only in one section of the book do demonic forces appear; and this section is plainly from a separate source. For it is concerned not with timeless contemplation, but with history—albeit history in legendary form. It tells of a terrible Thursday when word came from Rome that four great scholars and eight thousand disciples had been arrested. R. Nehuniah ben Hakanah ascended to heaven and learned that Ten Martyrs had been given into the power of Samael. But through their immolation, a horrible fate would ultimately come upon Rome. Samael agreed to this condition and eagerly wrote it down. When R. Nehuniah returned to earth with the news, the imprisoned rabbis did not consider death by torture too great a price to pay if the downfall of wicked Rome was thereby assured; and they held a festal celebration. Then, by a heavenly miracle, Rabbi Hanina ben Teradyon (one of those marked for execution) was placed on the throne of Caesar Lupinus, while the latter died a felon's death. Thus R. Hanina was enabled to execute all the foes of Israel.[28]

Note that while the death of the Ten Martyrs was to be consummated by Samael, the guardian angel of Rome, it was approved by God and His court. In a striking passage, God answers the plaints of Israel by admitting that He has been unduly severe in His judgments upon them. The mystics evidently preferred to ascribe human fallibility to God rather than suggest that His power is limited by Satanic opposition.[29]

The legend of the Ten Martyrs, alluded to above, is told at length in a number of special writings.[30] It deals with famous tannaim who did indeed die as martyrs at the hands of the Romans; in the legend they all die at the same time and for the same extraordinary reason. Their death is to atone for the guilt of the ten sons of Jacob who kidnapped Joseph and sold him into slavery. The wicked Roman king uses this charge as a mere pretext to destroy the Jewish leaders; but God and His court consider the decree valid. Throughout the centuries God's Attribute of Justice had been demanding satisfaction for the wrong done Joseph. Never before had there been in a single generation ten men as great as the ten culprits, and therefore capable of expiating their sin.

Still, the heavenly guardian of Rome, Samael, had authority to drop the complaint. God warned him, moreover, that if he insisted on pressing the charge, a horrible leprosy would be decreed on Rome. Heedless of the consequences for his own people, Samael insisted on the death of the sages. All this was learned by Rabbi Ishmael (a central figure in the mystical writings of this age) when he ascended into heaven to inquire if the decree was irrevocable. And he and his fellow-martyrs were comforted by the assurance that their sufferings would be visited upon Rome.

The reference to Samael is not found in all the versions of the story. Some of them ascribe the decree to God alone. This view appears in the touching *piyyut* recited during the Additional Service on Yom Kippur, a composition of the seventeenth century. As this poet tells the tale, Rabbi Ishmael went up to heaven and met "one robed in linen." The angel said to him: "Accept the decree upon you, O righteous and beloved ones! For I have heard 'behind the curtain' that ye are entrapped in this thing!"

Mysticism has often been associated with magic, though they are in fact quite different. The aim of mysticism is spiritual bliss; that of magic, control over the material world. Yet the two are often intertwined. A text from our period which is more magical than mystical is the still unpublished *Habdalah of Rabbi Akiba*.[31] The booklet is an expansion of the traditional *habdalah*, the ceremony for the outgoing of the Sabbath. The added material consists of formulae and imprecations to ward off various evils— forgetfulness of the Torah, evil spirits and, especially, magicians, against whom our exorcist waxes quite violent. The devices include prayers in the conventional style; they also include arbitrary and magical procedures. The first word of the *Shema* is recited, then the first word of Psalm 91, then the second word of the respective passages, and so on.[32] Angelic names are also used, and that of Metatron is singled out for special attention.[33] For our purpose, the most important section tells of Uzza and Azzael, who revealed the secret of their Master. Their punishment was to have their noses pierced and to be suspended upon the mountains of darkness, where the sun's light never comes and no refreshing breeze ever blows upon them. May He, the passage continues, who frustrated the design of Uzza and Azzael frustrate the designs of all who rise up against us! [34]

This document reveals a tendency toward dualism more in its general character than in any specific item. It frankly recognizes a demonic area in life which must be dealt with by magical procedures. Characteristically, these superstitions are connected with Saturday night, which for some reason was through the ages a focus of such infection.[35]

CHAPTER NINETEEN

New Paths: The Later Aggada

A sharp line of demarcation cannot be drawn between the apocalyptic and mystical writings and those that are purely aggadic; but the classification is a convenient one. This chapter deals with Midrashim that depart in some respect from the older standpoints; for, as we have seen, some later Midrashim are entirely in the spirit of the classical sources.

The mystical and eschatological booklets we have been examining never attained great authority in Jewish life. A few, such as the story of the Ten Martyrs, circulated among the people but hardly acquired the dignity of Jewish classics. The rest were known only in limited circles, and remained buried in manuscript till recent years. The same is true of most of the aggadic documents we shall consider now. They include short accounts of single episodes, such as the Story of Abraham and Nimrod, and the Passing of Moses. There are also some larger collections—Sefer haYashar and the Chronicles of Yerahmeel—compiled in the latter part of the Middle Ages. Such books made pleasant reading for the masses, but did not profoundly affect the development of Judaism.

The one notable exception bears the name Pirke d'R. Eliezer. This extensive Midrash contains much standard rabbinic aggada and is dotted with the names of the great talmudic teachers. But these ascriptions are not reliable; the author (who lived in the eighth or ninth century) scattered famous names through his book to lend it authority. The book itself is, to quote Dr. Gerald Friedlander, "polemical and unorthodox—polemical in opposing doctrines and traditions current in certain circles in former times, unorthodox in revealing certain mysteries." [1] It contains numerous parallels to the old pseudepigraphs and the Church Fathers, while departing in some instances from talmudic teachings.

But despite its slightly heretical tone, the book acquired great influence, since it bore the honored name of R. Eliezer the Great. The Palestinian Targumim, the late Midrashim, the medieval commentators on the Bible, the cabalists draw constantly upon it. Even Maimonides, the great rationalist, who disposes cavalierly of the mystical literature, quotes some bizarre aggadot of R. Eliezer with the remark that they are to be understood as allegories. Material from this source is therefore of special importance.

SINFUL ANGELS. We have already cited a seventh century Midrash which mentions that Azza and Azzael, though of fiery substance, sinned when they descended to earth. This document had been written before Moslem influence could have been felt in Israel— the notion that there were only two sinful angels was apparently familiar to the Jews before the Mohammedans told the story of Harut and Marut. Indeed, the one cryptic reference in the Talmud to Azza and Azzael does not suggest that they had any companions in crime; perhaps the tendency to limit the number of apostate angels was very old.[2]

The later aggadot occasionally mention our story. When God summoned the soul of Moses, it protested at being removed from the body of one so continent and pure, whereas "Azza and Azzael, two angels, descended from the nearness of Thy *Shekinah* on high and desired the daughters of earth; and they corrupted their way till Thou didst suspend them 'twixt earth and firmament."[3]

The Palestinian Targum to the Pentateuch (Targum Pseudo-Jonathan) consists of an ancient core, with numerous embellishments, some of the latter very late. In Gen. 6.2, *b'ne Elohim* is rendered "sons of the chiefs," just as in the standard Targum. But in verse 4, the words "the Nefilim were in the earth in those days" are paraphrased: "Shemhazai and Azzael fell from heaven and were on the earth in those days"—obviously a later addition.[4]

Seder Eliahu Zuta is a midrashic work, with an obscure history which we need not discuss for the sake of one brief excerpt. The passage concerns the attempt of Nimrod to destroy Abraham in a fiery furnace, and of God's decision to descend and save His faithful servant. The angels doubted the wisdom of this; for, they argued, Adam had been greatly blessed by God, and he had transgressed. God replied: "What, then, did Azza and Uzzi and Azzael, of your kind? They descended to earth, lusted after the daughters of man, led them to sin and taught them witchcraft by which they brought down the sun and moon, the work of My hands!" Abraham, however, had given proof of his fidelity to God's law.[5]

Aggadat Bereshit is a late Midrash to Genesis composed largely of standard material. The Oxford manuscript of this work has an opening chapter not found in the old prints and first published by Salomon Buber. Here we find two interpretations of Genesis 6, both of which depart from the classical tradition of the rabbis. One holds that the "sons of God" and the Nefilim (their identity is assumed) were the descendants of Cain, distinguished for their superior beauty and their ruthlessness. This seems to be a confused echo of the tale, long cherished in Christian circles, that the "sons of God" were Sethites who married the shameless daughters of Cain.

The other interpretation states that the "sons of God" were Uzza and Uzzael, who dwelt in the firmament and brought themselves down to earth for testing. For they had expressed their contempt for sinful man and had been stung when God replied: Were you on earth, like the sons of man, and were you to see their beautiful women, the evil inclination would enter you and cause you to sin. So they descended to earth; but when they beheld the beauty of the daughters of men, they sought to return to heaven, saying: Lord of the world! We have had enough of this trial. He, however, replied: Ye are already defiled and cannot become pure again. (This seems to mean that the angels were contaminated merely by gazing on women.) Our Midrash identifies Uzza and Uzzael as the Nefilim. They are suspended by a chain of iron upon the mountains of darkness. But they still instruct in witchcraft those who chose to defile themselves thereby.[6] This is perhaps the oldest Hebrew source which states that the angels could not return to heaven after being sullied by desire—a notion first suggested by one of the Church Fathers and held also by some of the Moslems. From the latter, apparently, comes the view that even after their imprisonment the fallen angels continue to teach sorcery.

The most elaborate of all the Hebrew versions is a Midrash preserved in several medieval sources.[7] Asked the meaning of Azazel, R. Joseph told how God was disappointed with the sinfulness of mankind and how Shemhazai and Azzael reminded Him that they had predicted man's wickedness in advance. They, however, were sure that they were proof against all worldly temptation and descended to earth for testing. At once they were overwhelmed by desire for the daughters of men. Shemhazai made his addresses to a beautiful woman named Istahar. But she would not yield to him until he should disclose the Explicit Name by the use of which he could fly up to heaven. At length her lover revealed the secret; whereupon Istahar escaped from his arms, pronounced the name and went up on high, where God rewarded her by placing her among the Pleiades. But the angels consoled themselves by marrying other women and begot giant sons; those of Shemhazai were named Hiva and Hiyya. Azzael became an authority on the dyes and cosmetics women use to make themselves alluring. But the Deluge was imminent and Metatron was sent to warn Shemhazai that punishment would soon come. The angel was greatly distressed for the sake of his children; their great stature might enable them to escape drowning, but the desolation of the Flood would leave them without food to satisfy their enormous appetite. One night Hiva and Hiyya dreamt similar dreams portending the destruction of all flesh save Noah and his family. They told the dreams to their father, who offered them strange consolation in the moment of doom. Their names would be immortal. For when in the future men should work together, heaving weights and the like, they would shout: Hiyya! Hiva! Shemhazai, repentant, hanged himself head downward between heaven and earth; and he is there still. But Azzael was incorrigible. He still leads men astray through the dyed garments of women. And he is identical with Azazel to whom the scapegoat is sent on Yom Kippur.

This Midrash has clearly drawn on the Mohammedan traditions about Harut and Marut. But here the temptress is called by the name Istahar—which calls to mind at once Ishtar-Astarte, the famous Semitic mother-goddess. She is the better known counterpart of Zuhra and Anahit. Our author either had access to written sources unknown to us, or more likely he drew upon mythical traditions still current among the people of his time.[8] But he combines them with other elements peculiar to the Jewish tradition and adds new items of his own. Professor Spiegel has pointed out, indeed, that one of the Phoenician deities mentioned in the Ras Shamra texts is sometimes called Heyyin; and according to Sanchuniathon, an ancient Phoenician historian, this deity was the first to practice navigation. (Moreover he had a brother, whose name is not given.) The cry "Hiyya, Hiyya," used by the sailors in hauling their boats in or out of the water, may have been in the first instance a sort of invocation to the patron deity of seafaring.[9] This is only conjecture, but it is far from implausible. The American youngster who exclaims "Jiminy!" in surprise or annoyance is quite unaware that he is calling upon Castor and Pollux, the ancient *Gemini,* who by the way were also nautical deities. So it is not improbable that faint recollections of the old Canaanite myths still persisted among the Jewish people well into the Middle Ages.

One cannot read this particular version of the story, however, without a suspicion that it is not entirely serious. The humorous touches do not seem to be accidental. One doubts that this is really meant to explain the Yom Kippur ritual. The atmosphere of grimness and terror which once surrounded the story of the fallen angels has evaporated; little more remains than an amusing folk tale.

We have postponed the version of Pirke d'R. Eliezer till now, not because it is the latest—it is not—but because it is not in line with the usual development of our myth in later Jewish literature. This development, we have seen, knows only two or three fallen angels, whose names vary slightly from source to source. But the Pirke d'R. Eliezer, which takes the matter quite seriously and devotes a whole chapter to it, tells of a large group of fallen angels. No proper names, however, are given.

The account opens with the startling statement that Cain was not of Adam's seed. (In another passage, the work states plainly that Samael was Cain's father, while Adam begot Abel.) The righteous descended from Seth; Cain was the progenitor of the wicked. This reminds us of the Christian view that "the sons of God" were Sethites and the "daughters of men" were Cainites; but the Midrash makes different use of the notion. The shameless Cainite women, strutting about naked, with painted eyes, caused the angels to sin. Now angels are of flame. How then could they have consorted with mortal women without burning their mates? The reply is: When the angels fell from their holy estate, they suffered a reduction in stature and strength, and their fiery substance was transmuted into earthy material. From the union of

angels and mortals were born giant offspring—the Anakim—
proud and violent.[10]

When the Flood threatened, the giants were confident that
they would escape. Their heads would rise above any level rain-
fall might produce, and their enormous feet would hold back
water rising from below the earth. But God heated the waters of
the abyss until the feet of the giants were scalded; and so they
met their doom. This episode is unique; perhaps it is a reminis-
cence of the hot springs in the Book of Enoch.[11]

The myth so long suppressed by the rabbis thus came to light
in the Middle Ages. It had, indeed, never been forgotten. But it
could now be tolerated even publicly because it was no longer
dangerous. Only the author of the Chapters of R. Eliezer seems
to take it seriously, and even to him the fall of the angels is not
one of the major events of history, certainly not the basic cause
of evil in the world. The other medieval writers treat the tale as
a minor episode, and the fullest version has a certain flavor of
comedy. The cosmic significance is gone.

Nevertheless, the standard non-mythical explanation of Genesis
6 was not displaced. We shall find the Bible commentators and
philosophers adhering to it; so did many aggadists. Thus the late
work, Sefer haYashar, which includes many untraditional legends,
paraphrases Genesis 6.2: "Their judges and officers went unto all
the daughters of men, and took them wives by force—even from
their husbands—of all whom they desired." [12] The Chronicles of
Yerahmeel are a heterogeneous compilation. One chapter contains the long legend of Shemhazai and Azzael we have sum-
marized above. But another introduces into Jewish literature the
view, hitherto confined to Christian writings, that the good men
of the tribe of Seth were lured into marriage with the sinful
daughters of Cain, fell from grace and engendered the giants.[13]

THE FALL OF SATAN. Talmudic literature nowhere contains the
slightest hint that Satan is a fallen angel. He holds his position
as prosecutor by divine appointment and never was anything
else. The view of certain apocryphal writings, that Satan was an
angel who rebelled against his Master, became standard doctrine
in the Church and was later adopted by Mohammed.

In the Middle Ages, however, some Jewish writers revived the notion. Here again the most notable instance is Pirke d'R. Eliezer. (This work, by the way, always calls the Devil "Samael"; the word Satan occurs only in biblical citations.) Samael was the great prince (*sar*) in heaven. The *hayyot* had four wings and the seraphim six; but Samael had twelve. Now the angels were envious of the honor accorded by God to the newly-created man, and they were still more irritated when Adam proved his wisdom by naming the animals, a feat they could not match. Most of the angels did no more than grumble. But Samael went the length of open rebellion. Descending to earth with his followers, he looked about for an agent to encompass Adam's ruin. The cunning serpent met his requirements. Samael mounted the serpent (which in those days looked something like a camel) and directed his actions, as an evil spirit takes possession of a man and compels his obedience. The Torah cried out in warning to Samael; but the warning went unheeded.[14]

The Chapters of R. Eliezer do not follow this view consistently. In the rest of the Paradise story, Samael is not mentioned, and the snake appears to be acting on his own initiative. But before the rather detailed account of the serpent's punishment, we read that God cast down Samael and his troop from their holy place in heaven. As Samael fell, he seized Michael by the wing and tried to drag him down too; but God intervened to save the archangel.[15]

Another passage in this remarkable work states that "he who rode on the serpent" had relations with Eve and became the father of Cain. This is another radical departure. The old aggada knew indeed of sexual contact between Eve and the serpent, but did not explicitly identify the latter with Satan; moreover, the consequence of this contact was the defilement of all Eve's posterity, but not the engendering of particular offspring. The new account, which is taken up by many later writers, makes Cain and his family more demonic than human.[16]

But this view of the Devil is rare in pre-cabalistic literature. An aggadic manuscript which Dr. Schechter brought to light connects Satan's fall, not with Adam, but with Job. Satan appeared before God and, admitting that Job was extraordinarily devout, undertook to turn his heart away from piety. But his repeated efforts failed. Thereupon God rebuked Satan (Zech.

3.2) and scornfully cast him out of heaven, as it is said, "Ye shall fall as one of the princes" (Ps. 82.7). This is the first—and almost the only—instance in Jewish literature which sees in Psalm 82 a reference to superhuman malefactors. Generally this Psalm is interpreted as condemning human kings, or Adam, or Israel in the desert.[17] In this aggada, also, Satan is not a good angel prior to his fall; he is the usual tempter and accuser, and he is cast out for excess of zeal in his job.

Rabbi Moses haDarshan lived at Narbonne, in France, during the eleventh century. He compiled an extensive collection of aggadot to the Book of Genesis. Among them is the following: When God had created Adam, He summoned the angels to worship His new creation, and the angels came to obey. Satan was the greatest of the angels in heaven, and he protested against the order that he, who had been created out of the radiance of the *Shekinah,* should bow before one formed from the dust of the earth. God replied that this earthly creature had superior wisdom and could give more appropriate names to the animals than could Satan. Satan was eager to be put to the test; but when he was faced with the different creatures, could not give them a name. Adam was able to perform this feat, though he profited by hints which God graciously gave him. Thereupon Satan cried out so loudly that his complaint was audible even in heaven. When asked the reason for his lament, he said: "Why should I not cry out, since Thou hast formed me from Thy *Shekinah* and hast formed man from the dust of the earth, yet hast given him such wisdom and discernment!" God replied: "O destructive Satan, why art thou astonished? Now man shall behold his remotest descendants and shall give names to them all!" [18]

So far our text as preserved in a manuscript abridgement of Rabbi Moses' work. But a famous Spanish monk, Raymundo Martini, in his learned treatise against Judaism, called *Pugio Fidei* (The Dagger of Faith), quotes a different version which is briefer and concludes with the words: "When Satan would not worship (man) and would not hearken to the words of the Holy One (blessed be He!), He thrust him out of heaven, and he became Satan; and concerning him Isaiah (14.12) says: 'How art thou fallen from heaven, O day star, son of the morning!' " [19]

Obviously these aggadot reflect Christian and Moslem influence. Even though the stories may have originated among

Jews, they had long vanished from Jewish belief and thought
and were now reintroduced from the outside.

SATAN'S MALICE. In most of the later aggadot, Satan continues to
play his traditional role of tempter and accuser; but his character
is somewhat blacker. His redeeming traits have vanished, and he
is gleeful when he can stir up trouble.

A legend to which there is no exact parallel in early writings
deals with Enosh whose generation, according to an old tradition,
was the first to practice idolatry. Enosh made an idol and
breathed upon it, whereupon Satan entered the image and caused
it to move. Thus the people were led to believe that it was indeed
a divinity.[20] A similar story in the Chapters of R. Eliezer tells
that when Israel made the Golden Calf, Samael entered the
image and caused it to bleat.[21] In such instances, he does not go
far beyond his old occupation of *agent provocateur*.

Nor was Satan utterly wicked when he helped Noah plant a
vineyard and fertilized the soil with the blood of a lamb, a lion,
a monkey and a pig. (That is why men behave like these animals
in the successive stages of intoxication.) This story goes far back
into oriental folklore; in Jewish literature it appears in only a
few late sources.[22]

But Abraham roused the worst of Satan's malice. Very old is the
story of Abraham's struggle with Nimrod and his deliverance by
God from a fiery furnace. One of the medieval versions of this tale
—which seems to have been translated from the Arabic—gives
prominence to Satan. He first advised Nimrod to arrest Abraham.
Then, when the heat of the furnace killed the executioners before
they could cast their victim into it, Satan devised a catapult to
hurl Abraham into the flames. Just before the sentence was to be
carried out, the tempter assumed a human form and urged Abraham to worship Nimrod and save his life. But the patriarch saw
through the disguise and rebuked his opponent.[23]

We have seen in the earlier Midrash that the command for
the sacrifice of Isaac resulted from a complaint that Abraham was
lax in his devotion to God; but there is some uncertainty as to
whether Satan or the angels or the Justice of God made the
charge. There is similar disagreement in the later sources.[24] According to Sefer haYashar, Satan was the plaintiff. In this single
episode, the Accuser plays a prominent role; throughout the rest

of Sefer haYashar, Satan is not even mentioned! There seems to be no logical explanation of this odd phenomenon.

Sefer haYashar describes the heavenly assize in terms obviously borrowed from the Book of Job. Satan expresses his opinion that men are pious only when they have a material benefit in view; once they get what they want, they forget God and His goodness. The case of Abraham proves this: before Isaac was born, he built many altars; but since he has a son, he has not offered a sacrifice, not even at the great feast he made when Isaac was weaned. The summons to Abraham follows immediately.[25]

Satan tries to direct events so that his contention will be proved. He attempts to dissuade Abraham and Isaac from their resolve; he changes himself into a stream to keep them from reaching Mount Moriah. (These events are known to the classic Midrash, but in less elaborate form.) [26]

But the malevolence of Satan is more clearly revealed when Abraham has demonstrated his fidelity. Satan tries to lead astray the ram that is caught in the thicket, in the hope that Abraham will not be able to catch it, and will be forced to sacrifice his son.[27] Since Satan has already lost his case, this is sheer vindictiveness. Even worse was his device to cause Sarah's death. According to Pirke d'R. Eliezer, she died of horror when Samael reported that Isaac had been slaughtered. The Sefer haYashar adds a more delicate psychological touch. After crushing Sarah with grief, Satan admitted that his story was untrue and that Isaac was really alive—and Sarah expired from excess of joy.[28]

The death of Moses is the subject of several aggadic writings. These tell at length of a struggle between Moses and the Angel of Death, who is here called Samael. These Midrashim display a curious uncertainty as to whether this Samael is a faithful servant of God or an evil being.

God first ordered Michael, Gabriel and Zanzagiel to fetch the soul of Moses; but they declined. Gabriel felt himself too feeble; Michael wept silently; Zanzagiel, the Angel of the Torah, pointed out that Moses had been his pupil, and he hadn't the heart to take away his life. But Samael gleefully accepted the commission when it was offered to him. He confronted Moses wrathfully; but the lawgiver refused to surrender his soul and called Samael "wicked one." (Yet Samael protested that he was sent by "Him who created the worlds and the souls; and into my hands are delivered all souls since Creation.") Terrified by Moses, Samael returned to God and confessed that he could not deal with the situation. God replied: "Thou wicked one! From the fire of Gehenna wast thou created, and to the fire of Gehenna shalt thou return! At first thou wentest forth from My presence in great glee; now that thou hast seen his grandeur, thou art returned in shame. Go, fetch Me his soul!" But on the second attempt, Samael again proved to be no match for Moses; he received a drubbing with the heavenly staff, and his eyes were blinded by the radiance of Moses' face. At length Moses prayed that he might not fall into the hands of Samael, and he surrendered his soul to God Himself.[29] In another form of this legend, Satan prevented Elazar, the nephew of Moses, from pleading for his uncle's life. What mean you, said Satan, by pushing aside the words of the Lord? The people prayed that the lawgiver might be spared to them; but ministering angels snatched the prayers away. Then a great angel named Lahash (Is. 26.16) tried to lay these intercessions before God, whereat Samael bound him with fiery chains, flogged him with seventy stripes of fire and expelled him from the divine presence.

Thus far he is the stern executor of God's will; but later on he appears as a malicious demon, gloating over Moses' approaching end, while Michael weeps in impotence. "Among all the accusers (*mastinim*) there is none like Samael the wicked." In the struggle with Moses, the latter even denied that Samael is a creature of God. At this, not unreasonably, Samael was indignant; but he still could not take away the soul of Moses. He returned to God with his mission unaccomplished; but God threatened to replace him with a more competent agent, and he went back to the conflict. This time Moses was about to slay the death-angel; but a heavenly voice was heard: "Do not harm him: mankind have need of him." Moses surrendered his soul to the kiss of God; thereafter Samael made a long and fruitless search for the soul of the great prophet.[30]

A late legend tells how Satan tried to tempt R. Matya b. Heresh to sin, assuming for the purpose the guise of a woman as beautiful as Naamah the sister of Tubal Kain, "after whom the angels went astray." But the noble scholar was proof against his wiles.[31] In this story, too, Satan acts with the permission of God.

When the Torah was given to Israel—so states the Pirke d R. Eliezer—Samael complained that God had given him power over every nation but Israel. God replied that over Israel, too, he would have control on the Day of Atonement—if they put themselves in his power by sinning. That is the reason for the scapegoat—it is a sort of bribe to Azazel, here identified with Samael. In the sequel, Samael testifies that Israel on Yom Kippur are sinless and pure as the angels. This passage strangely contradicts the usual view of the aggada, that it is precisely on Yom Kippur that Satan has *no* power over Israel.[32]

SAMAEL AS PRINCE OF ROME. We have already seen instances where the belief in the heavenly patrons of the Gentiles is combined with the belief in Satan as the arch-fiend. Satan-Samael thus becomes the patron angel of Edom, that is, Rome. Just as the Armilus legend suggests that the Roman power is the Antichrist, so this other fusion of originally independent myths makes Rome the earthly representative of all the powers of evil, and her *sar* their heavenly embodiment.[33]

The earliest expression of this view in aggadic literature is found in the printed Tanhuma, which states that the "man" who wrestled with Jacob was Samael, the Prince of Edom.[34] While the material of the Tanhuma is drawn largely from classical sources, it was not redacted till the Gaonic period. In fact, there are a number of divergent forms of the Midrash Tanhuma of which the printed version is not the earliest; and these versions occasionally reveal later influences.[35] Such influences account for the identification of Samael as guardian angel of Rome; for in talmudic literature, Samael is a name of Satan and has a cosmic rather than a national significance.[36]

This new outlook explains several passages in the late Midrash Abkir. When Jacob and Esau, still unborn, struggled within the body of their mother, Samael sought to kill Jacob. Michael rushed to the rescue and was about to burn Samael to nothingness when God intervened and subjected them both to legal discipline.[37] Samael here is undoubtedly the patron angel of Esau; for Midrash Abkir regularly calls the tempter Satan.

Likewise at the Red Sea, Samael protested against the deliverance of Israel, on the ground that they had worshipped idols while in Egypt. Moreover, he roused the Prince of the Sea to such a rage that the latter tried to drown the Israelites. (Here, apparently, the Satanic role of accuser is combined with the zeal of the angel of Edom attacking the enemies of his people.) But God answered him: Arrant fool! Did they worship idols deliberately? Was it not through servitude and mental confusion that they did so? Thou judgest inadvertent sin as though it were intentional, and what was done under duress as though it were voluntary. Thereupon the Prince of the Sea turned upon the Egyptians the wrath he had been directing against Israel.[38] Elsewhere, as we shall see at once, Abkir ascribes the attack on Israel at the Sea to Uzza, the angelic patron of Egypt.

UZZA THE PATRON ANGEL OF EGYPT. In the Book of Jubilees, Mastema, a cosmic demon, makes desperate efforts to prevent the redemption of Israel from Egypt, so that God and the angels must restrain him. In rabbinic aggada, the national angel of Egypt plays this role.[39] The episode receives its greatest elaboration in the Midrash Abkir.[40] The *sar* of Egypt was named Uzza—another case of the tendency to identify the authors of cosmic wickedness with the princes of the Gentiles. Uzza summoned Michael, the representative of Israel, to judgment before God. He argued that God had condemned Israel to four hundred years of servitude in Egypt (Gen. 15.13); this term had not yet expired, and Israel should be brought back in order to complete it. Michael was unable to answer his argument; but God pointed out that the verse in Genesis makes no mention of Egypt: it simply says that Abraham's descendants shall be slaves in "a land not theirs." Moreover, the period of slavery should be reckoned from the date of Isaac's birth and is therefore ended. God now determined to drown the Egyptians; but Uzza protested. It is unjust, he argued, to impose a capital sentence for mere enslavement, especially since Israel had been compensated for their labors by the treasure they took out of Egypt. Thereupon God assembled His heavenly court and laid the case before them, dwelling at length on the insolence and cruelty of Pharaoh. The angels all agreed that the sentence on the Egyptians was a just one. But Uzza still did not give up. He admitted that his people were guilty and begged God to be merciful to them. This plea might have been successful had not Gabriel displayed one of the bricks made by Israel in Egypt; and this evidence of Egyptian cruelty led God to act with unswerving justice.

In a variant of this legend found in the same source, the guardian angel of Egypt is not given a proper name. His plea for mercy toward his people is supported by all the angels in council. Thereupon Michael summons Gabriel, who lays before God a brick in which an Israelite infant had been embedded, and the Attribute of Justice urges God to punish the Egyptians.[41]

The forensic form of this tale is noteworthy. Uzza, though partisan, does no more than any attorney, assigned to defend a criminal, deems proper. The element of angelic rebellion is altogether missing.

THE GUARDIAN ANGELS OF THE NATIONS. There are also more general references to the guardian angels. Here, too, Abkir is more dramatic and interesting than the other works. It tells that the princes of the Gentiles sought to kill Jacob as he slept at Beth-El. They were like courtiers, resentful because a commoner has constant access to the king. "This one," they said, "is destined to inherit the world and cause the kingdoms to pass away; let us kill him!" And Jacob survived only by the special protection of God.[42] An older aggada had told that the angels sought to injure Jacob while he slept, because his face resembled the human face on the heavenly chariot and they were indignant that a mortal should receive such honors. This earlier story reflects the belief that angels in general are neither very intelligent nor unselfish.[43] As refashioned in Abkir, the story stresses the antagonism of the angelic patrons of the Gentiles to the people of Israel.

Incidentally, Abkir explains in a novel way how Michael became Israel's guardian. Some of the old aggadists had held that Michael was the angel who wrestled with Jacob at the Jabbok. Abkir adopts this and adds that, to compensate for the injury he had inflicted on the patriarch during their struggle, Michael was assigned thenceforth to care for him and his descendants.[44]

The accounts of the national angels do not always emphasize their hostility to Israel. A medieval Midrash relates that, when God created the seventy national princes, each wanted to be the patron of Israel, until it was decided by lot that the Jews are the peculiar concern of God—this, oddly enough, in a work which on a preceding page speaks of Michael as the advocate and spokesman of Israel.[45] A mystical booklet represents the patrons of the Gentiles as assembling before God to hymn his praise.[46]

A more rationalistic Midrash seeks to emphasize the balance in creation. God provided each nation with a guardian angel and gave Israel as its protectors Michael and Gabriel. When Israel sins, the patrons of the Gentiles make accusation before God. Then Michael and Gabriel plead for their people, and so God is enabled to show them mercy and reduce the power of the other *sarim*.[47]

A medieval version of the Hanukkah story uses this concept in a unique manner. When the Jews and Greeks joined battle, God seized the seventy guardian angels of the Gentiles, pierced them with an awl of fire and commanded them to slay their "relatives." If one of them escapes, He warned the angels, your life will be in place of theirs. So the guardian angels of the heathen perforce turned the weapons hurled by the Greeks back into the hearts of those who cast them; and pillaging the Greeks, they deposited the spoil in Jewish homes.[48]

ENOCH. Outside the specifically mystic literature, medieval Jewry does not display much interest in Enoch. The Chapters of R. Eliezer mention him with respect as one who transmitted the secrets of the calendar and the miraculous staff from Adam to Noah; and a lesser work mentions him as the heir of the wondrous garments of Adam.[49] Another document states that Enoch walked in the ways of heaven; to him may be applied the Scriptural words: "Happy is the man whom Thou choosest and bringest near, that he may dwell in Thy courts" (Ps. 65.5). The text adds that God took Enoch and hid him (*genazo*)—language suggesting that God took Enoch because of his superior piety, not, as early aggadists held, because of his unstable character.[50] The Alphabet of R. Akiba, which is really a mystical work of a mild sort, makes several references to Enoch-Metatron. The most interesting is the statement: when Moses stood against God to protect the people from the plague, he did something surpassing the power even of Metatron.[51]

LILITH. About the tenth century, a work of popular wisdom was composed, bearing the name The Alphabet of Ben Sira. A mixture of proverbs and tales illustrating them, it quotes a few authentic lines from The Wisdom of Ben Sira, the apocryphal book also called Ecclesiasticus. Somewhat later another Alphabet of Ben Sira appeared. Here the moralizing tendency is almost wholly absent; it is an extraordinary compilation of folk tales, not all of them edifying. In this work we encounter for the first time the story of Lilith, Adam's demon wife, which has passed into the European literary tradition.

The name Lilith has a very ancient history. A spirit or demon bearing this title appears in Assyro-Babylonian texts. A Bible passage, describing a scene of utter desolation, says "Lilith shall repose there" (Is. 34.14). The Bible translators generally translate Lilith by "the night-monster," on the supposition that the name is derived from *layil*, "night"—an etymology probably incorrect. The Talmud too mentions a female demon named Lilith and a whole class of spirits called *lilin*. It tells also that Adam and Eve once had demon lovers.[52]

Nevertheless, the tale in the second Alphabet of Ben Sira is altogether new. When God perceived that it was not good for man to be alone, He first created a mate for Adam out of the dust of the earth. But the two did not get on at all; for Lilith had no feminine submissiveness about her, since her origin was identical with Adam's. She soon left him and, by pronouncing the Ineffable Name, flew far away. Adam complained to God, Who despatched three angels to force her to return. They found her among the billows of the Red Sea and threatened to drown her, especially when she declared her intention of molesting infants during the early days of their lives. But finally they let her go on this condition: if children were protected by an amulet bearing the names or pictures of the three angels, she would do them no harm. She had further to accept the penalty, imposed by God when she refused to return to Adam, that a hundred of her own children should die every day.[53]

This legend was disseminated more widely among Jewish readers and students by the great cabalistic masterpiece, the Zohar; and the use of amulets to protect babies against Lilith became a regular feature of Jewish life. It is remarkable that a tale originating in so obscure a source should have become so well known to Christians. Johannes Buxtorf, a Christian Hebraist of the 17th century, is said to have introduced the story to the European public.[54] Goethe used it in *Faust;* Browning, in a dramatic lyric,

Adam, Lilith, and Eve. It was to be expected that when John Erskine came to disclose the private life of Adam and Eve, Lilith should play a great role in the primordial domestic drama. Further literary allusions could readily be supplied. But for the history of Judaism, the Lilith story is of little importance. It is simply an illustration of that old belief in demons which survived through the centuries and was accorded a certain tolerance without being allowed to undermine the absoluteness of Jewish monotheism.

SUMMING UP. In reviewing the literature that lies between the close of the Talmud and the later Middle Ages, one is struck by the extent to which the talmudic resistance to dualism is maintained. The silence regarding fallen angels is broken; but a myth which dealt with the destiny of the world and mankind has now shrunk to a mere folk tale. The myriads of fallen angels are reduced to two rather commonplace malefactors. And the sinfulness of Shemhazai and Azzael is connected only in a small degree with the existence of sin and evil among mankind.

Satan occasionally takes on a darker and more sinister character than the talmudic rabbis ascribed to him; but for the most part he retains his traditional role of tempter and accuser under God's direction. Only in the Chapters of R. Eliezer does he appear as a great angel who rebelled against God and encompassed the fall of man. This work (which also gives more weight to the myth of the angels who married mortal women) was indeed to have exceptional influence, but the fullness of this influence came about only with the efflorescence of the Cabala.

There is a marked tendency in this period to fuse the concept of the Devil with that of the wicked angel-princes of the Gentiles. This tendency indicates how far removed the medieval aggadists were from the circumstances out of which these originally separate conceptions emerged. Enoch, neglected and disparaged by the rabbis, becomes a cosmic figure in certain mystical circles; but he does not attain any great stature in medieval aggada. Armilus, the Jewish version of the Antichrist, appears repeatedly in late apocalypses and a few other writings; but he does not appear to have bulked large in the consciousness of the Jewish people.

The medieval sources speak of demons, of punitive and destructive angels, of the functionaries of hell. These beings, how-ever, are all creatures and agents of God, not rebels against Him. The successors of the talmudic teachers maintained without essential change the monistic position of their forebears. But they were less stringent about excluding myths, the dualistic charac-ter of which had been obscured with the passing of centuries.

PART SIX

Medieval Judaism

CHAPTER TWENTY

The Rationalists

After a long journey on dim and misty paths, we emerge into clear daylight. The last two chapters dealt with writings that occupy a marginal place within Judaism; their origin is obscure; their influence, with a few exceptions, was limited. From them we now turn to famous works by illustrious men of Israel.

Some explanation and even apology must be given for the title of this chapter.

During the Middle Ages, Jewish writers began to adopt new methods. While heterogeneous and anonymous compilations—somewhat like the Talmud and Midrashim—continued to appear, we find an increasing number of systematic works on specific topics by individual authors. Henceforth we need not survey an entire literature to see if it contains something for our purpose.

We can disregard a vast body of secular Hebrew writings—poetry and prose, scientific, grammatical and literary treatises. Nor need we examine the legal codes, commentaries and responsa.

Of non-legal religious writings, we set aside a large group—works on mysticism—for treatment in future chapters. Here we shall examine literature in which cabalistic elements are slight or altogether absent.

These "rationalistic" works fall into two general classes. There was a distinguished group of Jewish thinkers during the Middle Ages who are properly called rationalists. They affirmed (more or less absolutely) the supremacy of reason, which they identified rather closely with the logical methods and the philosophic outlook of their age. They were convinced also that Judaism teaches nothing repugnant to reason; and hence they were under the necessity of reinterpreting such biblical and talmudic passages as, taken literally, contradict the laws of science or the dicta of philosophy. In this group are numbered some of the greatest names in Jewish history—R. Saadia Gaon and R. Moses ben Maimon.

But there is another group of sages whom we venture to include among the rationalists. They are the scholars who adhered unphilosophically but very accurately to the teachings of the Bible and of tradition. The outstanding representative of this trend is Rashi, the great commentator on the Bible and Talmud. He and his confreres were insensitive to the problems that troubled the philosophers. Had they been told that the plain sense of the Bible contradicts the findings of logic, they would have concluded simply that the logicians were mistaken. But they studied the authoritative texts with keen analytical intelligence; and they often understood the classic sources better than the philosophic exegetes, who were sometimes driven to distort Jewish doctrines in order to harmonize them with the teachings of Aristotle.

Our classification is not absolute. Even such intellectualists as Saadia and Maimonides had their mystical moments; and all the rationalists were compelled at one point or another to bow before biblical and traditional authority. Abraham ibn Ezra, a brilliant intellect with moments of cynicism, was also a dabbler in the occult. Chasdai Crescas used the double-edged blade of philosophic criticism to attack philosophy and to vindicate the claims of orthodox literalism. Moses ben Nahman was a cabalist; his

Torah-commentary is dotted with cryptic allusions. But the dominant spirit of the work is traditionalist; it contains many paragraphs of rational theology, and we shall consider it in this chapter.

There is another reason why we can consider the philosophers and the traditionalists together. However these two groups may have differed on many questions, they were substantially agreed in rejecting the belief in fallen and rebel angels. The orthodox traditionalists did so because they followed the guidance of the Talmud. The philosophers did not diverge from talmudic doctrine without strong reason: in the present instance their own philosophic outlook coincided with the traditional view.

For when the philosophers discussed the problem of evil, it was in an abstract, reflective fashion. To many of these thinkers, notably Maimonides, evil is not a positive force but merely the absence of good, as darkness is the absence of light. Since evil is unreal, God—the positive Force in the universe—is not responsible for it. Other thinkers ascribe a greater measure of reality to what we call evil and admit that it comes from God; but they hold that this evil is not absolute. It has some purpose in God's universal providence. Moreover, divine reward and punishment in the next world will restore the balance that to us appears disturbed.[1]

To such thinkers, a mythological explanation of evil is not to be thought of; even to refute such a view is unnecessary. Only Hillel of Verona, in the thirteenth century, found it desirable to discuss the belief in fallen angels, in answer to Christian theologians.

The other philosophers touch on the matter only when discussing biblical or rabbinic passages that seem to refer to rebel angels or to the Devil. Our task, therefore, is to gather the comments on a few biblical sections we have repeatedly considered.

THE "SONS OF GOD." The rabbinic sources, notably the Targum, state that the "sons of God" who married the daughters of men were merely human beings of exalted social station. Some medieval Jewish exegetes depart from this slightly and hold that the "sons of God" were outstanding for physical or mental endowment and not merely for noble rank. But all the standard biblical commentators give some human explanation as the primary meaning of the phrase. The list is impressive: Saadia, Rashi,

Lekah Tob, Midrash Aggada, Joseph Bekor Shor, Ibn Ezra, Maimonides, David Kimhi, Nahmanides, Hizkuni, Bahya b. Asher, Gersonides and Abrabanel.[2] The Karaite scholars, too, though they rejected rabbinic tradition, adopted this interpretation of Genesis 6.[3]

Rashi adds the alternative explanation: "The sons of God are the sons of the heavenly princes (*sarim*) who perform the missions of God—for these also had mixed with (humanity)." Elsewhere he seems to prefer this view of the matter, for which indeed he had precedent in a few talmudic allusions and in the writings of his master, R. Moses haDarshan.[4] And R. Moses b. Nahman (Nahmanides), the cabalist, avows openly his preference for the Midrash given by R. Eliezer the Great in his Chapters and mentioned also in the Gemara. "To expound the secret of the matter," he adds, "would be too lengthy." These remarks, however, are appended to a rationalistic exposition of the passage which we shall examine in a moment.

But the other commentators eschew the mythological interpretation. Kimhi says the legend of Azza and Azzael is far fetched. Abrabanel will not accept it, even though it fits aptly the language of Genesis 6.2, and has apparent warrant in traditional sources.[5] The trouble is that the story cannot be reconciled with the entire context. How could the sin of angels occasion the moral decline and punishment of humankind? Nor is it believable that a spiritual being should become so earthy as to have relations with mortal women. The aggadot about the fallen angels, says Abrabanel, must refer to some secret doctrine; we should not take them literally, as do the Gentiles.

But this scholar, like a number of his predecessors, wishes to find some more adequate reason for the phrase "sons of God." Ibn Ezra had, indeed, offered four explanations of the term: 1) The traditional view that they were sons of the nobles. 2) They were men of holy character (cf. Deut. 14.1). 3) The sons of God were Sethites; the daughters of men were Cainites. This originally Christian interpretation had gradually become known among Jews. 4) Ibn Ezra's own view is that the men in question possessed the divine power that comes with astrological knowledge. Thus they could choose women of nativity similar to their own and beget offspring of unusual size and strength.

Nahmanides puts it this way: Adam and Eve were properly

called children of God, since they had no earthly parents. Their immediate offspring, who must have shared their physical perfection, were called by the same name. But when men began to worship idols (according to tradition, in the days of Enosh), a decline set in. The survivors of the older generation chose the more robust women for their wives; but they also consorted immorally with feebler mates. The sin became known when these puny women bore unusually large children. The latter were mighty men in comparison with average men, but fell below (*nefilim*) the stature of their fathers. This physical decline continued till the Flood.

This view seems to have been suggested by Genesis 6.3, in which God mentions the frailty of man and sets one hundred and twenty years as the limit of his life. The commentators inferred that the mixture of racial stocks led to physical degeneration. The ultra-rationalist Levi ben Gerson adopted this idea; and Abrabanel elaborated two versions of it. The second is substantially that of Nahmanides. The first, however, is concerned more with moral heredity. The Sethites yielded to lust and married women of Cainite stock, who were ethically inferior; but men should only choose wives whose background is good and who therefore give promise of bearing righteous children. In punishment, God gradually reduced their life span to one hundred and twenty years. These Sethites supposed that their children would inherit all their good qualities, as if the male principle—the form —were alone hereditary. But the children inherited also the female—material—factor, and so "fell below" their fathers.

A new type of Jewish literature in this period is the philosophic sermon. A number of Jewish preachers utilized the allegorical method in order to find abstract metaphysical truths in the pages of the Torah. Jacob Anatoli is the first of these whose writings have been preserved; and he applies his method in considerable detail and with marked ingenuity to the story of the "sons of God." He sees in this passage an account of the imposition of forms upon matter. The forms are the sons of God; the daughters of man are the two orders of material being, sensible and insensible; they are called daughters of man since the creation of the material universe has as its goal the existence of the human race. But though the production of man is the end of the creative process, man is none the less composite, and therefore mortal (Gen. 6.3). The goal of creation is not, however, the human race as such, but the best kind of human individuals. The importance of the individual is suggested by the reference to *Nefilim*. These are of two kinds: *Gibborim*, mighty men—those, namely, who achieve intellectual and moral greatness by the practice of self-control ("Who is a hero? He who conquers his passions") and the *Anshe Shem*, men of renown—those who are by nature wise and good.

Anatoli admits, with disarming frankness, his satisfaction with this original interpretation which is one of the arcana of the Torah. He knows that many scholars will consider it sheer fantasy, and he is quite ready for their abuse. For, says he, "the opinions of the commentators on this passage are untenable; and I have based myself on statements of our sainted rabbis, who declared that the 'sons of God' mentioned in this passage are angels who fell from heaven." [6] This is indeed a strange situation: an ultra-rationalist adopts the old myth, but uses it to find Aristotelian philosophy in the Bible!

Something similar is offered by Isaac Arama, the most famous of the philosophic preachers. He adopts the view that the "sons of God" were Sethites who married the daughters of Cain. But he has already explained that Cain, Abel and Seth (though he does not question their historic reality) are symbols of the three elements in the human soul—the sensual, the practical intellect, and the speculative intellect. Our episode describes allegorically the debauching of man's higher nature by lust. [7]

ENOCH. From the preceding it is clear that the medieval authorities, though they followed the talmudic tradition and generally avoided mythological interpretations, were no longer keenly aware of the old controversies and their meaning. In the same way, the association of Enoch with the fallen angels had disappeared from their minds. Rashi alone, following the old Midrash, repeats the derogatory opinion that God took Enoch from earth before his unstable virtue collapsed. This opinion is also quoted in the Midrash Aggada, but only after this laudatory statement: Jared was so called because in his days the angels descended and taught men the service of God. Enoch walked with the angels in Eden for three hundred years and learned many sciences from them, including astronomy and the computation of the calendar. At length, God rewarded him for his righteousness by translating him to heaven; and he became Metatron. "And there is a controversy between R. Akiba and his colleagues on this point." [8]

This, of course, is the view of Enoch given in mystical tradition. Other medieval scholars, however, join in the praise of Enoch; and it seems that they were influenced not so much by these mystical trends as by the plain sense of Scripture. For clearly the words "Enoch walked with God, and was not—for God took him" seem to suggest that Enoch was a man of lofty qualities, not the reverse.

Thus, Ibn Ezra says that "God took him" means that Enoch died. But, he adds, there is a hidden meaning, implied also in Ps. 49.16 and 73.24, which only the wise will comprehend. In his commentary on these Psalm-passages, however, his mood is less reticent. To be taken by God means that the human soul is united with the angelic spirit-forces, thereby attaining eternal bliss.

Kimhi, a disciple of the rationalist Maimonides, is one of Enoch's admirers. Enoch, he explains, raised himself to so high a spiritual level that God removed him from earthly life in the middle of his days, without sickness or suffering. Some of our sages held that God brought Enoch and Elijah alive into Paradise.[9]

Gersonides states that at first Enoch did not walk with God; later, he came to the recognition of his Creator through the study of nature and devoted himself to the quest of perfection. At length he attained so high a level that he was placed in Paradise.

Abrabanel quotes the unfavorable opinion of Enoch found in the Midrash; he is puzzled by it, for the biblical text hardly accords with the view of the rabbis. His own explanation is as follows: Originally Enoch was lustful, as shown by the very early age (for an antediluvian) at which he begot his first born, Methuselah. Thereafter he "walked with God," that is to say, he sought spiritual perfection. But he was still tormented by the flesh ("and begot sons and daughters"); God therefore released him from the burden of bodily desire and admitted him at once to heavenly bliss.

Thus the rationalists and traditionalists are not afraid to glorify

Enoch; while Nahmanides the Cabalist does not even comment on this episode.

AZAZEL. We have noted one early rabbinic passage which regards the Azazel-goat as a propitiatory sacrifice to Satan.[10] Usually, however, the talmudic authorities explained Azazel as the name of a place to which the scapegoat was sent. This view is maintained by Saadia (as cited by Ibn Ezra), Rashi and Lekah Tob. Samuel ibn Hofni (also quoted by Ibn Ezra) states that even the Azazel goat is offered to God.[11] But, says Ibn Ezra, this statement is superfluous: the scapegoat is not a sacrifice, for it is not slaughtered. And then he adds these cryptic words: "If you can discern the mystery that follows the word Azazel, you will know its mystery and the mystery of its name; for it has analogies in Scripture. And I will reveal part of the mystery to you by hint: you will know it when you reach thirty-three!"

A variety of explanations have been given for this remark by the supercommentators.[12] Few of these explanations attempt to account for Ibn Ezra's extreme reticence. Of the "arcana" which are mentioned elsewhere in his commentary, some deal with evidences of post-Mosaic material in the Pentateuch—where the reason for his discretion is obvious—and some concern the contact of the soul with divine influences, and hence are too sacred for open speech. Neither consideration seems to apply here.

But we must include one explanation of his riddle, not because it is necessarily the correct one, but because it comes from the great R. Moses b. Nahman. With delightful irony, Nahmanides, the cautious conservative, changes places with the radical Ibn Ezra whose audacities he has so often criticized. "Lo," says he, "Rabbi Abraham is 'faithful of spirit, concealing a matter' (Prov. 11.13), but I, the gossip, shall reveal his secret since our rabbis have already revealed it in many places." Such are a midrashic identification of the goat (*sair*) with Esau, the hairy man (*ish sair*), and the plain statement in Pirke d'R. Eliezer that the scapegoat is intended to propitiate Samael.[13] Nahmanides then adds by way of explanation: "The worshippers of other gods, that is, of angelic beings, offer them sacrifices, which is strictly forbidden by our Torah. God has commanded us, however, to send a goat on Yom Kippur to the ruler (*sar*) whose realm is in the places of desolation. From the emanation of his power come destruction and ruin; he ascends to the stars of the sword, of blood, of wars, quarrels, wounds, blows, disintegration and destruction. He is associated with the planet Mars. His portion among the peoples is Esau, a people who live by the sword; and his portion among the animals is the goat. The demons (*shedim*) are part of his realm and are called in the Bible *seirim;* he and his people are named Seir. The scapegoat is not (heaven forfend!) an offering from us to him, but an act of obedience to God. If one entertains a king at dinner, and the king asks his host to give a portion to one of the royal servants, the host obeys. He honors the king, not the servant, by his action. Of course, the king makes the request so that all his servants may praise and not dispraise the host. To avoid even the appearance that we ourselves give an offering to Azazel, the priest does not himself select or dedicate the scapegoat; this is decided by lot, leaving the matter altogether to God. For the same reason we do not slaughter the scapegoat." From careful scrutiny of the language of the Targum, Nahmanides concludes that one goat is for the name of the Lord, but not for the Lord (that is, it is sacrificed in God's honor, but God does not really consume it), while the second is for Azazel, but not for the name (that is, the honor and worship) of Azazel. Ibn Ezra's cryptic mention of "thirty-three" refers to Leviticus 17.7, the thirty-third verse after the mention of Azazel, which forbids the practice of sacrificing to *seirim.* Nahmanides declares further that the existence of disembodied spirits may be known on the one hand by necromancy (which strangely, he seems to sanction) and by the mystic interpretation of the Torah. He closes his comment with a blast against the Hellenists who follow Aristotle in denying the existence of anything inaccessible to sense, who assert that whatever their small minds fail to comprehend is not true!

Here, indeed, we have left the firm ground of rationalism for Cabala; but the passage belongs in this chapter because Nahmanides is trying to keep his foothold in tradition if not in logic, while at the same time he yields to his mystical impulses. We see him troubled by the conflict between his conviction that the demonic world is real and his fear of compromising his monotheism. Not all the Cabalists were so careful.

Nevertheless, none of the other classical commentators would go so far in recognizing a Realm of Evil. Gersonides and Abrabanel explain the entire scapegoat ceremony in terms of allegory and symbol.

JOB. The ultra-rationalism of Saadia is fully evidenced in his inter-pretation of the Job story. He explains that the Satan was a hu-man being who happened to dislike Job; he had considerable prestige in a religious fellowship whose members were called "sons of God." This personal enemy of Job was permitted by God to harm him, in order to test Job's righteousness; the early trials were due to his plottings. The sickness which Job later suf-fered came, however, from God alone; it is to Him that the words "He smote" (Job 2.7) must refer.[14] This interpretation is so obviously forced that none of the other commentators adopted it. Ibn Ezra cites the opinion of Saadia only to refute it. In stat-ing that the angels are never subject to jealousy and strife, the Gaon overlooked several biblical passages, notably the conflict between angels mentioned in the Book of Daniel. No volume, says Ibn Ezra, can contain all the profound mysteries on this subject; but he who knows about astral influences will compre-hend the essence of Satan. In any case he is an angel; but when Scripture speaks of Satan enticing God to harm Job (2.3), we must take the language figuratively.

Maimonides devotes two chapters of the *Guide* to a brilliant summary and exposition of the Book of Job. One of the talmudic rabbis has already declared that Job was not an historical char-acter, and that the book is a parable. Though other teachers disputed this view, we may be sure, Maimuni insists, that the book was written not to record events, but to teach profound truths. The scene in heaven cannot be taken literally. The adver-sary is inferior to the "sons of God." Their relation to God is more permanent and constant. His activity is limited to earth, and he has no power over the soul (Job 1.7; 2.6). He is identified by our sages with the evil inclination and the angel of death.[15]

This talmudic statement is fundamental to Maimuni's exposi-tion. Satan is the personification of the evil and sinfulness in-herent in matter and morality. Since evil is essentially negative, it is not caused by the Creator. Job and his friends supposed that his sufferings came from God; but we know from the opening chapters that they really were due to "Satan." (In his systematic discussion of the problem of evil, Maimuni insists on its essentially unreal and privative character. Man's sufferings are due to the accidents inherent in matter, to the wickedness of others and chiefly to his own foolish self-indulgence.) [16]

Job ultimately learns that true felicity is not to be found in earthly things, but in knowledge of God. Divine providence cannot be judged by the human mind.

Maimuni's interpretation, says R. Levi b. Gerson, is the only useful treatment of the subject by earlier writers. Most of the commentators have been content to try to explain the difficult language of the book. And even in this they have been far from successful, for the single passages can be understood correctly only if we grasp the content of the work as a whole. These remarks are found in the preface to Gersonides' own commentary, in which he follows the same general method as Maimonides. The scene in heaven is figurative; Satan an allegorical symbol.

So far the rationalists. The more orthodox commentators, Rashi and R. Samuel b. Masnuth, stick closer to the Talmud. Satan is a member of the heavenly economy; the assemblage of the "sons of God" was the assize of Rosh haShanah, at which Satan regularly plays the role of accuser. His motives were of the best; he acted only as God's servant and agent.

The traditionalists, in short, preserve Satan's essential respectability. The more extreme rationalists (except Saadia) reduce him to a figure of speech. Only the Cabalists, with some hesitation, begin to ascribe a genuinely diabolic character to Satan. This trend may be seen in the *Kad haKemah* of Bahya b. Asher. Bahya was a follower of Nahmanides, both in his devotion to the Cabala and in his equal devotion to rabbinic learning. The *Kad haKemah* ("Jar of Meal") is a collection of homilies, containing little or no mystical material and drawn chiefly from talmudic and midrashic sources. The section dealing with Providence (*Hashgahah*) contains an analysis of the Book of Job, in which Bahya avowedly follows Nahmanides. He cites the opinion of Saadia that Satan was a man; and then continues: "The opinion of R. Moses b. Nahman and of most commentators is that this Satan is an angel, and so are the 'sons of God.' That they should have been envious of Job's prosperity and donned the lusts of the body in places of drink and amusement is not surprising; for we find an explicit statement to this effect in Genesis 6.2. *And it is known that these angels were not men;* yet they clothed themselves with bodily passions and descended from their holy station in heaven. So in the case of Job: the sons of God and Satan were angels drowning in the sea of physical desire, and they donned the traits of man, such as jealousy, hatred, lust and anger. And Nahmanides has written: It is known in our tradition that he (Satan) is an angel created to oppose and to harm man." [17] Again we have followed these moderate mystics to a position far more extreme than even the talmudists—much less the philosophers—would accept. The rest of this development belongs in a different chapter.

HILLEL BEN SAMUEL AND THE CHRISTIANS. It remains to consider a short essay by the thirteenth-century philosopher Hillel of Verona, which forms an appendix to his chief work, *The Rewards of the Soul*.[18] In it he directly attacks the belief in fallen angels, or rather in the fall of Satan. This argument is part of his polemic against Christianity; apparently the belief in rebel angels found little credence among the Jews with whom Hillel associated. Hillel agrees that the notion originated in Israel, through mistakes in interpreting such passages as Genesis 6 and Isaiah 14.12. It is to be found in "a few homiletical works." The Gentiles borrowed the concept and made it one of the pillars of their doctrine. They declare that the angels sought to be the lords of the world, or sought the pleasures of lust, or were guilty of such sins as hatred or jealousy, or criticized God's conduct of the world. They were therefore dispersed through earth and air; they are the demons and devils who stir up war and all manner of evil. They fill hell; but some can ascend close to the angelic level, and thus they have a knowledge of the future.

Before we reproduce Hillel's criticism of this doctrine, it should be noted that he states it in a form much closer to that of the Christian than of the Jewish sources. Moreover, he is surprisingly bold when he refers lightly to the "few homiletical works" in which Jews have embodied the doctrine. One of these works was the Pirke d'R. Eliezer, which in that age was unanimously believed to emanate from the great Tanna, Eliezer b. Hyrkanos. Even Maimonides regards it as authoritative and, citing some of its more grossly mythological statements, declares that they must be interpreted allegorically.[19] Hillel, however, does not trouble himself with the explanation of difficulties in Jewish literature; instead he adduces philosophic reasoning to prove that sinful angels are an impossibility.

The argument is that the angelic substance is an emanation from God. God being a simple Substance containing no contradictions, nothing that emanates from Him can contain contradictory qualities—as, for instance, that the angels should be both good and sinful. We speak of various angelic degrees; but this refers only to differences of function. Since angels are all immaterial, they are alike in essence. It does not matter for our argument whether the angels emanate directly from God, or whether there are intermediaries between God and the angels. At any rate there must be some intermediary produced directly by God, who must be a simple substance devoid of contraries; and no matter how many stages supervene, this could only produce simple substances without contraries.

It is argued that, in a system of emanations, deficiency and imperfection increase with increasing distance from the source. But this only applies when an emanated quality mingles with some material or quasi-material substance as light mingles with darkness; and indeed it applies only to bodies in space and time. But the angels are themselves the emanation, and they are entirely immaterial. Yet even if we should admit this line of reasoning, and say that some angels are inferior in goodness to others, this would not prove that any are positively wicked. One king may be less rich or powerful than another, but he is just as royal. The capacity to do evil is an accident that befalls the soul because it is joined to a physical body. This cannot be predicated of angels, whose substance is one and simple, and therefore impervious to sin.

This, says Hillel, was the argument that I presented to a group of Gentile scholars. One of them answered as follows: Good and evil exist in various degrees: good, better, best, and the reverse. Angels are to some degree composite, since they have both will and intellect; therefore there can be various degrees of perfection among them. As it is possible that angels should choose a higher or lower degree of good, it is not impossible that some should even choose evil. The combination of will and intellect in the angels is illustrated by the behavior of the guardian angels of the nations, as described in the Book of Daniel.

But the Jewish savant was not impressed. You have dived into deep waters—he tells his opponent in talmudic language—and come up with a potsherd. Variability in the reception of moral influences is possible only for beings located in time and space, in short, for corporeal beings. Good and evil, however, can be ascribed only to the "practical soul," which angels do not possess. The "contemplative soul" may attain higher and lower degrees in the apprehension of truth—but not of goodness or evil.

Hillel then enters upon an analysis (the details of which are not all clear) to prove that angels do not have a will separate from their intelligence. Their existence and their intellect are but two names for the identical essence. The Christian notion that the lower angels were led to sin because of their proximity to earth is not as plausible as it seems. For they are closer to the heavenly spheres than to the sublunar world, and so would be more subject to spiritual than to material influences.

The argument from the Book of Daniel is dismissed by our philosopher with the statement that the passages in question cannot be taken in literal anthropomorphic terms. The angelic influences, ordained of God from Creation and working through the heavenly bodies, control climate and natural forces in the various quarters of the earth. Thus our sages say: Every blade of grass has an angel appointed over it to make it grow.[20] But we must not ascribe human passions to these angelic rulers of the physical universe. How this rarefied theory is to be accommodated to the plain text of Daniel, R. Hillel does not attempt to show.

But he refers in closing to the Christian theory that man was created to supply the deficiency left in heaven by the fall of the angels.[21] This view, he says jocosely, leads to the wildest consequences. If human souls attain to angelic status, it will follow that at the resurrection angels will have to put on physical bodies. Moreover, if the souls of the righteous become angels in heaven, it is but logical to suppose that the souls of the wicked will become demons in hell. But then, in view of the prevailing wickedness, the devils would multiply more rapidly than the angels. "See, then, how we profit by this doctrine—the Lord save us from it!"

Yet while this enlightened Jewish thinker was caustically attacking the mythological doctrines of another religion, similar myths were taking stronger hold than ever before upon his own coreligionists. Hillel was one of the last of the philosophers in an age when the influence of the Cabala was rapidly advancing. And here begins a new and important chapter in our inquiry.

PART SEVEN
Jewish Mysticism

CHAPTER TWENTY-ONE

The German Cabala

ystic piety, the sense of immediate communion with the divine, is strongly evidenced in many pages of the Bible. In post-biblical times, mystical movements were not infrequent. Groups of aspiring individuals perfected and transmitted techniques for entering the "Paradise" of spiritual ecstasy. Side by side with these practices there developed also a mystical theology, in which insights often profound were cloaked, sometimes grotesquely, in myth and symbol. We have found the belief in rebel angels chiefly in literature of this sort, emanating from conventicles of intense but slightly heterodox pietists.

So far as we know, Jewish mysticism flourished for many centuries only in the East. The secret lore was first brought to Italy in the ninth century, where it circulated among a very small group. About the year twelve hundred it appeared in the Rhineland, and the family of Rabbi Judah the Pious became its fervid devotees. Although these contemplatives were chary about disseminating their doctrine, their "public" was keenly aware that something unusual was going on. Legends about the adepts spread rapidly; and a large mass of magical and superstitious lore, bearing only a slight relation to true mysticism, was soon developed and compiled. Meantime, another center of esoteric study emerged in southern France and northern Spain. Here, apparently for the first time, the name of Cabala, tradition, was given to the mystic doctrine. Some of the Spanish Cabalists had studied philosophy; consequently their teaching assumed a more abstract and intellectual form. The interest in Cabala was greatly enhanced by the terrible persecutions which burst upon the Jews of Spain in the fourteenth and fifteenth centuries, culminating in the expulsion of 1492. So desperately did the people need spiritual fortification and solace that the old restrictions against revealing the mystic secrets could no longer be fully maintained.

The appearance meantime of the *Zohar*, the "Book of Splendor" (about 1280), was one of the decisive events of Jewish history. This bulky compendium of cabalistic lore acquired an influence almost as great as that of the Bible and the Talmud. Thenceforth, until the dawn of the modern era, all Jewish life was suffused with the cabalistic spirit. Even those whose chief interest was in Rabbinics, and the occasional students of philosophy, were learned in mystic lore.

This part of our investigation is peculiarly difficult; and our presentation is incomplete and tentative. The Cabala never entirely lost its secret character. Though several thousand cabalistic works have been printed, a far larger number remain in manuscript. Many of the mystical writers deliberately adopted a cryptic style, so that the uninitiate should *not* understand. Again, many Cabalists, feeling the inadequacy of ordinary discursive language to convey their inner experience, had recourse to symbolisms both obscure and strange. Finally, there are few works of reference, indices and compendia to assist the student; and the scientific investigation of the subject is still in its beginnings.

Now it is precisely in this area that dualistic trends and mythological fantasy had their most ·extreme development within Judaism.

We start with the mystics of the German school. The initiates of the group were few, their doctrines rather closely guarded.

The specifically mystic writings of R. Judah the Pious survive only in fragments; those of R. Eleazar Rokeach (of Worms), who most fully expounded the speculative teachings of the school, remain largely in manuscript. But these men were notable, not chiefly as mystical philosophers, but as devout pietists. Their moral austerity and devotional zeal greatly influenced the entire world in which they lived. Their most notable production, *Sefer Hasidim* (the *Book of the Pious*), is not technically a mystical work. It is a voluminous compilation for general use, containing ethical exhortations, tales of saints and sinners, ritual prescriptions and rather amateurish but earnest discussions of theology and theodicy—all gathered together with only the slightest system. More than any other Jewish classic, the *Book of the Pious* reflects the popular faith; or more correctly, the Hasidim had their own esoteric doctrines, but they held them in addition to the popular faith, which they accepted uncritically even to its foibles and superstitions.[1]

And here we come to a very striking fact. There is a marked relationship between this German Cabala and the mystical movements in contemporary German Christendom. Non-Jewish influence, for example, has strongly colored the notion of penance in the Jewish writings. Furthermore, the *Book of the Pious* borrows many a tale and superstition from German folklore. But Christian theology as such seems to have had little effect upon those who compiled this work. And this applies especially to our theme. Fallen angels are not mentioned at all. No hint of a wicked Devil, as conceived by the Church and as imagined with utmost terror in medieval Germany, appears. *Sefer Hasidim* on this point upholds the simple, naive, but essentially rational position of the Talmud.

Satan is mentioned infrequently, and pictured as a perfectly respectable prosecutor.[2] He is identified with the Attribute of Justice. When God purposes to confer great blessings on a man, Satan urges that this person be subjected to trials to prove himself worthy of the projected benefits. With God's permission, Satan then tempts the man to sin—this is depicted realistically—but, if he resists the temptation, Satan approves his reward.[3]

In contrast to the meager treatment of Satan is the extensive material on demons. Here the *Sefer Hasidim* seems to draw less upon the Talmud than upon the living superstitions of the German environment. There is much about ghosts, too—a topic which the Talmud seldom mentions.[4] If two men make a compact that the first to die shall communicate with the survivor, the revenant may be distinguished from a demon by administering an oath. Moreover, a dead person cannot pronounce the holy name Yah. If one has a bad dream, or sees a spirit or demon, he will avoid injury by not discussing the matter. If a demon appears in the guise of one dead, you may drive it away by spitting and saying, "Unclean, unclean, begone!" Other protective measures are the "fig" gesture and to touch coals before speaking.[5] It is permissible to bribe a demon (or for that matter, a human sorcerer) not to do one injury.[6] A parent should not force his child to go out alone at night, if he is afraid of demons.[7] And—characteristically! —one who copies a sacred text should repeat it aloud, for then the demons will hear and bless him.[8] As in the Talmud, then, they are not opponents of God, but His creatures. They are dangerous, but not absolutely evil.

When a new settlement is established in a forest, the demons who dwell there may resent the intrusion and send illness upon the newcomers. The *Sefer Hasidim* provides a ritual, partly religious, partly magical, to expel demons from such a locality.[9] But such procedures do not always succeed. The inhabitants of a certain village in Hungary were dying off, despite repeated public fasts. One day a villager encountered a host of demons; and their chief gave him a message to the Jews. They must move away, for their dwellings were built on the dancing place of the demons. This story is told—be it noted—to illustrate that some of God's decrees are inexorable and cannot be changed through human merit.[10] Demons are a sort of "natural force" like earthquake or storm. We may not understand why God utilizes them, yet He and no one else is their Master.

But the authors of *Sefer Hasidim* make one thing plain: a Jew has no business dealing with the evil spirits. All conjuring, whether of angels or demons, is sharply condemned. If a Jew becomes an apostate without discernible worldly motives, you may be sure that he or his ancestors had dabbled in the magic arts; and in punishment, God has let him go astray altogether. Divination through the agency of demons may be permissible for Gentiles; but it is not for Jews, who have the resource of prophetic revelation.[11]

A woman had hidden some money and, even on her deathbed, refused to tell her son where she had concealed it. After her death, the son engaged a witch to locate the treasure. The witch trapped a demon and plunged a dagger into his heart, which did not kill the demon, but inflicted unbearable pain, for he could not remove the weapon. The demon and his son then summoned the spirit of the dead woman and pleaded with her to reveal the secret, that he might be released from suffering. At first the woman objected: When I was alive, you ruled the soil on which I sojourned; now that I am dead, you have no authority over me. At length she consented to disclose the hiding place of the money. But she warned her son that horrible retribution would come upon him for exploiting occult powers.[12] The Hasidim, in short, did not question the efficacy of these supernatural procedures; but held them sinful.

It is thus clear that the German Cabala, despite a marked ascetic trend, is not dualistic in any philosophic or mythological sense.[13] The common notion that it is "practical Cabala," concerned only with spells and incantations, is altogether unfair. The masters of German Cabala were genuine mystics, and their chief written document strongly condemns magical practices. Nevertheless the predilection for such activity could not be restrained, and soon found literary expression. The *Book of the Angel Raziel* (which probably includes some material from R. Eleazar of Worms), deals with amulets, incantations and the like. All such devices, which aim at controlling the physical environment through supernatural forces, are in essence the very opposite of mysticism, which seeks spiritual benefits only. Yet magic and mysticism are often intertwined, and it is easy to understand why. Rationalism, with its cold and critical logic, is the natural foe of superstition. But mysticism tends (not invariably, but often) to repress the critical faculty and strengthen the will to believe. A strange doctrine, which the rationalist would pitilessly dissect, may be accepted without challenge by the mystic; in his humble faith, he will not pass judgment on a matter that may contain deep mysteries as yet unrevealed to him. Thus mysticism may absorb superstitious elements to which it has no affinity, which indeed are in essence the denial of mysticism. In this sense it is true that German Cabala became at length more theurgic than mystical.

There is, however, a basic difference between the magic of medieval Jewry and that of contemporary Christians. Dr. Joshua Trachtenberg, whose fascinating *Jewish Magic and Superstition* draws largely on *Raziel* and similar sources, points out that the Jews practiced white magic, that is, they used angelic and divine names to attain material benefits. This may have been an illegitimate use of spiritual forces, but the forces themselves were good. Gentile sorcerers, however, usually practiced the black art, consciously allying themselves with the Devil and his hosts against God and the Church.[14]

In the German Cabala, for all its luxuriant superstition and its speculative inexpertness, the demons remained no more than dangerous powers, like wild beasts, created by God and serving His purposes. But the Spanish Cabala, far more profound on the philosophic side, produced a dualism so thorough-going and extreme that its compatibility with the fundamental doctrine of Judaism may well be called into question.

CHAPTER TWENTY-TWO

The Spanish Cabala

The "Spanish" Cabala began, not in Spain, but in Provence, where the book called *Bahir* ("Radiance") was composed in the twelfth century. It is said to mark the transition from the older Gaonic mysticism to the later Cabala.[1] Here we find in considerable development (though the expression is fragmentary and obscure) the doctrine of the Ten Sefiroth —the forms or channels, to speak in crude and inadequate terms, through which Divinity manifests itself. In setting forth the interrelations of the Sefiroth, the emanations of the primal light, the *Bahir* adopts the ancient symbolism by which the structure of the cosmos is compared to that of the human body. The Ten Sefiroth in their organic unity constitute the Archetypal Man: the first emanations correspond to the head, and so on. This symbolism leads inevitably to a distinction between right and left, those Sefiroth which exemplify God's benevolent aspects being on the right, those which manifest His stern justice on the left. This provided the basis for a revival of both the spirit and the expression of Gnostic dualism.[2] In the *Bahir* itself, these notions are advanced only in brief and enigmatic hints. One passage describes Satan as a quality (*middah*) of God, whose name is evil, and which is on His northern (i.e., left) side. He is further compared to a king's officer who is appointed over the rock-pile and who tries to persuade the king's subjects to buy his stones instead of the food supplied by the officials in charge of the granaries. In a subsequent parable, however, Satan is compared to a servant who rebels against the king, refusing to serve in the place appointed to him and seeking by force and guile to lead both his fellow servants and the king's children into disobedience.[3]

The trends here indicated led, as we shall see, to extreme dualistic conclusions. But though they are implicit in the very configuration of the Sefiroth, these consequences were not immediately drawn. The first important Spanish Cabalist, R. Azriel (1160–1238), who studied under the Provençal mystics and brought the secret doctrine back to his own country, presented his views in abstract and quasi-philosophic form. Moreover, the problem of evil does not occupy a large place in his writings. The most famous of his disciples was R. Moses ben Nahman, a great talmudist and Bible commentator and the outstanding Jewish leader of his day. Nahmanides wrote comparatively little on the Cabala; but the fact that so eminent a scholar and so beloved a personality was an initiate gave to the secret doctrine a prestige it had not previously enjoyed in Spain. The progress of the mystical movement may be measured by the following circumstances: In his Torah commentary, Nahmanides refers to cabalistic ideas in brief and intentionally cryptic remarks, which he flatly tells the reader will be intelligible only to the adept. Two generations later, R. Bahya ben Asher (whose teacher had been a follower of Nahmanides) composed a Torah commentary which achieved great popularity and which draws largely on the work of R. Moses. But R. Bahya expounds at considerable length and with little reticence those cabalistic interpretations which his spiritual grandfather touched on so hesitantly.

These authorities (and certain others) are loosely grouped as the school of Gerona, the town where R. Azriel lived. Most of them were well grounded in the sane, balanced literature of the Talmud, and had some acquaintance with philosophy—despite their distrust of Aristotelianism. Yet even these thinkers display what is apparently a natural connection between cabalistic speculation and dualistic myth.

We saw above that Nahmanides took the scapegoat ceremony to be a propitiatory offering to Satan, though the ceremony is commanded by God and performed in obedience to His will. R. Moses enlarges on the rationalistic interpretation of the "sons of God" in Genesis 6; yet he indicates his preference for the view that they were fallen angels. Another revealing passage is his comment on Genesis 4.3, about Naamah, the sister of Tubal Kain. Here he cites three opinions: Genesis Rabba, a classical Midrash, states that Naamah was a righteous woman, who became Noah's wife. Another Midrash depicts her as a beautiful and unprincipled woman, who lured angels to ruin. Still others say that she was the wife of Shamdon and the mother of Ashmedai, for so it is recorded in the *Writings on the Use of Demons.*

In explaining the fall of Adam, Nahmanides adheres to traditional views and does not identify the serpent with Satan. At the end of his exposition, however, he insists that the narrative has also an inner meaning. For, he says, serpents now do not have the power of speech. Were the story to be taken only in its literal sense, mention should have been made of the chief curse laid upon the serpent, namely, that he was made dumb. But here Nahmanides stops short, without revealing the inward significance of the tale.

Bahya, the pupil of his pupil, added nothing new to cabalistic doctrine, but represents opinions that were widely diffused in Spain prior to the appearance of the *Zohar.* (Bahya indeed quotes a few passages from the *Zohar,* which came to light in the later years of his life, but does not seem to have been profoundly influenced by it.) Like his masters, Bahya tried to find a place within the monotheistic scheme for a realm of evil; but his attempt was not entirely successful. His Torah commentary combines mythological and rationalistic materials; for this catholic scholar delighted in all four methods of biblical interpretation—literal, midrashic, philosophic, and mystical.

Thus he gives a lengthy allegorical explanation of the fall. Adam symbolizes the intellectual soul; Eve is matter. The serpent is the evil inclination which leads the soul astray by seducing the body. The punishment upon the serpent is a prophecy that at the end of days the evil *yezer* will be completely subjugated.[4]

Less homiletical is the statement that prior to his sin, Adam was completely intellectual and had no evil inclination. He ate the fruit out of desire to increase his knowledge, though the intellectual faculty should have kept him from disobeying God's decree. The evil inclination could reach him only through Eve; but after he had eaten the fruit, it entered his own being in the form of sexual desire. This notion that Adam could sin before he possessed the evil *yezer* should occasion us no difficulty; for the angels, disembodied intelligences though they be, have been known to turn away from God: and Bahya provides illustrations from Scripture and rabbinic books.[5]

The chief instance is that of Satan himself. He was a heavenly power, but he began to slander his Creator and was therefore driven from his high abode and brought down below the Sefiroth. The serpent was but the instrument of the power of evil: thus alone can we understand the declaration of eternal enmity between mankind and the serpent (Gen. 3.15), for we have no special hatred for literal snakes. Bahya also notes as significant that both angels and serpents are called in Hebrew *serafim*.[6]

Eve, the passive feminine principle, whose soul is from the north, succumbed readily to the blandishments of Satan. Cain was not the son of Adam, but was sired by the serpent. Therefore the Cainites were called "sons of god"—since they were begotten by the power of the "strange god" Samael. But Bahya also gives the traditional view that the "sons of God" were eminent human beings.[7]

Another mythical section discusses Naamah, quoting first the Midrash that she was Noah's wife. "But some say she was the wife of Ashamdon and the mother of Ashmedai, and that the demons were born of her. Four women were mothers of demons: Lilith, Naamah, Agrath and Mahlath. Each has camps and bands of the spirit of uncleanness, beyond all numbering. They say each rules over one of the seasons of the year. They gather on a bare mountain near the mountains of darkness.* Each rules during her season from sunset to midnight, they and all their camps. Solomon controlled them all, calling them servants and handmaids (Eccl. 2.7), and used them to do his own will. These four

* Is this a hint of the *Walpurgisnacht?*

are the wives of the heavenly prince of Esau; correspondingly Esau married four women, as stated in the Torah." [8]

This last paragraph is especially instructive because practically all its elements are drawn from the talmudic aggada; but the total effect is quite different and much more ominous than anything in the early sources.

Nevertheless Bahya is at pains to stress the Divine Unity, lest the implications of these dualistic myths be carried too far. We have seen that Satan was of heavenly origin. In a cabalistic passage, Bahya states that the good and evil inclinations have a common root in the "Middle Line" (*Kav haEmtzai*), a name given by the mystics to the sixth Sefirah, usually called *Tifereth* (glory) or *Rahamim* (mercy). And again he declares: "Good and evil have a single root, which is entirely good." [9]

An anonymous work of the same period is *Sefer Temunah*, the "Book of Likeness." Here too we have the theory of the Sefiroth, some of which represent the harsher, some the milder aspects of the divine nature. This is combined with the doctrine that world history consists of seven periods, each lasting seven thousand years, until in the Great Jubilee, the fifty-thousandth year, the process of cosmic development will reach its culmination. We are now in the period dominated by the Sefirah of strict justice—this explains the existence of suffering and wrong. [10] In the next period, all evil will disappear. In such a scheme, evil is only one element in God's preconceived plan, and the idea of a rebellion against the divine rule is irrelevant. Yet the book *Temunah* likewise speaks of angels who mingled with external and unholy forces, fell from their sanctity and united on earth with alien powers. [11] The tale was of no importance to this (or indeed to any) cabalistic system, but it was adopted because it fitted the prevailing mood of the Cabalists.

It is evident then that even the moderate Geronese Cabala displayed a strong tendency toward dualistic myth. But as the thirteenth century drew to a close, a much more extreme doctrine came to the fore, which Dr. Scholem calls the "Gnostical" Cabala. The source of evil is no longer merely in those Sefiroth which represent the severe justice of God: now there is an entire series of evil emanations, the Sefiroth of the "left side," which largely parallel the divine Sefiroth. This is the doctrine of the *Zohar;* but it is fully set forth in several earlier writings.

In the middle of the thirteenth century—contemporary with Nahmanides—lived two brothers, Isaac and Jacob haKohen, in the Spanish town of Soria. Ardent devotees of mysticism (they were not distinguished talmudists), they studied in southern France, where the secret lore was still expounded in its older Oriental and German forms, without the philosophic subtleties which the Spanish contemplatives had added. The writings of the two brothers were not published at length until recent years: the most important is an essay on *The Emanation of the Left Side,* by R. Isaac haKohen.[12] It consists largely of extracts from earlier sources and contains a dualistic doctrine more extreme than anything we have yet encountered. Perhaps Gnostic tendencies were stronger in the older tradition than our previous studies have indicated. Or perhaps R. Isaac and his brother, because of personal predilection, collected and concentrated tendencies which were more scattered and (so to speak) diluted in the older sources. At any rate, both R. Isaac and his successors stress the "top secret" character of the doctrine, which is unknown even to many Cabalists.

According to R. Isaac, the first two Sefiroth (and certain secondary emanations from them) constitute a world of pure goodness. But from the third Sefirah (*Binah,* Discernment, called by R. Isaac "the Power of Repentance") the leftward emanation began. First a dividing partition (*Masak Mavdil*) emanated from the third Sefirah; it had a personality and was named Mesukiel. But before an orderly process of emanation from Mesukiel could start, worlds of horror and destructive imaginings came forth. Three times, therefore, the emanational process had to be reversed—as when a burning wick is extinguished by thrusting it deep into the reservoir of oil. These three abortive "worlds" are hinted at in Job 22.15, and in the midrashic report that God created and destroyed many worlds before He made this one.

Thereafter the double emanation began, consisting of seven successive groups of pure angels on one side, and seven camps of dark spirits on the other. Between them there is constant warfare, yet their intention is toward the Lord of all, Who created them, and to the performance of His will.

The first and chief of the forces of jealousy is Samael. He is not, indeed, wicked in essence, but in his desire to come into contact with an emanation not of his own kind. The other leaders of the "left side" bear names suggesting their wrathful and jealous nature. The occasion for conflict in these spheres is a being called Lilith, who stands to Samael in the same relationship as Eve to Adam. She is, in fact, called "the old Eve," and also Zefonith—"the one from the North." Yet Samael and Lilith emanate from beneath the Throne of Divine Glory, the legs of which are somewhat shaken by their activity.[13]

R. Isaac is at some pains to indicate that none of these powers is material. The bright and dark angels are like forms of man depicted in "appearances of great fire," but are genuinely spiritual.[14]

This work also presents the doctrine that there are three "atmospheres"—levels of existence—on high. The first is apparently that inhabited by angels; below it is the area through which prophets receive their inspiration; lowest is the "air of the utilization of demons," through which one may gain foreknowledge of events, travel from place to place instantaneously, and so on.

This lowest level is itself divided into three levels. The first is ruled by Ashmedai who, though called King of the Demons, is subject to Samael. The mate of Samael is Lilith, while Ashmedai mates with the Lesser Lilith. The middle level is controlled by Kafkefoni, whose two wives are called Little Leprous One and Dreary One. From these unions issue horrible creatures with bodies, which war against one another and cause comets and quakes. These beings are all subject to Ashmedai, and they transmit their supernatural knowledge to those beneath them.

The lowest of the sub-levels is inhabited by injurious demons (*mazzikin*), which take various forms, such as dogs and goats. Azza and Azzael belonged to this latter class, but they alone had human form. When they fell from heaven—that is, the level just mentioned—they donned materiality and their offspring were distinguished by their great size and strength. Other demons appear regularly in human form, both male and female. Only falsehood prevails among them; they are jealous of humanity and constantly seek its harm. Indeed, they would obliterate everything they encounter, were they not subjected to the control of a great angelic prince, named Yofiel. To this angel the king of the *mazzikin*, by name Kafzefoni, must submit. His children can leap from one end of the "air" to the other; sometimes they perform actions that benefit human beings. Thus they reveal the future if he who questions them is worthy. When summoned by an unsuitable inquirer, they appear in response to his incantation, but are not allowed to reply to his questions.[15]

The destruction of the evil emanations and of Edom, which will occur at the appointed time, is announced in several passages. One such asserts that in the physical world there are two kinds of Leviathan—one a clean, the other an unclean beast. Likewise in the celestial world there are a clean and an unclean Leviathan. The latter acts as the "groomsman" who effects the union of Samael and Lilith, and is therefore called Taninivver, blind dragon. The future extermination of this being is predicted in Isaiah 27.1.[16]

These excerpts give some notion of the world of dark mythology in which R. Isaac moved. He himself was conscious of the difficulty these ideas involved for the faithful Jew, and he tried to fit them into the monotheistic system. The leftward emanation does not proceed directly from the Godhead, but from the third of the emanated beings or Sefiroth. The earliest of the evil emanations, being too virulent, were not permitted to endure. Samael is not absolutely, but only relatively evil. The entire leftward process is ordained of God for His own purposes. "It was the decree of His wisdom to create a world which should be entirely evil, in order to chastise the erring, that they might repent completely and thus receive benefit and, if they do not repent, to destroy them. Concerning these two worlds, the Bible says of God that He forms peace and creates evil" (Is. 45.7). "Though the evil emanation has no share or inheritance in the world that is all good, the beginning of its emanation is not evil." Why God chose that evil should emanate from good is beyond our comprehension. "Our intelligence cannot conceive the depth of the hidden mystery, for it is sealed up." [17]

A similar spirit pervades the writings of R. Moses of Burgos, a disciple of Isaac haKohen. There are a number of differences both in the cabalistic doctrine and in its presentation. R. Moses gives a connected and rather wordy account of the matter, adorning it with talmudic and cabalistic citations and imparting a strong moralistic tone. His chief work, *The Left-hand Pillar*, insists that the dualistic system was willed by God because the world can exist only through the interplay of opposing forces, and because reward and punishment both are essential to the divine justice. In his description of the ten evil Sefiroth, R. Moses departs considerably from his teacher. According to R. Isaac, the leftward emanation begins from the third Sefirah, and there are only seven existent spheres of evil—the number ten being made up by the three worlds that were destroyed. R. Moses, however, states that the leftward emanation starts from the fifth Sefirah, "the great fire of *Geburah* (Might)," and there are actually ten evil Sefiroth. The eighth in this series bears the name Samael; Lilith is the tenth. This is the scheme later adopted in the *Zohar*.[18]

The writings of Moses of Burgos, like those of Isaac haKohen, have been published in full only of late years. But his outlook was shared substantially by R. Todros Abulafia, who seems to have been his pupil, though they were nearly of an age. Unlike the scholars just mentioned, R. Todros was a leader of the Jewish community and an accomplished talmudist. His book, *Ozar haKabod* ("The Treasury of Glory"), is the first systematic effort to interpret talmudic aggada in cabalistic terms. In this work he speaks clearly, yet reticently, about the double emanation, a subject unfamiliar even to the mystics. Despite the parallel character of the two emanations and their correspondence, there is nevertheless "a difference in their existence and persistence" at which Abulafia dares not even hint. Yet dark and bright forces alike yearn to fulfill the purpose of their Possessor. What this purpose is, we cannot guess. It belongs to the things of which it was said: "Be silent! Such is My plan." [19]

CHAPTER TWENTY-THREE

The Zohar

In the last years of the thirteenth century, the book called the *Zohar* began to circulate among Spanish Cabalists. It is a kind of rambling commentary on the Pentateuch, together with sections based on Ruth and the Song of Songs. Its contents are not exclusively mystical; much of it has an ethical or devotional character. Elaborate aggadic sections, derived only in part from the old sources, adorn its pages. The *Zohar* is not only the greatest sourcebook of Cabala, but the last monument of creative aggada.

The *Zohar* consists of alleged discussions between the second century Tanna, R. Simeon b. Johai, and his disciples, with stories of their spiritual experiences. Most cabalists have revered it as an authentically ancient work. But from the time of its appearance, it has been connected with the name of a well known mystic, Moses de Leon; and some people suspected that he had written it himself.

The historian Graetz, who detested the Cabala, insisted that the *Zohar* is a forgery, the work of the "charlatan" Moses de Leon. Other scholars, however, held that Moses merely assembled and edited materials gathered from many places—so that the work has some claim to be considered ancient. It is, indeed, made up of various documents, bearing different names.

The fullest analysis of the problem, by Professor Scholem, indicates that Graetz was not far from wrong. Except for two documents (the *Ra'ya Mehemna*, or Faithful Shepherd, and the *Tikkunim*), the *Zohar* is the work of a single author, who was almost certainly Moses de Leon. The earliest sections are those entitled *Midrash haNeelam*, or Esoteric Exposition. The fact that certain aggadot appear in different versions is not to be explained as due to various sources. The author returned repeatedly to certain themes, developing them each time in a different way. Graetz was mistaken only in branding Moses de Leon as a fraud who foisted his work on the public for his own gain. Moses was influenced by the same reasons which led the apocalyptic authors to ascribe their writings to ancient worthies.[1]

To confirm or refute Dr. Scholem's arguments is outside the scope of our undertaking. But the material we shall now present fits in well with his thesis.

THE FALLEN ANGELS. One passage in the zoharic literature does *not* see in Genesis 6 an allusion to the fallen angels. It is found in the *Midrash haNeelam*, which Scholem regards as the earliest portion of the great undertaking. Here the "sons of God" are said to have been "sons of prominent personages," and the fathers are blamed for their failure to restrain their children. Another explanation is that the "children of God" were Adam and Eve, since God created them directly; they are called *Nefilim* because they fell (*nafelu*) from grace.[2]

But the author soon gave up this approach and interpreted the passage in accordance with the familiar myth. The story is told and re-told many times; as in most late versions, the *Zohar* knows only of two angels who married mortal women and invariably calls them Azza and Azzael. One cannot trace exactly the development of the legend in the *Zohar;* some of the accounts differ little from those in the older sources,[3] others add mystical overtones, or bring the fallen angels into association with Balaam and Solomon, or with Naamah and Lilith. We shall cite only the most interesting examples.

R. Simeon expounded to his companions: When the *Shekinah* proposed to the Holy One (blessed be He!): Let us make man, a number of the angels objected, and Azza and Azzael were particularly vehement. They argued: Why make man, when it is known in advance that he will sin through his wife who is darkness? (For light is male, darkness female; the left side is the darkness of creation.) The *Shekinah* replied: You yourselves will fall through the one you now accuse. For these very angels later went astray after mortal women, and the *Shekinah* cast them down from their holiness.—Here the disciples interrupt the discussion to point out that Azza and Azzael spoke truth just the same. To which R. Simeon answers: The *Shekinah* objected to their airs of superiority. Adam sinned with but one woman, the angels with many. Moreover, God had provided Adam in advance with the capacity to repent.—A general discussion of the problem of evil follows. Why, instead of creating man with two inclinations and freedom of will, did God not make man sinless, eligible neither for reward nor punishment? R. Simeon can only answer that the Torah, which was created for man's benefit, contains promises of retribution: God creates nothing to no purpose.[4]

Fuller details appear in the following: Azza and Azzael were two angels who criticized their Lord (for making man) and were cast down to earth. Usually, when angels descend to earth, they clothe themselves with air and take on a temporary matter, of which they divest themselves when they are ready to go back on high. But the two angels were so eager to remain among women that they became more completely material; and when they had been on earth for seven consecutive days, they could not return again to heaven. They begot children upon their mortal wives; then God chained them in the mountains of darkness with iron chains which are fixed to the great deep. Were it not for these bonds, they would obliterate the world. Even fettered, they can still weaken the celestial family by the magic spells they know and which they teach to all who resort to them. These angels draw their vitality from the north, the "left side." They are the *anshe shem* (literally, "men of name") because they use the holy names in magical incantations. (The usual interpretation, "men of renown," is also mentioned.) [5]

Prominent among those who have learned supernatural arts from Azza and Azzael was the enchanter Balaam. For the latter testified (Numbers 23.7) that he came from the "ancient mountains" (or "mountains of the east"), which were readily identified with the mountains of darkness where the fallen angels are chained. The *Zohar* speaks several times of Balaam's dealings with the imprisoned pair; the most fantastic version runs as follows:

Balaam, practicing the black art in Egypt, realized that his spells could not prevent the liberation of Israel. In trepidation he went to the mountains of darkness and reached the chains which fasten the fallen angels. Now Azza who, even when punished, continued to rage against God, is shrouded in complete darkness. Azzael was a little more submissive; he was therefore permitted to see. Consequently, when a visitor arrives at the top of the mountains, Azzael can inform Azza about it. The two then set up an outcry and are soon surrounded by great burning serpents. They send to the visitor an *unimata*, an animal something like a cat with a snake's head, two tails and small paws. The newcomer must cover his face and produce smoke by burning the carcass of a white cock. Tamed apparently by the smoke, the *unimata* guides the visitor till he reaches the end of the chain which is fixed in the earth and reaches down into the deep, where it is securely fastened to a bolt (*samik*) set in the lower abyss. The man must kick the chain three times; the angels call him; he must bow, then climb up to them with his eyes closed. The visitor sits before them, serpents surrounding them on all sides; when he opens his eyes, he is filled with terror. They instruct him in magic for fifty days, after which the monsters escort him from the mountains of darkness. Balaam, however, knew a word of special power, so that he could remain with them for a longer course of study.[6]

Solomon likewise had dealings with Azza and Azzael—of a more legitimate sort. Each day he would ride on an eagle to Tarmod in the desert of the mountains. This is not the earthly Tarmod (Palmyra-Tadmor), but a place where spirits and beings of the "other side" gather on the mountains of darkness. The eagle could reach this place in an hour's flight and hover above it while Solomon dropped an amulet he had prepared to ward off harm from evil spirits. Then espying the place where the angels are chained (a place which no one but Balaam could enter), the eagle would swoop down, holding Solomon securely under his left wing. Solomon would produce a ring engraved with the Holy Name, and place it in the eagle's mouth; and by this means the angels were constrained to answer his inquiries.[7]

NAAMAH, LILITH, THE RULERS OF ARKA. Naamah is frequently mentioned as the temptress of Azza and Azzael; but the *Zohar* presents her in other roles as well. One passage connects her existence with fundamental concepts of zoharic Cabala. When the Primeval Light was concealed, a husk was created for the "marrow," that is, the good reality; the husk extended and produced another husk. (This symbol of negative and demonic forces will be discussed below.) The latter sought to cleave to the *Anpe Zutre* (literally, "the Impatient," the configuration of the Sefiroth expressing the quality of severe justice), but this God would not allow. When Adam and Eve were created, the same husk again sought contact with the "Impatient," but God cast her into the sea. After Adam fell, God brought the husk forth from the sea and gave her the power to injure those who have incurred punishment through the sins of their fathers. She hurries through the world, and wherever she finds children appointed for punishment, she mocks at them and kills them. When Cain appeared, she could not at first cleave to him; but afterwards she bore him demon children. A little later in the passage, Naamah and Lilith are mentioned; they appear to be descendants of the original "husk," the ancestress of the evil spirits, whose qualities are so akin to theirs.[8]

Elsewhere it is emphasized that Naamah comes from the "side" of Cain, who was really the offspring of the primeval Serpent. She is the mother of demons and bears rule by night, wielding the terrible weapon of croup. She rouses the passions of men in dreams and sometimes has spirit-children by them. These spirits in turn beget demon children upon mortal women, and the children become the charge of Lilith. Sometimes Naamah rouses a man by a sexual dream; he awakens, and embraces his own wife. The child is then begotten from the "side" of Naamah and, instead of becoming a victim of Lilith, becomes Naamah's charge. Though most demons (according to talmudic report) are mortal, Naamah, Lilith and Agrath bath Mahlath will continue to exist until the Messianic day when God shall extirpate the spirit of uncleanness. Naamah's regular abode is among the waves of the sea.[9]

The *Zohar* also speaks repeatedly of Lilith. She acts as the nurse of demon children; but she seeks to kill human infants and draw away their souls. The souls, however, are rescued and brought to God by three holy spirits. The Jew who leads a sanctified life need not fear Lilith; for these holy spirits will protect his child. If he neither sanctifies nor deliberately defiles himself, the protection will extend only to the soul of the child, not to its body.[10]

One of the most grossly mythological passages in the *Zohar* concerns a subterranean area, one of the seven "earths" below, where the Cainites dwell. When Cain was driven off the face of the earth (Gen. 4.14), he descended to this place, which is called Arka. It is a land of mingled darkness and light, each of which has its ruler; and previous to Cain's arrival they had been in conflict. But when Cain descended, the rulers composed their differences; and the two-headed offspring which Cain sired participate both in darkness and light. The two rulers of Arka are named Afrira and Kastimon. In appearance they resemble the holy angels, each having six wings. They both have one face like an ox, and one like an eagle; when joined, they have a human countenance, and in darkness they are changed to the appearance of a two-headed snake. They enjoy swimming through the deep to plague the imprisoned Azza and Azzael. Thence they go by night to visit Naamah; but she evades their embraces, preferring to rouse the passions of men. They flutter about the world, then return to their underground domain to awake the appetites of the Cainites, that the latter may beget progeny. The "heavens" where Afrira and Kastimon rule are not like ours, nor is their "earth" productive. Jeremiah 10.11 refers to such "gods," who did not make heaven and earth.[11]

THE PATERNITY OF CAIN. We have noted a single talmudic statement that Eve suffered sexual defilement by the serpent, and thereby a moral taint was transmitted to mankind. Israel, however, by accepting the Torah, was purged of this "original sin." Another aggada declares that Seth was the first to be begotten in Adam's likeness; and later homilists drew rather far-reaching deductions from this. The Chapters of R. Eliezer boldly declare that Cain was not the son of Adam, but of the serpent.[12] This kind of mythology would naturally appeal to the mystics, and it occurs repeatedly in the *Zohar*. The distinction between Satan and the serpent, which had been maintained even by the more sectarian aggadists, now breaks down completely.

An extended discussion of this theme ascribes the fall of man to the "heavenly serpent," from the "side" of which all deaths have occurred save only those of Moses, Aaron, Miriam and (by implication) Sarah. All magic is ultimately derived from the side of the primeval serpent—therefore all enchantments, including divination by the chirping of birds, are called *nehashim*, from *nahash*, snake. Magic is a peculiarly feminine art, because it was the woman, Eve, whom the serpent defiled.[13]

The statement that the serpent sired Cain seems to contradict the biblical report that Adam was his father. Actually, the serpent did defile Eve, begetting an evil spirit which sported within her, but had no body with which to enter the world. The marital relations between Adam and Eve provided this spirit with an outer covering, and so Cain was born. That is why Eve says "I have gotten a man with the Lord" (Gen. 4.1).[14]

The purification of Israel by the acceptance of the Torah was only temporary; the worship of the Golden Calf defiled the men again. The women had never completely lost the taint; for woman comes from the left side, the side of strict justice, and is therefore the more susceptible to defilement. During her menstrual periods, an unclean spirit rests upon her, and the magical spells she works at such a time are particularly efficacious. Hence the drastic necessity of avoiding contact with a menstruous woman.[15]

SAMAEL-SATAN. There are innumerable references to Samael-Satan, by these and other names. As he is identified fully with the Primeval Serpent in some passages, so he is elsewhere fully identified with the Prince of Edom—but now Edom likewise is a symbol more cosmic than national.

Sometimes the *Zohar* reproduces the material of the old aggada with slight cabalistic overtones. For example, he who celebrates the festivals in joy, but does not give a portion to God by sharing his good cheer with the poor, incurs the enmity of Satan. The Accuser lays the matter before God and brings punishment upon the selfish offender. He is always making the rounds of festal celebrations to discover if the poor are received hospitably. At the feast Abraham gave when Isaac was weaned, the poor were neglected; and it was Satan's consequent complaint that led to the command for the sacrifice of Isaac.[16]

One of R. Simeon's disciples held that the serpent in the Eden story is but a symbol of the evil inclination; another, that it was a literal snake. The master decided: It is all one. Samael appeared upon the serpent; the image of the serpent is Satan: it is all one. Samael descended from heaven, rode upon the serpent and terrified the creatures. They (*sc*. Samael and the serpent) seduced the woman by their words and brought death into the world. By his malevolent wisdom Samael brought curses on the world and destroyed the "primal tree" created by God. But later another holy tree—Jacob—appeared and took the blessings, so that Samael should not be blessed in heaven or Esau on earth.[17]

The "man" with whom Jacob wrestled was Samael, the prince of Edom. According to the *Midrash haNeelam*, the heavenly patrons of some nations are at times given power over others; especially is this true of the ruler of Edom. The words (Gen. 32.25) "Jacob was left alone" mean that Israel had no angelic defender. Though all the other heavenly princes sought to take his part, God restrained them, saying: He needs none of you. The merits of Jacob enabled him to defeat Samael single-handed, but the latter succeeded in touching Jacob's thigh—that is, his offspring. When Israel neglect the Torah, Samael is permitted to enslave them.[18] The *Zohar* proper declares that Samael attacked Jacob on Wednesday, the day of the week on which the sun and moon were created and, according to a familiar exegesis, a day of ill omen. (For the command *Yehi meorot*, "let there be luminaries," is written defectively and can be construed *Yehi meerot,* "let there be curses.") Hence Jacob was "left alone," for when the moon wanes, the power of the evil serpent is increased. As Samael tried to destroy Jacob, he was protected on the right by the power of the "side of Abraham" (representing mercy) and on the left by the power of the "side of Isaac" (representing strict justice). Samael could therefore not injure his body, but only one of his extremities.[19]

When Israel stood at the brink of the Red Sea, the angel of God went behind the Israelite camp to guard against the Egyptian advance (Ex. 14.19). But attacks from on high as well as from human enemies threatened Israel. The heavenly patron of Egypt had gathered six hundred chariots, each manned by six hundred attacking "princes." There is something odd in the biblical phrase (Ex. 14.7): "He took six hundred chosen chariots and all the chariots of Egypt." Were not the six hundred chosen chariots Egyptian too? No, replies the *Zohar;* they were a loan to the patron of Egypt from Samael. God retaliated in the days of Sisera, when these chariots were delivered into the power of the *Matronitha* (or "mistress," a name given to the last of the Ten Sefiroth). They will finally be destroyed when Edom falls.[20]

MYSTICAL DUALISM. The material we have been presenting—which could be enormously expanded—reveals the exuberant imagination of the author of the *Zohar*. Utilizing old materials freely and fancifully, and combining them with creations of his own, he greatly augments the mythological trend within Judaism. But he is also a serious and in many ways a profound thinker, and he is deeply troubled by the problem of evil. To this problem the *Zohar* provides several solutions.

The conception of the double emanation—of good and evil Sefiroth, balanced against one another—is ubiquitous in this work. The *Zohar* is studded with references to the right and left "sides," especially to the left as the "other side." We have already encountered this idiomatic use of the word "side." The "side" of Cain, of Samael, of strict justice, and so on, are (in Zoharic language) "all one." The concept of the double emanation, which in the *Zohar* is taken for granted more than it is expounded, systematically is close to that which Moses of Burgos had taught.[21]

Another doctrine of the *Zohar* was foreshadowed in the writings of Isaac haKohen. It is the myth that God created and destroyed many worlds before making this one. The debris of these previous worlds seems to be a kind of poison that infects our now existent creation.[22]

Related to this concept, surely, is another which pervades the *Zohar* and all subsequent Cabala. Demons and evil beings in general are known as *Kelipoth*, "husks," and Samael himself is sometimes called the *Kelipah*. This symbolism is most significant. For, however dry, tasteless and bothersome the husk of a fruit or the shell of a nut may be, it is part of a normal growth, and without it there would be no ripened kernel. Evil, then, is declared to be a kind of waste product which results from the processes of God's world. This imagery is utilized with great precision by Moses Cordovero, whose life was devoted to setting forth the Cabala of the *Zohar* in systematic form and interpreting it in conformity with Jewish monotheism. The most thoroughly bolted and purified flour, says Cordovero, when eaten and digested, leaves a residue of excrement. Did the flour then contain filth? Certainly not. The excrement was produced as a by-product of the process in which the valuable nutritive elements were extracted from the flour. A more exact analogy, adds Cordovero, is that of semen, which according to his physiology is derived from the brain. Certainly the mucus and slime that befoul a new-born baby were not present in the brain itself. There is no evil in the ultimate Source of Reality; it manifests itself only in the process of cosmic development.[23]

But the *Zohar* goes even farther in the attempt to penetrate this process of cosmic development, or, to use the other symbolism, of emanation both to right and to left. The earlier writers are content to interpret the leftward emanation in moralistic terms—it is to provide chastisement and warning and, if necessary, final punishment for sinners. But this is a circular form of reasoning, which does not account for the emergence of sin itself. The *Zohar* pictures a sort of upheaval within the very Godhead. Evil results from the division or, if you prefer, the differentiation, of the divine powers. "Power and wrath were aroused on the left by division, until they could not rest. Thus was Gehenna created." [24] This concept is closely related to the doctrine taught centuries later by Jacob Boehme, the great Protestant mystic, who emphasized the existence of dynamic and negative aspects within God, as the only possible explanation of the flux, the tensions and the conflicts of life.

One may well question whether such dualistic concepts of Deity are ultimately to be reconciled with the stubborn monotheism of Israel. And we shall see how Cordovero attempted this synthesis and ran into difficulty. Indeed, all inquiries into the processes, the natural history of divinity, such as are involved in the doctrine of Sefiroth—good as well as bad—may be criticized as incompatible with the true spirit of prophetic Judaism, which does not seek to penetrate into the secrets of God's existence, but only to discover His will and His commandments concerning us. But one cannot lightly dismiss the struggle of the Jewish mystics to find a satisfactory answer to the problem of evil. However grotesque their forms of expression may be, and however unsatisfactory their conclusions, they did not simplify their own task by minimizing the seriousness of the problem. They never failed to reckon with the vast and terrible power of wickedness in human life.

CHAPTER TWENTY-FOUR

The Later Mystics

The *Zohar* quickly achieved enormous influence and its teachings were widely accepted as authoritative. The doctrines of the "other side," "the husks," and the fallen angels, and the general consciousness of a satanic element in the world, are familiar in post-Zoharic Jewish literature. Even those writings which are not primarily cabalistic are touched by the mystical temper of the age.

Such, for example, are the Torah commentaries produced in these centuries. We saw earlier that the medieval expositors, influenced both by rabbinic tradition and by philosophic rationalism, explained that the "sons of God" in Genesis 6 were human beings distinguished for rank or for some physical or mental superiority; and they gave "safe" interpretations to the Azazel ceremony of Atonement Day. Now we find just the opposite. Such well known commentators as the Italian Menahem Recanati (early fourteenth century), the Spaniard Abraham Saba and the German Menahem Ziuni (both of the fifteenth century) take for granted that the "sons of God" were fallen angels; and they give a more frankly diabolic explanation of the Azazel ritual. Saba admits unblushingly that the scapegoat is a sacrifice to Satan. God advised us to appease the Accuser, that he may not attack us too harshly when we appear before the divine court.[1]

A curious variation of the Azazel story is preserved by Jacob di Illescas, an Italian scholar of the fourteenth century: Azazel was a prince of one of the angelic orders, who used to accuse Israel on Yom Kippur and call for their complete annihilation. God declared: Were you among them, you might be as sinful as they. Azazel called for a test; but when he descended to earth, soon fell prey to the charms of Naamah. Thereupon God proclaimed: Since he has sinned, let him never return to heaven, but let him dwell in the desert until the end of the world. In the long run, Azazel's malice redounds to Israel's benefit: the punishment he received deters other angels from accusing Israel with undue harshness! [2]

The sixteenth century saw the rise of a new and creative mystical movement centered in the little Palestinian town of Safed. Here, among other extraordinary personalities, lived Moses Cordovero, who clarified and systematized the cabalistic doctrine of previous generations; at almost the same time Isaac Luria was directing the Cabala into entirely new channels.

Cordovero was the great theorist of Jewish mysticism. In expounding the heritage of the past, especially of the *Zohar,* he made a mighty effort to harmonize cabalistic teaching with the fundamental concepts of Judaism. We have already seen his explanation of the "husks," in which he is at great pains to deny that the root of evil is in the Godhead.[3] In all his discussions of evil, the mythological materials are an inheritance and—so to speak—a problem. Cordovero's own contribution is the attempt to fit such materials into the monotheistic scheme.

This effort proceeds along two lines. One is to limit the parallel between the good and the evil emanations. This is already suggested in the earlier sources, which state that the leftward emanation proceeds from one of the Sefiroth, not from the *En Sof.* Cordovero goes further and declares that the ten evil Sefiroth bear the same resemblance to the real Sefiroth that an ape bears to a man. Again, there are seven "chambers of impurity" which provide garments for the ten stages of evil, just as there are seven chambers of purity which clothe the ten good Sefiroth. But there is no basic impurity beyond the seven chambers of evil, whereas above the seven chambers of purity are the different levels of the divine throne.[4]

We must not misunderstand aggadic passages which depict the "husks" entering the realm of holiness while in an unregenerate state—for instance, evil angels accusing Israel before God. What is meant is that the accusations arouse God's wrath and result in judgment against Israel, and thus it is said figuratively that the husks entered the holy presence. Elsewhere Cordovero puts the matter differently: the husks can penetrate the realm of holiness only in the world of *Yetzirah* (Formation), the world of Metatron; but they are excluded from the higher levels of *Azilut* (Emanation) and *Beriah* (Creation).[5]

In addition, Cordovero repeatedly declares (and this is also foreshadowed in earlier writings) that the evil forces serve a useful purpose of the divine economy. The "outside powers" exist by divine intent. Speaking figuratively, we may say that a portion of the divine emanation, clothing itself in garment after garment, is transmitted to them, and by this means they survive. Were there no spark of divinity within the husks, they could not exist at all. But their activity does not require us to impute change or impurity to the First Cause. They are called "other gods," impure, destroyers and similar names, not to suggest that they are outside His will or act without His permission, but because they are not united with Holiness in a bond of unity. God willed them into being so that man might receive his moral deserts, which would be impossible were he created (like the angels) without the capacity to do wrong. The "husk" is a necessity of heaven, suitable for the righteous and suitable for the world. Without it, there would be no possibility for man, by his good or evil actions, to influence the upper spheres.[6]

One should therefore not minimize the value of the "outside" powers. They may be compared to dust which, if fructified by water, becomes the soil for the cultivation of plants. Thus the sexual impulse, disciplined by the Torah, leads to the consecrated union of marriage. Jealousy can be sublimated (to use a modern term) into zeal for the faith; the appetite for food is transfigured at a festival celebration.[7] "Though the husks are unclean below, they are pure on high." [8]

This is admirable indeed, whether or not it is adequate. Yet the author of these philosophic statements is constrained by his faithfulness to the tradition to reproduce the personalized names of the evil *Sefiroth* and the gross legends about the two Liliths and their several consorts.[9]

Cordovero, however, exerted little influence on the subsequent development of the Cabala. It was the personality and outlook of Isaac Luria which dominated the next century. Here again, as in the case of German Cabala, one should distinguish between the actual doctrine of the master and the atmosphere of superstition which enveloped the masses. But both represent a challenge to the classic affirmations of Judaism.

Luria himself wrote little; the works of his disciples are voluminous and difficult. We shall rely chiefly on Dr. Scholem's exposition of the Lurian doctrine. The problem of evil is directly connected with the basic concepts of Luria's system—namely *Tzimtzum,* the contraction of the divine essence, and *Shevirath haKelim,* the bursting of the vessels through which the divine essence was channeled. Most interpreters have stressed this latter event as the source of evil. The divine light should have been contained in vessels, corresponding to the *Sefiroth* of earlier Cabala. But the light overflowed and broke through these receptacles. Thereupon sparks of goodness, scattered, detached from the whole, moved about the universe in confusion. This is evil; and the process of redemption must consist in the withdrawing of the sparks from their mixture with the "husks" and the reintegration of the divine goodness into a perfect and unmixed unity.

Actually, Dr. Scholem declares, a more searching examination of the Lurianic doctrine indicates that the beginnings of evil existed even before the "breaking of the vessels," and were, indeed, "latent in the act of *Tzimtzum.*" For this "contraction" means the withdrawal of the Infinite God into Himself, in order to make room for the processes of Creation. And this is an act of limitation, of "strict justice." Luria held, moreover, that the withdrawal of divinity did not leave a complete vacuum; traces of the divine, called *reshimu,* remained in the space actualized through the withdrawal of the *En Sof;* and the origin of the "husks" is connected also with this phenomenon.

Without probing more deeply into these difficult speculations, it is sufficient to remark that there is an unmistakable connection between Luria's doctrine of the "breaking of the vessels," and the older notion that evil is a kind of waste product of the cosmic process. In all these concepts, the root of evil is somehow in divinity itself; and it consists not so much in rebellion as in detachment from the central purposes of the Godhead.[10]

The ideas of Luria (of which we have mentioned only as much as we need for our purposes) had a wide influence. But the atmosphere of mystic awe, generated among the adepts, spread more widely still. Like the earlier cabalists, the Lurian mystics revealed their doctrine only to those they deemed mentally and spiritually ready for it. Nevertheless, they greatly stirred the imagination of the masses, as the German Hasidim had done in their time. In the mild climate of the Holy Land, Luria and his followers conducted many of their gatherings out of doors; and their comings and goings were no doubt closely and reverently observed by their fellow-villagers. Even more important was the new emphasis in the Lurian Cabala. The goal of mystic effort was no longer the personal bliss of inner vision, but the hastening of the Messianic redemption. This was an aim that appealed directly to all Jews of every degree, learned and unlettered. Lurian mysticism brought about considerable changes in the liturgy of the synagogue; it encouraged asceticism even among those who were not cabalistic initiates; and it heightened the mood of uncritical faith in which superstitions could flourish. However profound may be the concepts of Concentration and the Fracture of the Vessels—by which Luria accounted for the presence of evil—these processes were held to issue in a multiplicity of fiends and demons which were vividly real in the minds of plain people.

Characteristically, the Lurian school revived an old Sabbath ceremony which the rabbinic scholars had allowed to decline. Two bouquets of myrtle were placed on the Sabbath table; the celebrant walked twice around the table, carrying the bouquets on the second circuit. The myrtle plant was generally thought to have supernatural virtues; and this ceremony, among other purposes, was intended to protect the household against evil spirits.[11]

Another evidence of the mood created by the Lurian Cabala is the popular legend of Joseph della Reyna. This subject has been investigated by our mentor, Professor Scholem, and in essence it has nothing to do with Luria and his ideas.[12] The real Joseph della Reyna was a cabalist who lived probably in Egypt (certainly not in Palestine) a century or more before Luria was born. About the beginning of the fifteenth century a legend began to circulate about him, which has survived in several forms.

One tells that della Reyna, with ten associates, sought to gain control over Samael and Ammon of No, his servant, in order to destroy their power. The procedure they were to follow was to force the devils to materialize, by the use of a ring engraved with names, together with certain conjurations. Then each of the mystics was to place a brass crown, engraved with the Forty-Two Letter Name of God, upon the head of Samael, exclaiming: Thy Master's name is upon thee! This would break the power of evil. The preliminary procedures were efficacious; and amid natural convulsions the demons appeared in the form of serpents. Della Reyna's associates fled in terror; he alone stood his ground and placed the crown on the head of Samael. Samael informed his captor that he might complete his conquest (since the others had failed to do their part) by entering a certain house and burning incense. But this was an act of idolatry. Della Reyna succumbed to Samael's ruse; the demons regained their liberty; and the exile, instead of being cut short, was prolonged forty years.

A second version of this tale states that Joseph sinned by evoking the devils while he was in a waking state, instead of in a dream. For demons cannot be materialized by a waking person without the use of incense—which is forbidden as idolatry.

Later on the legend was completely recast into the form more familiar to us. Here Joseph della Reyna appears in the Galilean country as a member of the Lurian school; and the tale—written in a self-consciously literary style—was published as an appendix to a booklet, *Likkute Shas*, ascribed to Luria. The author, in Dr. Scholem's opinion, was one Solomon Navarro, who adopted the Christian faith in 1664!

According to this tale, R. Joseph hoped to bring about the redemption at once by conquering Samael. He first came into contact with Elijah, who discouraged him from the attempt, but finally told him how to summon the angel Sandalfon. Sandalfon appeared amid awful terrors, and Joseph invited him to join in fighting against Amalek and his "prince." Sandalfon replied: "If you knew the heights which Samael and his host have attained, you would not embark on this venture. None can prevail against him save the Holy One, until the time set for his downfall arrives." But Joseph della Reyna was determined to press on; and so Sandalfon, who did not know the secret of Samael's power, explained how the angels Akteriel and Metatron could be summoned.

The latter, after many misgivings, imparted the information which Joseph sought. He and his disciples were to perform lengthy and arduous purifications, then go to Mount Seir, while the angels (in company with his soul) were to parallel his progress in heaven. The use of imprecations and holy names would drive off the dogs which defended the stronghold of evil. By the same means Joseph and his fellows were to remove a mountain of snow, dry up a sea and cut a door through an iron wall. Having passed these obstacles, they would find Samael and Lilith in the shape of black dogs hiding in a ruin. They were to capture them by means of two inscribed leaden disks; and were to give no heed to their requests for food.

All these instructions were successfully carried out. But after the demons had been leashed, R. Joseph was near to fainting from his violent exertions and from the fasts which had preceded them. He refreshed himself by smelling a grain of incense. Samael pitifully asked that he too be given a sniff; and since no food was involved, Joseph felt that he could grant the plea. At once a spark issued from Samael's nostrils and consumed the incense! R. Joseph had performed an idolatrous act. The demons regained their freedom with savage glee; the whole undertaking had proved futile. Two of the disciples died, two went mad, only one returned to tell the tale. Joseph himself became the paramour of Lilith, used his cabalistic powers to gratify his bodily lusts, and came to a violent end.

In essence, this tale is un-Jewish. It draws upon popular traditions related to the Faust legend. In it we meet a Satan who is a mighty enemy of God and Israel, and who exults in evil; moreover, he is to be overcome only by magical devices. The fact that this story could become so popular, and that it could be associated with the practitioners of Lurian Cabala (though the doctrines of Luria had no resemblance or relation to it) is extremely instructive. It indicates the extent to which dualistic notions had penetrated into the lives and minds of Israel in the sixteenth century.

The direct result of the later cabalistic development was the Messianic movement of Sabbatai Zevi in the latter half of the seventeenth century, and the Sabbatian heresy which persisted in parts of Europe well into the nineteenth. This is not the place to tell the story of the fascinating young Jew of Smyrna who proclaimed himself Messiah in 1666, creating an uproar in world Jewry which had many echoes among the Christians, and who finally lost his nerve and saved his own life by adopting Islam. But it is clear that the way for Sabbatai, and even more for those who continued his cult after he had become an apostate, had been prepared by the cabalistic speculation that had preceded it. One might argue that the Sabbatian heresy (in at least some of its manifestations) would have appeared even had there been no Sabbatai. Not that Luria and his spiritual heirs intended anything like the consequences which the heretical cabalists drew. Undoubtedly they would have been horrified at the subversive doctrine of the sectaries. Nonetheless, it was from both the mood and the doctrine of Lurian Cabala that the followers of Sabbatai drew many hints for their new system.

First and foremost, the final redemption which Sabbatai hoped to achieve, and of which his successors did not despair, was the basic aim of Luria's teaching. Second, the doctrine that "sparks" of holiness have been dispersed among the "husks" and that the process of redemption consists in drawing out the sparks and uniting them with the central holiness was taken over by the Sabbatians—with an important addition. It is not enough for pure personalities to exert—so to speak—a magnetic attraction upon the sparks that have been scattered. So deeply are the good elements embedded in the husks that, to release the sparks, the righteous must enter the domain of evil. This, then, was why Sabbatai adopted Islam—not out of cowardice or weakness, but because as the redeemer he must enter the "side of evil" in order to rescue the elements of holiness trapped therein. The result of this doctrine was a more or less open antinomianism, a kind of sacramental violation of the precepts of the Torah, and in the case of extremists like Jacob Frank, an unrestrained licentiousness. It was consistent with all this that many Sabbatians followed their messiah into Islam, while other heretical groups were baptized *en masse.*

These messianists also elaborated a heretical theology. Like the ancient Gnostics they distinguished between the Hidden God and the Demiurge, whom they called "the God of Israel." But whereas the Gnostics considered the Demiurge to be evil, and the Hidden God alone worthy of worship by the enlightened, the Sabbatians regarded the First Cause, the God of the philosophers, as too remote for worship, which should be addressed only to the "God of Israel." [13]

We need not pursue this subject further. No critical eye is needed to see that such doctrines are a repudiation of everything essential and sacred in Judaism. The rabbis who hunted out the Sabbatian heresy may have displayed a touch of fanaticism; and their zeal in destroying sectarian documents has made the historian's task more difficult. But their attitude was basically sound.

CHAPTER TWENTY-FIVE

Mysticism for the Masses

The movement of Sabbatai Zevi was a natural outgrowth of Luria's Cabala; but the latter was not discredited in the eyes of the faithful because of its monstrous offspring. Jewish life continued to be dominated by the mystic mood, in the dark ascetic version of the Safed school. Comparatively few were concerned with the speculative aspects of Luria's teaching. Even for Luria himself, the interest in doctrine had been subordinate to the practical purpose of hastening the Messianic redemption. The chief means to this end were scrupulously ethical conduct and self-effacing piety. It was to these values that Luria's successors dedicated their efforts. R. Elijah di Vidas, a pupil of Cordovero, had already exerted great influence by his book, the *Beginning of Wisdom,* a handbook of morals and devotion. Though R. Elijah drew nearly all his material from talmudic-midrashic literature, his method of selection and presentation creates a darker atmosphere than that of the original sources. In the next century, no work achieved greater prestige than *The Two Tables of the Covenant* of R. Isaiah Horwitz. It is a sprawling compilation of counsels for every phase of the religious life, pervaded by the Lurian spirit, and with no pretensions to metaphysical system.

The seventeenth century saw likewise the wide distribution of simpler manuals of piety, which circulated both in Hebrew and in Yiddish translations. The *Kab haYashar* (*Honest Measure*) of R. Zevi Hirsch Kaidanover, and the *Shebet Musar* (*Rod of Rebuke*) of the Levantine R. Elijah b. Solomon Abraham quote Luria and the Lurians, as well as the older classics of Cabala. They often mention Satan, "the other side," "the husks" and the demons, now euphemistically referred to as "outsiders." But these popular writings do not attempt to explain the origin of evil or to define its place in the divine economy. Their aim is to arouse people—even to scare them—to repentance; and to this end they speak, now of Satan's wiles, now of God's grim justice. As the theoretical dualism of the great cabalists moves to the background, we hear again the suggestion that the forces of evil are somehow an integral part of the divine plan.

Kaidanover, for example, relates a bizarre occurrence in Posen. Some demons refused to vacate the cellar of a house, alleging that the former owner was their father and they were but occupying their inheritance. The case was actually tried before a rabbinic court, and the defendants are said to have presented their arguments within the framework of talmudic law! True, they had to be constrained by powerful conjurations to accept the jurisdiction of the court and to obey its decision; yet in some measure they recognized the validity of the Torah. This tale does not lead the author to any inquiry into the nature of demons or the possibility of their mating with mortals. He cites it simply as a warning against sexual license which, bad enough in itself, may even lead a man into the embraces of a demon.[1]

The *Rod of Rebuke* displays a similar moralistic approach. But sometimes we meet the notion (we found it expressed most dramatically in the legend of Joseph della Reyna) that Satan strives to prevent, or at least delay, the messianic redemption. This work quotes from Luria the opinion that one should follow his own inclinations in choosing a branch of Torah for intensive study. A strong desire to pursue a certain subject indicates that this was the purpose of his present incarnation. R. Elijah adds that one should disregard the critics who would persuade him to study something else than the theme his soul desires. For Satan is clothing himself in such persons in the hope that the man will fail to accomplish the goal of his incarnation and so doom himself to another needless death and rebirth.[2] In such a case Satan is not the tempter working within the framework of the divine purpose, but an opponent on the outside. But this viewpoint is not consistently maintained.

The popular pietism reflected in these writings was given an entirely new character in the Hasidic movement which arose in Eastern Europe in the middle of the eighteenth century. Jewish mysticism, which had so long been gloomy and ascetic in tone, was transformed by the spirit of joy and hope, rooted in simple and confident faith. This transformation was accomplished by a unique personality, R. Israel b. Eliezer, known as the *Baal Shem Tov* (Besht). The title is itself instructive. *Baal Shem* (master of the Name) was a term applied to those who could utilize the divine names for supernatural purposes, especially to control demons. The evil spirits who claimed the cellar in Posen submitted to the authority of the court only under the compulsion of a famous *Baal Shem*. R. Israel, however, was called "the good *Baal Shem*," as if to suggest that he was not a terrifying figure, like the other adepts, but someone kind and genial. His message brought light and vitality into the lives of masses broken by poverty and oppression, and unable to acquire the rabbinic learning which previously had been the pre-requisite for honor within the Jewish community. The Hasidic movement gave a heightened importance to the emotional side of religion, engendered a fresh awareness of the beauty of nature, stimulated the use of music and dance for religious expression and provided a more human and less bookish approach to the problems of daily living.

The Besht stressed the omnipresence of God almost to the point of pantheism. Since God is everywhere present and everywhere available, the proper mood of the pious man is one of joyous enthusiasm. How can one not be happy when he is near God? Gloom estranges man from the divine; even excessive anxiety over one's own sins is to be avoided, for it is a device of the evil inclination.[3] Such an outlook was calculated to minimize men's concern with the realm of active evil. The Hasidim, many of them simple unlearned folk, were connoisseurs of superstition; but (especially in the classic period of the movement) they had little concern with a cosmic war between God and the Devil.

The Besht is reported to have raised the question how good and evil can co-exist within the divine economy, which must be a unity, and to have replied "Evil is a throne for the good." This is immediately followed by moralistic examples: Suffering brings us nearer to God; those who live lives of rectitude experience satisfaction when they observe wickedness and reflect that they have escaped its temptations. Nay, by these means evil is itself transformed so that it is raised nearer to God.[4]

A later teacher, R. Naphtali Zevi of Ropshitz, put the matter in a different way. God is too pure to look upon evil (Habbakuk 1.13)—how then can the Accuser present our sins before the Divine Court? The answer is that even sin contains an element of holiness—the seed of repentance. Accusation is made against us in the form of a demand that we actualize the good potentiality of our evil deeds through penitence.[5]

The Hasidim therefore sometimes show a sympathetic attitude toward the forces of temptation, similar to that which we found in talmudic sources. "How," asks the Besht, "can a man hearken to the evil *yezer* to commit a sin? He ought to learn from the example of the evil *yezer* itself, which constantly performs the will of its Creator." [6] And he illustrates the matter with a parable: A certain king wished to test the loyalty of his subjects. So he designated a member of his court to simulate a rebellion and to urge others to join the revolt. The supposed rebel had some success; but a wise man reflected that the king would not have tolerated such behavior unless he had some deeper purpose in view. This story is told by R. Jacob Joseph, one of the Besht's early disciples, who finds the same truth indicated in the verse: "The Lord appeared unto him at the terebinths of Mamre" (Gen. 18.1). The name Mamre is connected with *marah*, "to rebel"— even in our rebellious instincts the divine reveals itself.[7]

The Hasidic authors (like most of their contemporaries) avoid the name Satan, speaking sometimes of the Accuser, the opponent (*baal davar*), the other side, the husks, and especially of the evil inclination. The latter term is applied not only to the tempter in the breast of the individual, but to the power of sin in general. The following legend is told of R. Elimelech of Leziensk, a leader in the second generation of the Besht's disciples: The "evil inclination" warned R. Elimelech to give up his efforts at regenerating his fellow-men. Were he to reform the entire world, nothing would be left for the evil *yezer* to do! Unless the rabbi desisted from his endeavors, the evil *yezer* would cease to tempt the rest of mankind and war against him alone. R. Elimelech replied: Whatever I do, you will surely tempt me with all your might— for you are no respecter of persons. And I too shall continue to do my very best.[8]

Sometimes, indeed, we meet suggestions that a malicious Satan is seeking to delay the redemption. In his younger days, an old legend reports, the *Baal Shem* had the duty of escorting children from home to school and back again. On these walks he taught the children to hymn God's praises with such fervor that Satan became fearful that his destruction was at hand. So he took the form of a Gentile enchanter, who appeared to the children as a ravening beast. No one was actually hurt; but the daily trips to school were interrupted until the Besht regained his self-confidence and persuaded the parents to trust their children to him. The next time the beast showed himself, the Besht struck him dead with a blow on the forehead. The following day they found the corpse of the sorcerer.[9]

This story displays not the power of the Devil, but the greatness of the *Baal Shem*. But occasionally we observe a darker note. The *Baal Shem's* great-grandson, R. Nahman of Bratzlav, was a gifted story teller. One of his tales concerns a young scholar who was dissatisfied with rabbinic studies: they failed to nourish his soul. In his quest for spiritual fulfillment, he decided to visit a certain (Hasidic) saint. But his father objected: the saint was inferior to his son in ancestry and learning, and it was beneath their dignity to visit him. But the son's desire was so strong that the father agreed to undertake the journey as long as no warning omen stopped them. On the way one of the horses fell and the cart was overturned; the father then decided that they must go back. The son insisted on a second attempt; but the axle of the cart broke, and again they turned homeward. On a third venture, they stopped at an inn; and there, in casual conversation, a trader informed them that the so-called saint was really a sinful fellow. Once more they went home, and soon thereafter the son died. Then he appeared repeatedly to his father in dreams, urging him to visit the saint; and at last the father set out on his mission. Stopping at the same inn, he met the trader again; and the latter now revealed that he was responsible for the obstacles that had prevented the young man from meeting the saint. For the saint had attained the rank of "great luminary," and the young scholar that of "lesser luminary." Had the two lights been joined, the Messiah would have come. "Now that I have got rid of him," ended the trader, "you may continue your journey." [10]

R. Nahman's story is obviously directed against the opponents of Hasidism; the conclusion is reminiscent of the legend about R. Joseph della Reyna. But nothing else of this sort is found in R. Nahman's stories, or in his recorded sayings. Under the heading *Kelipah* (husk), R. Nathan of Nemirov, R. Nahman's Boswell, has listed a dozen remarks—but they are all commonplaces about demons.[11]

It should be added that, while the founders of Hasidism did much to dissipate the atmosphere of terror which had been generated by the later Cabala, their successors did not always maintain the new mood of mystical joy. Some of the later Hasidim were inclined to the asceticism of the Lurian school; but they never abandoned entirely the hopeful and wholesome outlook which the Besht had commended.

Above all, we must remember that the Hasidim never cast their doctrine into systematic form. Their books are in considerable part notes of the informal instruction which the Hasidic saints gave their followers by word of mouth. In such collections, inconsistent elements are the more likely to appear. The most profound thinker of Hasidism, R. Shneor Zalman of Ladi, has little to say about evil forces. Dualistic ideas in Hasidic literature seem to be a survival of earlier doctrines rather than an integral part of Hasidic teaching. The key word of the latter is *yihud*, "unification," which is applied to every phase of existence from the creation of a unified fellowship in Israel to the uniting of the *Sefiroth* one to another and to the Infinite. No place is left for an independent area of the cosmos in rebellion against God. Satan resumes his old roles as tempter and accuser. Evil is a means for the revelation and triumph of the divine.

PART EIGHT
Christian Theology

CHAPTER TWENTY-SIX

The Devil of the Philosophers

Wͤe turn back to the Middle Ages to survey Christian beliefs concerning the Devil. A real development of the idea cannot be expected. The New Testament writings and the opinions of the great Fathers, notably Augustine, had fixed the doctrine of the Church rather clearly; and the Fourth Lateran Council, in 1215, defined the official teaching: "The Devil and the other demons were created by God with a good nature; but they themselves through their own agency became evil." [1] No change in this basic position could occur within the Catholic Church; and the doctrine was retained even by those who repudiated the authority of Rome. Not until, at the end of the eighteenth century, a new critical approach to both Hebrew and Christian Scriptures appeared, could there be substantial revision of the doctrine of Satan.

But though the idea underwent no inner development, it did express itself in a variety of new forms, some terrifying, all of them interesting.

The later Middle Ages saw the rise of great universities where philosophy was cultivated with increasing interest and skill. Aristotle reappeared in Latin translations made by way of Arabic and Hebrew; his Moslem and Jewish interpreters likewise became known in Christian Europe. The philosophers of this era—whether Jewish, Christian or Moslem—did not attempt to construct original or independent systems. Known as scholastics, they sought only by rational methods to clarify and defend the doctrines of their respective religions.

One of the most notable scholastics was St. Anselm of Canterbury (1033–1109). With resolute courage and great independence, he attempted to justify the doctrines of religion, not by appeal to the authorities of the past, but by reason alone. He formulated a famous proof for the existence of God; and in his *Cur Deus Homo* he attempted a rational account of the incarnation. Not only did God become man, as related in the New Testament, but, argues Anselm, the divine plan *had* to work out in this way and no other. The redemption of sinful mankind could be brought about only through a being who united within himself the human element (so that he shared the experience of those needing redemption) and the divinity by which he could rise above the fate of mankind. This thesis has some bearing on our subject. It precludes the view (already condemned by the Church) that the Devil and his minions may eventually be saved; for to redeem them, not a God-man, but a God-angel would have been required.[2] Anselm also, in the course of his demonstration, attacked the notion, held by several early Fathers, that the crucifixion was in the nature of a ransom paid to Satan and argued that "satisfaction" was due to God alone.[3]

In a short *Dialogue Concerning the Fall of the Devil*, Anselm makes plain the difficulties which this belief presented to the trained thinker. The angels are disembodied intelligences, completely spiritual, subject to none of the accidents or passions of the flesh. Their fall could not have been due to sensual impulse; their sin must have been a spiritual sin. But how could angels, created all good, have yielded to such sin? What was the difference by virtue of which some fell from grace, while others stood firm? Either there was some weakness in the original nature of the rebels—which means, God did not create them good—or else He did not bestow on them the same grace through which the others resisted temptation—in which case the fall was God's doing, not Satan's. Moreover, it is generally held that Satan's sin was the desire to usurp God's place. But even we mortals know that such an ambition was, not only wicked, but ridiculous; could not great angels, with their lucid minds, understand and refrain from such tragic folly? [4]

Anselm, it need hardly be said, stated the problems much more effectively than he solved them. We need not follow all the devious subtleties by which he and his successors—Peter Lombard, Albert the Great, Duns Scotus—attempted to reconcile tradition and reason on this point. Instead we pass at once to the man who digested and synthesized the work of all predecessors in the field. St. Thomas of Aquino, "the Angelic Doctor" (1225?–1274?), is still regarded by the Catholic Church as the authoritative expositor of its philosophy and theology. He frequently quotes the Jewish philosopher Maimonides; and there are many resemblances between the two. Both were rationalists, though not without mystical qualities. Both, saturated with the Aristotelianism of their age, re-interpreted in its light the received doctrines of their respective faiths. A comparison of the way these two men treat the problem of evil therefore provides an excellent insight into the essential divergence of the two religions.

Maimuni, it will be remembered, regards evil as something negative, the absence of good. It cannot therefore be ascribed to God the Creator. As for Satan and the demons, Maimonides speaks of them only as far as Scriptural references require, and explains such passages allegorically.[5]

St. Thomas, too, when treating of evil in the abstract defines it as a deficiency, not as a positive entity. Evil is "some absence of good"—it consists in the circumstance that a "thing fails in its goodness." [6] In one passage he even finds it necessary to prove logically that evil actions can occur, in the light of a statement by Dionysius "that evil acts not save by the power of the good." True, says St. Thomas, every action is good insofar as it has being. In this sense, too, God is the source of evil, since He alone can confer existence; but every evil, insofar as it has positive

existence, is good. What makes an act evil, however, is some deficiency, in order, measure, time, place and the like. Above all,
there is no first principle of evil, corresponding to and opposed
to the highest good.[7]

Such argumentation derives from Neo-Platonism, which was
partly retained by the scholastics even after the rediscovery of
Aristotle. The Platonists had always held the doctrine that evil is
non-entity. St. Thomas, however, clings to it the more emphatically because it provides a defense against extremes of dualism.
Several times he refers to these arguments as a refutation of the
Manicheans.[8]

But what about the Devil and his wicked hordes? Here
Thomas, the faithful Churchman, must reconcile the old myth
with his sophisticated rationalism. The problems Anselm had
tried to solve must be reviewed and settled. St. Thomas proceeds
as follows:

Angels are immaterial intelligences; but they are created beings, they have not always existed.[9] They possess free will—a
point much emphasized by Christian thinkers. For free choice,
argues Aquinas, is part of man's dignity; and since the angels
surpass man, they must all the more have the power of free will.
Again the angels are devoid of irascible and concupiscible appetites; for these instincts are assigned by Aristotle to the bodily
part of man, and the angels are bodiless.[10]

"To be established or confirmed in the good is of the nature of
beatitude." The angels were not so confirmed from the moment
of their creation; for we know some of them fell. They were
indeed created in a state of intellectual perfection, but had not
yet attained the supernatural vision of God. To turn to Him as
the object of beatitude, they required divine grace. Exercising
this divine power provided for his benefit, the angel might turn
to God; and he was beatified instantly after his first act of devotion to God's service. Having once made this choice, the angel
was not further subject to sin.[11]

But not all the angels made the same choice: some decided
wrongly. Here St. Thomas finds it necessary to introduce proofs,
from both Scripture and logic, that angels can be subject to sin.
They cannot indeed commit the gross mortal sin that comes
through ignorance or error, or through bodily passion. But there
is also another kind of sin, which results from choosing something

good in itself, but not according to the proper measure or rule. Such a sin does not presuppose ignorance, but merely the failure to consider things which ought to be considered. An angel might sin in this way, by turning freely to his own good without regard for the divine will. As Augustine long since argued, angels can have no other sin than pride or envy—sins in no way dependent on body or sense.[12]

When did the angels sin? The Fathers disagree. St. Thomas rejects the view that they sinned in the very instant of their creation, for in the first moment the angels must have acted through the agency of their Creator. He thinks it probable that the Devil sinned in the first moment *after* his creation; and he inclines to the view of Gregory that, previous to his downfall, the Devil had been the most eminent of the angels.[13]

From Isaiah 14.13-14, says Thomas, we have clear proof that the Devil actually desired to be as God. But how could he have wished such a thing? Surely an angel must know that for a creature to desire to equal the Creator is a logical contradiction!

True, says the wise doctor, the Devil did not desire to be absolutely equal with God, not only because he must have known it was impossible, but because it would have meant that he must cease to be himself. But the desire to be like God can take two forms. One is the proper desire to become godly through God's help. "In another way, one may desire to be like God in some respect which is not natural to one: e.g., if one were to desire to create heaven and earth, which is proper to God, in which desire there would be sin. It was in this way that the Devil desired to be as God. Not that he desired to resemble God by being subject to no one else absolutely; for he would thus be desiring his own non-being, since no creature can exist except by participating under God. But he desired resemblance with God in this: that he desired as the last end of beatitude something which he could attain by the virtue of his own nature, turning his appetite away from the supernatural beatitude which is attained by God's grace. Or if he desired as his last end that likeness to God which is bestowed by grace, he sought to have it by the power of his own nature, and not from the divine assistance according to God's ordering. This harmonizes with Anselm's opinion, who says that he sought that to which he would have come had he stood fast." Moreover he wished dominion over others.[14]

This is indeed an attenuated version of Satan's rebellion. It seems hardly worth the trouble to sin for such limited objectives! St. Thomas, however, is struggling to adjust an old crude myth to his own highly developed philosophic outlook; one cannot but admire how manfully he attempts a thankless and, indeed, ultimately impossible job.

Thomas goes on to state that the sin of the Devil served as an example and inducement for others to follow him; but the number of angels who stood fast is far greater than that of those who sinned. The fallen angels are identical with the demons.[15]

These beings remain essentially intellectual. They retain that knowledge of truth which derives from their original nature, and as much of the speculative knowledge obtained through grace as is needful. But they are utterly deprived of that grace-given knowledge "which is affective, and produces love for God." [16] They are not subject to bodily feelings and passions. When we ascribe fury or lust to the demons, we are speaking metaphorically, just as when we ascribe anger or regret to God.[17] The demons delight in carnal sin, but only as a means of hurting man. They derive, so to speak, a spiritual pleasure from human sensuality, not because it is pleasurable, but because it is wicked.[18] St. Thomas does not doubt the existence of incubi and succubi; but he holds that an incubus can beget a child only by utilizing human seed.[19]

Just as the blessed angels are confirmed in goodness and cannot sin, so the wicked angels, having chosen sin, are irreparably committed to it. They are sorry for having failed, but they are not sorry for having sinned.[20]

In St. Thomas' thought, the fallen angels subject to punishment are fully identified with the evil spirits now active in the world. Because of their sin, they deserve to be in hell. But God, using their evil inclinations for his own purposes, keeps most of them in the "cloudy atmosphere" as in a prison until the judgment day. This is the teaching of Augustine. Some of the demons are already in hell, where they torment those souls which they successfully tempted—just as some of the good angels are with the holy souls in heaven. After judgment day all the wicked, both angels and men, will be in hell forever.[21]

Meantime, detained in the cloudy atmosphere, the demons do God's work by tempting men. True, their intention is entirely

malicious; but God turns it to good use, for it is morally benefi-
cial for man to struggle with temptation. God, of course, knows
in advance what will be our reaction to the Devil's wiles. The
temptation ordained of God is not really for the purpose of knowing, but rather making known, the moral stuff of which we are
made. Sometimes, however, the demons assault us, not for temptation, but for punishment. In such cases—as when the lying
spirit was sent to lure Ahab to his death—we may say that the
demon is sent by God.[22] There is a sort of hierarchy among the
demons, based on the angelic status they possessed before their
rebellion.[23]

In the sense that he instigated the sin of Adam, we may call
the Devil the source of all sin. But individual sins have a variety
of causes, and are not all the work of Satan. Some of the causes
of sin are internal—ignorance, malice, passion. The external causes
of sin are said to be God, the Devil and human tempters. St.
Thomas denies that God can be the cause of sin. He is indeed the
cause of all acts, insofar as they possess being and activity; but
sinfulness is always in the nature of a deficiency, resulting not
from God's will, but from man's free choice.[24]

Thomas also limits the role of the Devil as a cause of sin. The
sins which result from inordinate physical appetites could occur
without any diabolic intervention. Though St. Jerome says that
"as God is the perfecter of good, so the Devil is the perfecter of
evil," his words must not be taken too literally. For God can move
the will inwardly; but the Devil can only stir the imagination and
the bodily appetites, thereby darkening the reason. The Devil's
role is limited to proposing sin and persuading us to it, just as
human tempters might do.[25] The root of sin is in man's freedom
of will.[26]

We must likewise be cautious in attributing miraculous powers
to the demons. God alone can perform true miracles. But men can
sometimes do astonishing works, and angels all the more. Some
of these performances are not illusory—as when the magicians
of Egypt, by demonic powers, produced real serpents and frogs.
(In such cases the demons do not actually transmute matter, but
utilize certain seminal principles resident in the material world.)
The more radical wonders produced by the demons are only semblance. They are accomplished either by working on man's imagi-

nation or senses, or by clothing the air with a corporeal appearance.[27]

Some features of this exposition of Thomas Aquinas were criticized by his contemporaries, especially his great antagonist Duns Scotus.[28] Nor has every detail been adopted by the Church. But in its main outlines, the satanology set forth above is still the doctrine of Rome.

CHAPTER TWENTY-SEVEN

The Devil of the People

The highly abstract conception of the Devil presented in the previous chapter was of interest only to a few exalted intellects; but the popular notions to which we now turn were not confined to quaint villagers. They were shared by laity and clergy alike; even men of vast erudition believed in a most realistic sort of Devil, whose workings they were sure they had experienced. Not a few were convinced that they had seen him with their own eyes, in a variety of dreadful forms. Medieval literature and art depict him as a horrible monster, usually equipped with horns and with the wings and claws of a dragon. He takes other forms, too, notably those of the goat and pig. He blights all life with his malice; he is the source not only of sin, but of every physical evil—sickness, storm, crop-failure, emotional disturbance.

Surprisingly, the consciousness of Satan was not at its height in the early medieval period, the so-called Dark Ages. The twelfth and thirteenth centuries, which witnessed the building of the great cathedrals, the rise of the universities, and the flowering of scholastic philosophy, were precisely the years in which the awareness of the Devil and his powers rose to a new and terrifying climax.

The belief in the reality and power of the Devil is indeed to be found in every age of historical Christianity. Tertullian, for example, was obsessed by the horror and danger of the spirit world. But the violent intensity of his feeling was, for his age, somewhat exceptional. More and more, however, as centuries went by, did this mood become characteristic. Bulky tomes were compiled by monastic writers, setting forth in minutest detail the innumerable activities and stratagems of the Devil and his hosts.

Nothing is too trivial for Satan's direct intervention. If the howling of the wind through the trees produces a momentary fright, if a headache distracts a brother from his devotions, or if an indolent mood prompts the postponement of some task, the Devil is at work in person. An endless store of tales in which the Devil appears visibly to torture the saints or to tempt the unsteady are solemnly set forth. No one doubted that Satan had unwisely approached St. Dunstan while the latter was working at his forge, and that the doughty saint had grasped Satan's nose with his red-hot pincers and forced him to an undignified retreat! Such tales were part of the stock-in-trade of the preachers and circulated freely among the people.

As in this last instance, there is sometimes a comic note in the stories about Satan.[1] I suspect that this is partly an inheritance from heathen antiquity. The relation between pre-Christian paganism and the demonology of medieval Europe has not been fully settled. The Christian teachers, we saw, identified the heathen gods and goddesses with the demonic fallen angels. Some modern investigators have taken a similar view and interpreted medieval witchcraft and diabolism as survivals of the old pre-Christian cults.[2] However this may be, we cannot doubt that many an old Germanic tale of forest demons, trolls and giants persisted after the tellers of the story had become Christian; and the evil spirit of the story became Satan or one of his lieutenants. Many of these old tales concern the outwitting of the demon by some clever human device. They may be the source of some of the jollier stories in which Satan comes off second best.

But by and large, there was nothing funny about the Devil in medieval Europe. A competent authority remarks: "It may almost be said that to the ordinary man during this period, the Devil was a more insistent reality than God Himself."[3] He darkened men's lives with his terrors. The love of God was too often obscured by the all-powerful fear of the Devil.

WITCHCRAFT. The consequences of this pervading terror were far more serious than the generation of a gloomy mood. The belief in witchcraft—universal in former ages—now took on a more dreadful aspect. The view gradually emerges that a person can enter into direct compact with the Devil, selling his soul in exchange for material benefits or supernatural powers. The earliest instance of this belief is the story of Theophilus, which appeared in a Greek writing of the sixth century and was retold later in many different versions.[4] Theophilus had been disappointed in his hopes of ecclesiastical preferment, and sold himself to the Devil in order to gain power; but, in the end, the Virgin intervened to release him from the power of Satan, and he died in sanctity.

At a later date this theme of a compact with the Devil became much more popular. The most famous example is the story of Faust, which has had such great fascination for creative artists. The older versions of this tale, incidentally, agree that Faust remained unregenerate, and in the end the Devil carried him off. So it is not only in the old folk-story, but in Marlowe's *Faustus* and in the musical setting of Berlioz, *La Damnation de Faust.* Even in Gounod's tuneful opera, Marguerite's soul is saved, but Faust remains in the clutches of Mephistopheles. Only Goethe's philosophic poem, and Boito's ambitious but not wholly successful attempt to transform it into music-drama, permit Faust to attain eventual salvation. Of course, to the modern writer it is precisely the outwitting of the Devil which is the chief interest. A beautiful instance is Stephen Vincent Benet's story, *The Devil and Daniel Webster.*

But this notion, unfortunately, did not remain mere legend, to be studied by folklorists and transfigured by poets. It is the root of the medieval Christian conception of witchcraft and of all the abominable deeds it brought forth. To comprehend this matter the more clearly, let us turn back for a moment to the Jewish views on the subject.

Sorcery, magic and divination are ancient beyond all reckoning. By many peoples they are regarded as transactions with dark and dangerous powers. In Israel especially they were condemned as illegitimate. The law (Deut. 18.10 ff. and elsewhere) briefly prohibits a number of occult practices. Some involved consultation of the spirits of the dead; other techniques can be illustrated from non-Israelite sources. There is more than one hint in the Bible that these practices are prohibited because they are akin to idolatry. Special mention must be made of the brief law in Exodus 22.17: "Thou shalt not suffer a sorceress to live." Later commentators remark, no doubt correctly, that the law applies equally to male sorcerers; but the Torah mentions women because they are specially addicted to this sin. It is reported that Saul was energetic in purging the land of witchcraft, though in desperation he himself finally resorted to it (I Sam. 28).

The Mishnah distinguishes between witchcraft—the actual performance of supernatural deeds—and illusion. If a man caused the cucumbers in a garden to pluck themselves from the vine and pile themselves in one spot, he would be liable to the death penalty; if he merely made people think they had seen this trick happen, he would be guiltless.[5] The Mishnah likewise reports that Simeon b. Shetah (a leading Pharisee, c. 70 B.C.E.) once hanged eighty witches in Askelon on a single day. The episode is mentioned as highly exceptional, since the Jewish criminal law forbids not only mass executions, but even mass trials. Simeon is said to have suspended the established laws because of emergency. It should be added that the detailed account of the incident in the Palestinian Talmud is altogether of legendary character; the real facts of the case are highly uncertain.[6]

This is the only recorded instance, to my knowledge, in which Jewish authorities are reported to have invoked the death penalty for witchcraft. From about the beginning of the Christian era, it is true, Jewish courts rarely had the right to try or punish major criminal offenders. But I have not encountered any case where even an accusation of criminal witchcraft was made. Jewish thought does not regard witches as constituting a special category of human beings; it simply condemns certain types of behavior.

During the Middle Ages, superstitious practices became somewhat more open and respectable. Even the talmudic sources, condemning many procedures as "ways of the Amorite," list others which are permissible, or at least pardonable.[7] The "practical Cabala" was a kind of magic; but as we have seen, it consisted chiefly in the use of divine and angelic names. It is not a rebellion against God, but a somewhat selfish and materialistic use of divine powers.

Christians, too, knew of what is sometimes called "white magic." One, Agrippa of Nettesheim, early in the sixteenth century, wrote a massive defense of what he calls "natural" or "celestial" magic.[8] But it was generally agreed among Christians that witches are persons who have made a compact with Satan, the father of evil; they are enrolled in his legions and are the avowed enemies of God and His people. They accomplish their supernatural deeds through the agency of the demons. They can be overcome only by the most alert resistance and the most ruthless prosecution.

Once more, the marked divergence between Jewish and Christian viewpoints can be illustrated by citing the two great rationalists, Moses ben Maimon and Thomas Aquinas. Maimuni summarizes the talmudic laws concerning witchcraft in the section of his code dealing with idolatry, and concludes as follows: "All these things are lies and falsehoods with which the ancient idolaters deceived the peoples, that they might follow them. It is not fitting for Israel, who are a truly wise people, to be attracted by these vanities, or to suppose that they are of value; for it is said (Num. 23.23) 'There is no enchantment with Jacob, neither is there any divination with Israel.' And it is said (Deut. 18.14) 'For these nations, that thou art to dispossess, hearken unto soothsayers and unto diviners; but as for thee, the Lord thy God had not suffered thee to do so.' Whoever believes in these things and the like of them, and supposes that they are genuine and a kind of wisdom, but that the Torah forbids them, belongs to the fools and the deficient in knowledge, in a class with women and children whose mentality is incomplete. Those who are possessors of wisdom and perfected in knowledge know by clear proofs that all these things which the Torah forbids are not wisdom, but empty vanity, after which the deficient in knowledge are drawn, who in consequence cast off all truth. Hence the Torah, in warning us against these follies, says: (*ibid.* v. 13) 'Thou shalt be whole-hearted with the Lord thy God.'"[9]

No such forthright skepticism is expressed by the philosopher of the Church. He is, indeed, far more cautious in relating the works performed by sorcerers than the writers we shall shortly mention. "*It is averred,*" he says, "that at the mere presence of a certain person all doors are unlocked, that a certain man becomes invisible, and many like occurrences *are related.*" And again, "*It is stated* that by the magic art a statue is made to move of itself, or to speak." Sometimes he is less wary. He remarks without qualification that "answers are given about stolen goods and the like." "Now in these apparitions and speeches that occur in the works of magicians, it frequently happens that a person obtains knowledge of things surpassing the capacity of his intellect, such as the discovery of hidden treasure, the manifestation of the future; and sometimes true answers are given in matters of science." But these variations of language are not very important. For even the items which Thomas mentions as mere reports are used to reinforce his argument that the magic art cannot be merely the employment of astral forces, that is to say, a kind of scientific technique, but involves recourse to the demons—demons whom he elsewhere has identified as the altogether depraved companions of Satan in rebellion against God.[10]

These two thinkers represent the maximum of enlightenment in their respective religious policies. There were many medieval Jews who did not doubt the reality of witchcraft and might have censured Maimuni for denying it. But just as there is a great difference between Maimonides with his flat denial and St. Thomas with his cautious affirmation, so there is a comparable gap between the most superstitious medieval Jew and the frantic witch-hunters of Christendom. Here again, it should be noted that the witch hysteria is a comparatively late development. It swelled toward the end of the Middle Ages and was at its height throughout the period of the Renaissance and Reformation. A modern Catholic writer can point with some satisfaction to the fact that Agobard, Bishop of Lyons in the ninth century, attacked the credulity which led to witch-prosecutions.[11] At a later date, Agobard might have suffered for his forthrightness. In 1453, the Prior of St. Germain, William of Edelin, who had preached against the reality of witchcraft, had to sue publicly for pardon; he had to confess that he himself had worshipped Satan and had renounced his faith in the Cross. His own sermons against the belief in witchcraft, he was forced to declare, were preached at the express command of the Devil, for the propagation of the Satanic dominion. Even this recantation did not save him from spending the rest of his life—a very short time—in prison.[12]

This episode reflects a trend which had been growing for years. The glorious thirteenth century witnessed the activity of Conrad of Marburg, an inquisitor who ferreted out heretics and witches throughout Germany with terrible ferocity. Another executive of the "Holy Office," Hugo de Beniols, burned a number of distinguished persons at Toulouse in 1275. Among them was Angèle, Lady of Labarthe, then sixty-five years old. It was alleged that she had been the paramour of Satan and had borne her lover a monster, with a wolf's head and a serpent's tail, which ate nothing but babies.[13] Such ghastly events were not infrequent; to multiply citations would only serve to nauseate the reader.

Although the initiative in witch-hunting was taken by workers "in the field"—sometimes the local clergy, sometimes the Inquisitors—they received substantial backing from headquarters. In 1437, Pope Eugene sent a circular letter to the Inquisitors, urging them to act swiftly and efficiently in the prosecution of witches, without the formalities of judicial procedure. Indeed, it was generally understood that the usual legal safeguards for the accused did not apply to witch-trials. Asseverations of innocence were regarded as *prima facie* evidence of guilt, and the flimsiest and most nonsensical testimony was treated as fully valid—so long as it served to condemn the suspects. In 1484, Pope Innocent VIII issued the bull *Summis Desiderantes,* which greatly facilitated the labors of Jakob Sprenger and his Inquisitorial colleagues who were busy hunting witches in Germany, and who had encountered some opposition from secular authorities. Later on, the successors of Innocent made similar pronouncements.[14]

Three years after the issuance of the bull of Innocent, a monumental work appeared entitled *Malleus Maleficarum* (The Witch Hammer). It is very probably the work of Sprenger. Here the various activities and characteristics of witches are described with unlimited fantastic detail, and full directions are provided for the successful detection and prosecution of witchcraft. In sum, the Inquisitor is advised to abandon all reason and justice. With complete assurance the author of this book declares that to deny the reality of witchcraft is the worst of all heresies.[15]

Not long after *The Witch Hammer* appeared, the Abbot of the Monastery of Sponheim, one Johann Trithemius, was requested by the Markgrave of Brandenburg for an opinion on the whole question. The reverend abbot accordingly devoted years of conscientious study to the subject and presented his findings in a four volume work, which began to appear when the author had reached the age of sixty-six. This *Antipalus Maleficiorum* distinguishes four classes of wizards and witches: those who hurt and kill others by poison and other natural means; those who commit injuries by the use of magical formulae; those who converse personally with the Devil; and those who have actually entered into a compact with him. And Trithemius gives his considered opinion that there is not a village which does not harbor at least one of the third and fourth classes! [16]

Armed with such convictions, the witch-hunters put thousands of victims to death, often with savage torments. The cruelty evoked by the belief in witchcraft is the accurate measure of the frantic terror which it inspired. Simple ignorance and normal brutality do not suffice to explain the atrocities. Certain classes of individuals were especially marked out for destruction. Those with odd, especially disfiguring, physical characteristics; neurotic and feeble-minded persons; old and solitary women; scientifically-minded students who expressed disbelief in some superstition were frequently the targets of denunciation, which almost invariably meant condemnation. At least occasionally, accusations must have been leveled out of sheer malice, since there was hardly a better way to get rid of an enemy than to charge him with witchcraft. Probably the greatest number of the accusations had no basis whatever except in the mental disease which was chronic in the population and acute in the prosecutors. And the root of the disease was dread of the Devil.

Yet it seems indubitable that the sins which the Church condemned so roundly and punished so terribly were not altogether imaginary. There must have been practitioners of black magic. It has been supposed that the cult of the Devil was a survival of the old paganism, which went underground after the triumph of Christianity. Perhaps the conventional picture of Satan with horns and hooves is somehow connected with the figure of the god Pan. It is easy to understand how those who continued to worship the old deities in secret would cherish a bitter hostility to the dominant religion, yet more and more they would accept its presuppositions. Thus an ancient pagan cult would become gradually a glorification of the Devil as the opponent of Christianity. This is still, however, only a plausible hypothesis.[17]

It has also been suggested that many a credulous soul may have been attracted to witchcraft and Devil worship through suggestions implanted by the official enemies of these practices: that, in short, the witch-hunters created the very terrors that haunted them. Such an explanation seems to fit well in the case of the famous Gilles de Rais (1404–1440), a scion of an ancient and noble family and Marshal of France. He had won great glory for his courageous support of Joan of Arc in the war of liberation against the English. Then, apparently because of financial stringency, he began to dabble in witchcraft in the hope of restoring his fortunes, meanwhile protecting his spiritual interests by various gifts to religious foundations. Gradually he became involved in ghastly and truly diabolic undertakings in which dozens of individuals were tortured to death. The detailed and voluminous evidence which was presented at his trial seems to preclude any doubt that the victims were actual sacrifices to the evil power whose favor Gilles sought to obtain.[18] But there are still many queer and unexplained things about the famous trial; and it should not be forgotten that in the next century, when a priest named Urban Grandier was tried on similar—though less sensational—charges, the original contract by which he disposed of his soul, bearing his own signature and that of the Prince of Darkness, was actually produced in court.[19]

At all events, there is little reason to doubt that the Sabbat—the gathering of witches for nocturnal rites, in which one of those present impersonated Satan—and the Black Mass, in which the central rite of the Church was obscenely burlesqued, were actually celebrated.

THE DEVIL'S PEOPLE—THE JEWS. Another tragic consequence of the lively belief in the Devil was the demonic conception of the Jews which evolved during the later Middle Ages. Here, again, the roots of the attitude go back almost to the beginnings of Christianity. There are bitter anti-Jewish elements in the Synoptic writings; and the Fourth Gospel explicitly identifies the Jews as children of the Devil (John 8.44). There is a great deal to the same effect in the writings of the Fathers.

When Rome became officially Christian, oppressive measures against the Jews were introduced, and from time to time active persecutions occurred. And yet, during the "Dark Ages" the Jews enjoyed a substantial measure of security and freedom, and there was often friendly social intercourse between Jews and Christians. Except in Spain under the Catholic Goths, who persecuted the Jews without mercy, this period was not altogether an unhappy one.

A new and terrible era was ushered in by the First Crusade, when in 1096 the Jewish communities of the Rhineland and elsewhere were systematically butchered. Thereafter massacres and expulsions became frequent and affected much larger numbers of people; and during intervals when violence subsided, Church and State collaborated in segregating and humiliating the Jews, and in subjecting them to all kinds of oppressive and discriminatory laws.

Concomitant with these overt acts was a new interpretation of the Jewish character. It was no longer sufficient to condemn the Jews for their rejection of the Christian gospel, to hate them for their alleged responsibility for the death of the Savior, or to charge them with all sorts of moral faults. They are now pictured as entirely devoid of normal humanity. Since they deny the truth of Christianity, they are obviously enemies of Christ. Therefore, they are allies of Satan. Therefore they are themselves devils. Such was the simple reasoning of the Middle Ages.

Dr. Joshua Trachtenberg, who has investigated this subject thoroughly, has drawn his materials not only from books but from the art and drama of the period. Jews were represented with horns, claws and tails (to this day, there are rustics in our own country who cannot be persuaded that Jews do not have horns), and in other pictures Satan appears among the Jews wearing the Jew-badge upon his garments and joining with them in the practice of usury. In the "mystery plays," the crucifixion is the result of a conspiracy in which the Jews and Satan are partners, and Jews and demons manifest equal glee over the sufferings they occasion.[20]

Particularly striking are the medieval Antichrist legends, for they resemble tales we have already encountered in Jewish sources of dubious authority. The idea of the Antichrist is found in New Testament writings; but a detailed legend about this sinister figure is said to have taken form only about the tenth century. The great scholastics, Albertus Magnus and Thomas Aquinas, discuss the matter; and for reasons readily understood, deny that the Devil himself is to sire the Antichrist, though they agree that the birth of the latter will be in some way influenced by Satan. But they could not eradicate the popular view. In one of the French Antichrist plays, a Jewish prostitute offers herself to Satan that she may bear a child who will destroy Christianity and restore Jewry to power. In another version of this drama, a Jewish voluptuary gives his daughter to the Devil for the express purpose that she may mother the Antichrist.[21]

Further details—and they are consistently appalling—may be found in Dr. Trachtenberg's valuable study, *The Devil and the Jews.* He has shown beyond challenge that the demonic conception of the Jew has greatly colored European culture and provided a deep-rooted emotional prejudice for the modern anti-Semites to exploit.

Once more, let us note a strange fact, which cannot be fully explained. The intense awareness of the Devil, the fear of witchcraft, and the dread of the Jew as a demonic being all reached their climax toward the end of the Middle Ages and the beginning of the Renaissance. These violent emotional disturbances were at their height precisely during the period when European culture and intellectual life were in a magnificent upswing.

THE HERETICS. As in its earliest days, so in the Middle Ages, the Church set limits to the degree of dualism that was allowable and condemned extreme doctrines as heretical. And from time to time the old Gnostic-Manichean themes were revived, generally in combination with a radical opposition to clerical authority and to the established institutions and rites of the Church. As early as the fifth century, there was a sect in western Asia known as the Paulinians or Paulicians, who distinguished between the good Heavenly Father and the evil Demiurge, the God of the Old Testament. (Yet they indignantly denied that they were Manicheans, and are said to have anathematized Mani!) They suffered fierce persecutions by the Byzantine emperors, but they were never completely conquered; they were rediscovered in the eighteenth century, after an underground existence of many hundreds of years.[22]

It is hard to trace the relationship of one heresy to another. We have some record of incidents by which the Paulicians moved westward into Europe; but it is not clear whether the Bogomils of Bulgaria, the Cathari of western Europe, the Paterines who appeared in Italy, and other similar heresies represent the direct continuation of Paulician influence or are parallel phenomena.

The Bogomil movement is especially interesting for our purpose because of its highly developed dualistic mythology. The
Bogomils taught that God had two sons: the elder Satanel, the
younger Michael. The elder son rebelled and became the spirit
of evil. He created the lower heavens and the earth, but was not
able to create a living man. At length he persuaded God to
breathe a soul into Adam. Once this was accomplished, Satanel
set out to corrupt humanity. According to one version, he permitted Adam to till the earth only on condition that mankind
should serve him (Satanel), the owner of the earth. Another account reports that Satanel seduced Eve and became the father
of Cain, the principle of evil in humanity. This principle prevailed over Abel, the good principle. Satanel imposed himself on
the Jews as the supreme God, and beguiled Moses into accepting
the fatal gift of the Law. In the fullness of time, Michael, God's
younger son, was incarnated as Jesus. Though Satanel was able
to bring about the crucifixion, he lost the limitless power he had
hitherto enjoyed. The last syllable of his name was taken away,
as an indication that he had lost his former rank: he is now mere
Satan. Yet he was still able to father the whole orthodox community with its churches, priests, monks, vestments and sacraments.[23]

A little later, western Europe saw the rise of a sect who called
themselves *Cathari,* the pure ones. Teaching a doctrine less
crudely mythological than that of the Bogomils, they drew even
more radical consequences from their beliefs. Opposed to the
true God, they held, is the evil God Satan, "who inspired the
malevolent parts of the Old Testament, is god and lord of this
world, of the things that are seen and are temporal, and especially of the outer man which is decaying, of the earthen vessel,
of the body of death . . . This world is the only true purgatory
and hell . . . Men are the result of a primal war in heaven, when
hosts of angels incited by Satan or Lucifer to revolt were driven
out and imprisoned in terrestrial bodies created for them by the
adversary."

Earthly life being so essentially evil, one who dies unregenerate is reincarnated in the first body, animal or human, which
the soul can find, in order to escape persecution by the powers of
the air. The only escape from this impasse is the way of spiritual
redemption taught by the Cathari. Churches, creeds and sacra-

ments are of no avail. Only the ascetic life of purification will do. Those who entered fully upon this course were known as *perfecti;* their sympathizers were known as *credentes.*

Such heresy was bound to evoke the fury of the Church, not only because of its unorthodox theology, but because of its clear challenge to ecclesiastical authority. It became very popular in southern France in the twelfth and thirteenth centuries, where its adherents were known as Albigenses. So serious did the threat seem to the Popes that an Albigensian Crusade was launched in 1209, and thousands of the heretics (together with many who were innocent even of heresy) were ruthlessly massacred.[24]

Less successful were the efforts to eradicate the Waldenses (or Vaudois), a related sect of northern Italy. Their doctrines were, however, not so extreme as those of the earlier sectaries, and their chief interest was in the reform of the Church. Under the stress of persecution, they withdrew into the mountain fastnesses of Piedmont, where they still survive, though with great difficulties. Ultimately they made common cause with Calvin and the Reformers, and it is as a Protestant group that they exist today. One of the many punitive expeditions against them called forth Milton's magnificent sonnet *On the Late Massacre in Piedmont:*

> "Avenge, O Lord, thy slaughtered saints, whose bones
> Lie scatter'd in the Alpine mountains cold." [25]

CHAPTER TWENTY-EIGHT

Protestant Christianity

LUTHER. The Protestant Reformation was not a modernist or liberal movement, though it eventually led to such developments. At the start it was a reaction against the corruption of the Catholic Church and a manifestation of the growing spirit of nationalism. Martin Luther was less of a liberal than such Catholic humanists as Reuchlin and Erasmus. He challenged the authority of the papacy, and he drastically revised certain doctrines; but he retained many elements of traditional Christian theology: among them, the belief in the Devil.

There is little or nothing about the Devil in the most important Protestant creeds, such as the Augsburg Confession, the Thirty-Nine Articles and the Westminster Confession. The men who composed these documents were not at all indifferent to the belief in Satan, still less were they sceptical about it. But they devoted their attention chiefly to controversial issues. Since everyone agreed about the existence of the Devil, they felt no need to discuss it.

A familiar legend tells that while Luther was confined in the Wartburg, Satan appeared to him; whereupon the doughty monk threw his inkwell at the fiend and drove him off. There seems to be no basis for the tale; yet rarely is a legend so apposite. Luther was not apparently subject to the grosser hallucinations. (He does report that Satan once kept him awake by tossing nuts at the ceiling of his room in the castle; but the episode became much more terrifying in recollection twenty-five years later than when it actually occurred.[1]) Yet few men have been more conscious of a personal Devil. Luther's emotional, impulsive and dramatic nature was well adapted to such a belief. His conversation and his letters were studded with references to Satan. After due allowance for figurative and facetious allusions, the number made in dead earnest is impressively large.

In his work on the *Unfree Will* (in which Luther solemnly set forth a basic element of his doctrine) he declared: "The human will is like a beast of burden. If God mounts it, it wishes and goes as God wills; if Satan mounts it, it wishes and goes as Satan wills. Nor can it choose the rider it would prefer, nor betake itself to him, but it is the riders who contend for its possession." [2] During the period of negotiations looking toward a reunion of Catholics and Protestants in Germany, Luther wrote his lieutenant, Philip Melanchthon: "I see they think this is a comedy of men, instead of a tragedy of God and Satan, as it is. Where Satan's power waxes, that of God grows rusty." [3] Such citations, from his published works, his letters and his table talk, could be multiplied endlessly. It goes without saying that the Pope and the papacy were closely associated with the Devil and the Antichrist in Luther's mind; and his other opponents, both political and religious, including Protestants with whom he differed, were the victims, when they were not the allies, of Satan. Particularly interesting is his view that gloom and discouragement, as well as an excessive preoccupation with one's own sinfulness, are devices of the Devil. Luther's exhortations to cheerfulness remind one strikingly of the advice given two centuries later by the *Baal Shem*. "Sometimes," writes Luther, "we must drink more, sport, recreate ourselves, aye, and even sin a little to spite the Devil, so that we leave him no place for troubling our consciences with trifles." [4] We have many reports of Luther talking to the Devil, generally in a most abusive and insulting manner.[5]

The crowning evidence is Luther's great hymn, "Ein' Feste Burg," which has become the musical symbol of the Reformation and is still widely sung in Protestant churches. After four lines praising God as the Mighty Fortress, the hymn turns to the glorification of Satan: [6]

> "Der alt böse feynd
>   mitt ernst ers yetzt meint,
>   gross macht un vil list
>   sein grausam rüstung ist,
>   auff erd ist nicht seins gleichen."

> "Our ancient foe accurst
>   Now means to do his worst,
>   Great power and craft are his,
>   And armed with them he is
>   On earth without an equal."

Only against the background of the power and majesty of the "Prince of this World" can Luther present adequately the redemptive power of the "righteous man."

As he retained the medieval conception of the Devil, so Luther clung to the practical concomitants of this belief. He denounced witchcraft repeatedly. Witches, he held, should be prosecuted with vigor and without too many niceties of legal procedure; though he was concerned that some positive evidence of guilt be adduced. Four witches were burned at Wittenberg, in June 1540, at the time when Luther's influence was dominant in that city. Consulted by the authorities regarding an idiot child, he decided that it must be a changeling, and recommended that it be drowned, as a body without a soul.[7]

There was a period in Luther's life when he adopted a sympathetic attitude toward the Jews. His book *That Jesus Christ Was Born a Jew* condemned persecution and slander of the Jewish people, and explained their failure to accept Christianity by the corruption of the Roman Church. It is apparent that Luther had high hopes of winning the Jews to his gospel. After these hopes were disappointed, he attacked the Jews with coarsest savagery, by both the spoken and the written word. His pamphlet *Concerning the Jews and their Lies* and his other anti-Jewish writings indicate that Luther's bitterness was not merely the result of personal pique. The whole medieval combination of hatred and fear, which he had consciously put aside when he wrote his more tolerant work, was again given full rein. He doubted that even baptism could redeem the demonic Jew. A Jewish convert to Christianity, Luther related, had his statue carved with a cat in one hand and a mouse in other, to hint that as the cat and mouse can never be at peace, so a Jew can never become a Christian. For Luther, too, the Devil and the Jews are closely allied.[8]

CALVIN. Luther's views about the Devil reveal in their expression the stamp of his unique personality, though in substance they are neither new nor distinctive. These same views were held by his colleagues and successors in the Protestant movement, however different their tone and manner of utterance. We need not examine tediously all that the Reformers wrote on the subject. It will be sufficient to refer to John Calvin—next to Luther, the most influential of the early Protestant leaders, and totally unlike Luther in temperament. Luther's religious doctrines must be sought through (literally) a hundred volumes, many of them turgid, abusively polemical, unsystematic, permeated by the scholasticism which he had repudiated but could not entirely escape. Calvin's ideas are clearly and systematically expounded in the comparatively small compass of his *Institutes of the Christian Religion.* He works with few tools except the authority of Scripture and a simple, common-sense logic.

These qualities are manifest in his chapter on angels. Calvin leaves no doubt that he considers speculation about angels a futile occupation. Such matters are of little practical consequence for religious living. The hierarchy of angels, their number and their names are not suitable subjects for our inquiry. Angels are not to be explained away as figures of speech; they are not merely "the notions which God inspires into men, or those specimens which He gives of His power." For such rationalism is contradicted by Scripture. These "foolish and absurd notions . . . were disseminated by Satan many ages ago, and are frequently springing up afresh." [9]

By the same token, we should not regard devils as "evil affections or perturbations, which our flesh obtrudes on our minds." [10] There are really evil spirits, and we must guard against their machinations. Indeed, this practical purpose pervades the Scriptural treatment of the subject; for our theoretical information about the demons is far from complete.[11]

There are many demons; but Scripture frequently mentions one Satan or Devil in the singular number to denote "that principality of wickedness which opposes the kingdom of righteousness. For as the Church and society of the saints have Christ as their head, so the faction of the impious and impiety itself are represented to us with their prince, who exercises supreme power over them. . . . He is everywhere called God's adversary and ours." He is the villain of the drama of Eden; he is "naturally depraved, vicious, malignant and mischievous." [12]

But this was not his nature from creation. It is the result of corruption. He once had truth, but did not hold to it. When Scripture calls him "the father of lies" (John 8.44), it is to preclude the supposition that God caused his depravity, which indeed originated wholly from himself. "Though these things are delivered in a brief and rather obscure manner, yet they are abundantly sufficient to vindicate the majesty of God from every calumny. And what does it concern us to know, respecting devils, either more particulars or for any other purpose? [13] . . . let us be content with this concise information respecting the nature of devils; that at their creation they were originally as of God, but by degenerating have ruined themselves and become the instruments of perdition to others." [14]

Calvin is careful to point out that Satan's evil acts occur with the permission and intent of God. Satan's purpose is wholly evil and rebellious. But whether he will or not, he must obey his Creator, who so directs his evil actions that they have a useful effect.

The activity of the evil powers, under God's direction, serves to "exercise the faithful with fighting," and to "subdue and lead captive the impious." The faithful—that is, from the Calvinist viewpoint, those whom the Divine Grace has foreordained to be saved—can never be permanently defeated by Satan. The victory of Jesus Christ over Satan is now, as always, complete; but in us, because of the flesh, only partial. Christ by his death overcame Satan, who had the power of death, and triumphed over all his forces, that they might not be able to hurt the Church; for otherwise it would be in hourly danger of destruction . . . God permits not Satan to exercise any power over the faithful, but abandons to his government only the impious and unbelieving, whom He designs not to number among his flock.[15]

It will be seen that Calvin, though he discouraged elaborate speculation regarding the Devil and his nature, did not for a moment doubt the existence of the Devil; and he had no hesitation in acting on the practical consequences of this belief. In 1545, thirty-four witches were burned in Geneva, where Calvin was an uncrowned monarch.[16] Calvin hoped for the ultimate conversion of Israel—but had no dealings with the Jews of his own time. Since, in the Genevan theocracy, even Christians were admitted only if they accepted the Calvinist doctrines, Jews could not even approach the sacred city. They did not constitute a contemporary problem.

ENGLISH LITERATURE. The basic belief in the Devil, as the enemy of God and man and the source of all evil, continued unchallenged in Protestant thinking to the end of the eighteenth century. It could not be otherwise, since it is so clearly defined in the New Testament. As long as the inerrancy of Scripture was accepted as a fundamental premise, there could be no revision of the belief in Satan and his evil hosts. Fundamentalist Christians, both Catholic and Protestant, still hold to the substance of these doctrines. During the progress of this book, the author has discussed its content with many acquaintances; and some orthodox Christian friends have expressed surprise that any one can doubt the reality of the Devil in a world where his work is so manifest!

Our theme has been extensively treated by later Protestant authorities.[17] But it may be more profitable to turn from the works of professional theologians to general literature. The consciousness of Satan became much more intense in English writers after the rise of the Puritan movement: in earlier Anglican thought the traditional views, though not challenged, were taken somewhat more calmly. But it was precisely the Puritan authors whose ideas on this subject had a profound effect on English readers long after the struggle of Cavalier and Puritan was ended.

At the very start of our inquiry we referred to Milton's *Paradise Lost*. It is unique among epic poems. Such writings are ordinarily classified as genuine folk epics, like the Homeric poems and the *Kalevala*, or as literary epics like the *Aeneid*. Now it is characteristic of the latter class that they deal with characters and events of a distant past, without much relevance for the time of the writer. They are thus invariably artificial and, with the exception of Vergil's masterpiece, have rarely been successful. *Paradise Lost* does not altogether belong to this class. For though the events it describes were thought to have occurred at the dawn of Creation, they were yet the stuff of the poet's own experience. The struggle of God and Satan; the fall of man, the redemptive power of the Savior, were all completely real and vital to Milton, a man of deep religious convictions and a profound, though somewhat heretical, theologian. Milton used literary devices to ornament the poem; but the poem itself is not a literary contrivance. It is the utterance of genuine beliefs. If the need to expound theological doctrine produces some dull passages in the epic, it also endows the poem with passionate intensity. Had Milton followed an earlier plan to write an epic about King Arthur, he would probably never have risen to such heights of feeling.

It has often been remarked that Satan "steals the show" in *Paradise Lost*. He is far more interesting than any of the angels and arouses our sympathy by his indomitable will in fighting a hopeless battle. Various explanations of this fact have been given by poets and critics; but no profound psychological interpretation seems necessary. It is almost always easier to create a plausible villain than an interesting hero. But Milton's heroes are God and the angels, whose very perfection renders them colorless from our standpoint; while Satan is invested with human weaknesses and emotions.

If *Paradise Lost* has appealed to the more cultured English readers, few books have enjoyed wider or more lasting popularity than *The Pilgrim's Progress* of John Bunyan. It is included among lists of "popular classics" and decked out with colored illustra-

tions. as a gift book for children. It was to be found, along with
the Bible, in many a home where books were few. Huckleberry
Finn, it may be recalled, discovered it on the library table of a far
from literary household and found it engrossing. It was "about
a man that left his family, it didn't say why," he reports . . . "The
statements was interesting, but tough."

A modern parent, schooled in contemporary psychology, might
hesitate to put the book into the hands of a child. He would
(perhaps mistakenly) attach diagnostic significance to the alter-
nations of depression and exhilaration that mark Christian's
journey.

Be this as it may, the book displays a lively consciousness of
the Devil. The most important section for our purpose is that in
which Christian, crossing the Valley of Humiliation, encounters
a foul fiend named Apollyon,[18] who appears as a monster with
wings like a dragon. Christian, in answer to his question, admits
that he is from the City of Destruction, whereat Apollyon claims
him as a subject and accuses him of desertion. Christian replies
that he was dissatisfied with the wages paid by his former master
—for the wages of sin is death—he has therefore bound himself
to a new lord. In the discussion that follows, Apollyon represents
himself as a rival of God for the loyalty of men, and he argues
that those who have abandoned his service for that of God have
fared badly, while the faithful followers of the Devil have been
protected and rewarded. Most striking are his words: "I am an
enemy to this Prince, I hate his Person, his Laws, and People."
He and Christian engage in a violent duel, in which Christian is
nearly worsted. At one moment he loses his sword, but desperately regains it and thrusts Apollyon through. "And with that
Apollyon spread forth his Dragon's wings, and sped him away,
that Christian for a season saw him no more." Thereupon Christian sings:

> "Great Beelzebub, the Captain of this Fiend,
> Design'd my ruin; therefore to this end
> He sent him harness'd out, and he with rage
> That hellish was, did fiercely me engage:
> But blessed Michael helped me, and I
> By dint of sword did quickly make him fly."

Apollyon then, is not Satan himself, but only his representative:
and elsewhere we read that Vanity Fair was set up long ago by

Beelzebub, Apollyon, Legion and their companions; and that Beelzebub, "the chief Lord of the Fair," had even invited the Prince of Princes to purchase his wares. The details of Bunyan's symbolism are not important. The real point is that the intense struggle between the powers of good and evil, between God and Satan, was a central element in his thinking.[19]

No doubt most of Bunyan's readers felt less violently about the matter, but basically they were in agreement. Professor W. E. Hocking, the American philosopher of religion (born 1873), describes the spiritual atmosphere of his own boyhood in the words: "Bunyan and Milton were understood to be fanciful enough, but not wholly false to the situation." [20]

And this remains the position of those Protestants who accept the literal inerrancy of Scripture. The witness of the New Testament is sufficient proof that the Devil exists; and this fact seems to them abundantly confirmed in personal experience.*

THE WITCHES. But the conclusions which medieval Christians drew from this belief have been greatly modified in Protestantism. Luther was the first and last Protestant leader of outstanding importance who can be regarded as an active anti-Semite. Anti-Semites, alas, have not been rare in the Protestant Church. Johann Andreas Eisenmenger (1654–1704), whose bulky *Entdecktes Judenthum* (Judaism Unmasked) has served as a sourcebook for anti-Semitic slanders ever since, and Pastor Adolf Stöcker, for many years court preacher at Berlin, are notable examples; but they are notable only as anti-Semites. The great figures in the Protestant Church, if they have concerned themselves with Jewish matters at all, either worked and prayed for the conversion of the Jews, or else labored for their emancipation. Some, it must be added, simply clung to old prejudices regarding

---

* Though William Blake was manifestly influenced by both Milton and Bunyan, his own outlook was diametrically opposed to theirs. Blake saw the source of evil in cold rationalism and codified morality which destroy the innocence of man's desires and choke the poetic and artistic imagination. Curiously reviving Gnostic notions, Blake identified Satan with "Urizen," the embodiment of reason, who is often associated with the Ten Commandments. Blake's own ideal, set forth in *The Marriage of Heaven and Hell*, is the harmonious union of reason and inspiration, in which reason no longer dominates. In this work he remarks: "The reason Milton wrote in fetters when he wrote of Angels & God, and at liberty when of Devils & Hell, is because he was a true Poet and of the Devil's party without knowing it."

Jews and Judaism, but made no special effort to inflame others. If the notion of the "demonic Jew" has survived in Christian circles, this is due to the persistent quality of folklore, rather than to the policy of Christian leaders.

Altogether different is the history of witchcraft within the Protestant Church. Consider Jean Bodin, one of the most remarkable figures of the sixteenth century. He was a man of great learning and intellectual brilliance, and his name appears in the more extended histories of modern philosophy. One of his principal works is a dialogue in which representatives of various faiths and philosophies present their viewpoints; among them is a Jew, who is depicted sympathetically and whose ideas are set forth cogently and effectively. Bodin was one of the early liberals.[21]

But on the subject of witchcraft he was a fanatic of fanatics. His views are expounded in a massive work, *De Magorum Daemonomania seu Detestando Lamiarum et Magorum cum Satana Commercio*. He argued that strict proof of guilt in cases of witchcraft should not be required—since by the very nature of these cases it would be difficult to produce. Therefore, said Bodin, no suspected person should ever be released, unless the malice of his accusers was plainer than day. Otherwise scholarly and critical, Bodin clung to every medieval superstition when dealing with this subject. Sorcery is the work of those who have sold themselves to the Devil. Witches and wizards can ride through the air; and so on. Johannes Weier, who challenged some of these views, was characterized by Bodin as "a true servant of Satan."[22]

The fact is that in his day there was an increasing current of skepticism about witchcraft, among both Protestants and Catholics. Nevertheless, the dominant view for a long time upheld the reality of witchcraft, and expressed itself not only in books and speeches, but in the actual condemnation and execution of hundreds of alleged witches. These persecutions reached a climax and conclusion in the seventeenth century, on the Continent, in England and in America. The Salem witch trials were the last of several such episodes in New England; and the mass hysteria which produced them was largely stimulated by theology. Increase Mather and his son Cotton, the exemplars of Puritan piety, were the soul of the movement; and Cotton Mather published a full account of the Salem trials. Later on, when a stop was put to this activity, Cotton Mather bemoaned the decay of the religious spirit and, to his dying day, regarded disbelief in witchcraft as an attack upon the glory of the Lord.[23] A century later, when witches were no longer put to death, John Wesley could still declare that giving up witchcraft meant giving up the Bible.[24]

Let us retrace our steps and see what had happened. Erasmus of Leyden, the great Catholic humanist, had ventured the opinion that compacts with the Devil were an invention of witch-hunters; Montaigne, skeptical about everything, naturally voiced his mild doubts on the subject of witchcraft.[25] More immediately effective were the objections raised by jurists as to the validity of witch-trials. The question was not whether witchcraft is possible, but whether accused individuals were actually guilty. Something of a storm was created when a Jesuit priest, Friederich Spee von Langenfeld, declared publicly that among two hundred condemned witches whom he had personally prepared for execution, he did not believe one was guilty—this despite the fact that Spee did not question the possibility of witchcraft.[26] About the same time, Johannes Weier, a Protestant, produced a bulky volume in which he denied the possibility of compacts with the Devil and of witchcraft based thereon. That the Devil exists, Weier did not deny; but as we have seen, Bodin, "Satan's attorney-general," regarded Weier's denial of witchcraft as evidence that he was on the Devil's side.[27]

Suddenly—considering how long the hysteria had lasted—the outrages came to an end. Witch prosecutions were abolished in Holland in 1610, at Geneva in 1632, in Sweden under the enlightened Queen Christina in 1649. Louis XIV of France decreed in 1672 that all witch cases be dismissed; but later on he had to make concessions to the still vigorous superstition. In England, King James I had written in defense of the reality of witchcraft and had committed to the flames the skeptical *Discovery of Witchcraft* by Reginald Scot. Yet the capital penalty for witches was abolished in 1682, a little less than a century later. The trials continued in Germany, until the middle of the eighteenth century, and the last victim in Spain was burned by the Inquisition about a hundred years later.[28]

Even after the legal prosecution of witches was abolished, the craze did not immediately disappear. We saw that Wesley still stoutly insisted on the reality of witchcraft; and by the same token the representatives of the modern spirit felt the need of continuing the fight. It is noteworthy that two of the most important of these fighters on the Continent attacked not only the prosecution of witches, but the basic idea by which it was justified. In *The Enchanted World* (1691–3), Balthasar Bekker, a Dutch clergyman of German descent, denied the existence of a personal Devil. A little later, Christian Thomasius, at Halle, denied the possibility that the Devil could be corporeal. Hence, he argued, no signed compact with him could occur. Thomasius developed this argument as part of his fight against the witch-craft mania.[29]

The psychology of this whole matter deserves more careful exploration. Why was it that, after centuries of unchallenged acceptance, the belief in witches took on such violent intensity and expressed itself in such frenzied terror? Why again did this violent feeling subside at a time when the authority of Scripture (which seems to affirm the existence of witchcraft) was still to all intents unchallenged? One can only guess that the influence of the rationalistic and scientific spirit gradually permeated the life of the people. Yet the dramatic contradictions in the mind of Jean Bodin should make us dubious about any simple explanation.

Of course, among the ignorant and superstitious these beliefs still persist. Not many years since, in York County, Pennsylvania, a man murdered his neighbor in the belief that the latter was "hexing" him. But such crimes are no longer given religious sanction, even by the most Scriptural of Protestants.

The Catholic Church, indeed, has never denied the substance of sorcery. Catholic writers have severely criticized those who see in the prosecution of witches mere hysterical aberration. Witchcraft, they have held, is rooted in apostasy and dis-obedience.[30] The somewhat apologetic article on "Witchcraft" in the *Catholic Encyclopedia* stresses the opposition of Agobard and others to the craze, minimizes the influence of the bull *Summis Desiderantes,* and reflects with some complacency on the atroci-ties of the *Protestant* witch-hunters. But the writer concludes in these measured terms: "In the face of Holy Scripture and the teaching of the Fathers and Theologians, the abstract possibility of a pact with the Devil and of diabolical interference in human affairs can hardly be denied, but no one can read the literature on the subject without realizing the awful cruelties to which this belief led, and without being convinced that in ninety-nine cases out of a hundred, the allegations rest upon nothing better than pure delusion." [31]

PART NINE

The Devil in Modern Dress

CHAPTER TWENTY-NINE

The Century of Liberalism

J ewish thought in the nineteenth century was dominated by rationalistic and scientific trends. This
was true not only of Reform Jews in Germany and
America but even of the more traditionally minded. The scientific
spirit was manifested in the critical study of Jewish history and literature (*die Wissenschaft des Judentums*), as well as in the movement of Enlightenment (*Haskalah*) through which secular knowledge and modern ideas were brought to the Jews of eastern Europe.
The growing sentiment of Jewish nationalism, despite romantic
overtones, was remote from all supernaturalism. The Cabala,
which had so long colored Jewish thought, was vehemently
rejected by all parties, save for a few scattered mystics and for
the largely decadent and obscurantist Hasidim of rural Poland.

This period, despite many tragic events, was a time of hope
for Israel. The French and American Revolutions ushered in the

emancipation of the Jews. Hundreds of thousands fled from the oppression of the Czars to the freedom of western Europe and especially of the United States. The prevailing faith in progress deeply influenced Jewish thinkers. Those who, under the impact of the new anti-Semitism, lost faith in political emancipation turned to socialism or Zionism as the hope of Israel—but hope remained.

Under such circumstances, the idea of a world of spiritual evil opposed to the realm of divine goodness was absent from Jewish thought, even in its more conservative expressions. Such beliefs, we have seen, were hardly typical of Judaism—save to some extent in the Cabala. Jews had repeatedly experimented with the idea of wicked or rebel angels, and had rejected the concept as incompatible with pure monotheism. Now in an age of enlightenment, of optimism, and (in some quarters) of secularism, such notions were altogether swept aside. If scholars mentioned them at all, it was only from the historical standpoint, as evidences of borrowing from Persian myth, as superstitions of a long dead past.

It was different with Christianity. Dualistic concepts were much more deeply rooted in the daughter faith, and held an important place in Christian teaching throughout all periods of Church history. But Christianity, too, felt the impact of rationalism and of the historical-critical method in the study of religion. How did the Churches react to these new trends, insofar as they challenged the doctrine of rebel angels?

The authoritarian groups stuck to their guns. The Catholic Church maintains the doctrine defined by the Fourth Lateran Council that the devil and other demons were created good and, by their own free choice, became evil. For the interpretation of this principle it abides substantially by the views of St. Thomas Aquinas. Certain details may be modified. A modern Catholic admits that Isaiah 14.12 refers originally to the King of Babylon, but adds: "Both the early Fathers and later Catholic commentators agree in understanding it as applying with deeper significance to the fall of the rebel angels." [1] Another Catholic writer regards it as unfortunate that such great schoolmen as St. Thomas and St. Bonaventura accepted the belief in incubi and succubi.[2] But though some of the picturesque trappings of the belief in demons have been tacitly dropped by modern Catholics, the basic notion of rebel angels and of a personal Devil remain unchallenged.

A striking evidence of this is the baptismal service. Before the infant is even brought into the church, the priest breathes upon its face and exorcises the evil spirit. And prior to the ablution, the catechumen makes the triple renunciation of Satan, his works and pomps. (The Anglican rite of baptism also requires the candidate to renounce the Devil and all his works.)[3] Nor are all these rites a mere survival from the past. In 1890 Pope Leo XIII published a form of exorcism of Satan and the apostate angels, first composed apparently for use in his own devotions.[4]

Among Protestant teachers, likewise, the more conservative have clung without flinching to the traditional concept of evil angels. A nineteenth century Lutheran, Dr. Sartorius, declared flatly: "He who denies Satan cannot truly confess Christ."[5] More recent handbooks of fundamentalist theology are not quite so blunt; but they maintain stoutly the correctness of the doctrine of Satan.[6] A confession of faith adopted in 1942 by a group of "Bible-believing" Baptists in New York State affirms the belief "in the personality of Satan, that he is the unholy god of this age, and the author of all the powers of darkness, and is destined to the judgment of an eternal justice in the lake of fire."[7]

Such utterances as these are frequently defensive. They are directed not only against the unbelievers who have rejected Christian theology as a whole, but even more against those who have been attempting to reconstruct Protestant thought in the light of the new science and philosophy. Among the first of these was Immanuel Kant. Despite the sophistication of his philosophic thought, he remained a loyal member of the Lutheran Church; but he explicitly rejected the old-fashioned, realistic Devil.[8] In this he was followed by Friederich Schleiermacher, one of the most influential of modern Protestant thinkers. Without denying absolutely the possibility that a Satanic power may exist, Schleiermacher held that the question is not essential to Christian faith. This he argued especially from the fact that some of the most important New Testament statements about sin and atonement make no mention of the Devil. Hence we infer that when Jesus and his followers speak of Satan and of evil angels, they are merely utilizing notions current in their time.[9]

Schleiermacher's philosophical and practical arguments against retaining this ancient belief were supplemented by an attempt at historical analysis of the concept of Satan. This effort was carried forward by other scholars. Study of Persian literature showed that the figure of Ahriman had greatly influenced Jewish, and especially Christian, ideas about the Devil. The recovery of the Babylonian epics revealed a dualistic myth still more ancient—the struggle of Marduk, the god of light, with the primeval dragon Tiamat. Along with the origins of the belief in the Devil, men studied also the fortunes of this belief through the centuries.[10] The history of witchcraft and satanism were also examined critically; Jules Michelet, the famous historian of France, was a pioneer in this field. Such studies were bound to have a strongly negative effect on the actual belief in Satan. The heathen origins of this belief and the fantastic horrors it had inspired combined to discredit it to modern men.

While some Christian thinkers challenged the belief in Satan, and others investgated it as a historical phenomenon, a good many others simply disregarded it. Dr. Edward Langton has listed a number of important doctrinal works, published during the past seventy-five years, which mention the Devil only in passing, in connection with New Testament or patristic quotations. The most remarkable instance concerns a distinguished Anglican, Bishop Gore. In his *Dissertations on Subjects Connected with the Incarnation* (1895), he argued strongly for the retention of the belief in good and evil spirits, stressing both the authority of the New Testament and the practical religious value of the doctrine. From 1921 to 1924, however, Bishop Gore published three volumes on *The Reconstruction of Belief*. "In none of these notable contributions to theological literature," reports Dr. Langton, "is any definite teaching given concerning the existence and operations of Satan." Only in a few incidental allusions does the Bishop touch on a belief he had once proclaimed to be essential! [11]

There were, however, individuals who were unwilling to see the liquidation of the belief by modernism, even though their thinking was too advanced to tolerate a simple literal Satan. Wide notice has been given the views of Bishop H. Martensen, a Danish divine whose work on dogmatics appeared in the middle of the last century. Martensen was apparently concerned to raise the dignity of Satan to a higher level, in keeping with the New Testament doctrine which calls Satan "the god of this world" and other titles which are honorific in a negative way. If Satan were no more than a disobedient underling, would it not be a ridiculous impertinence for him to try to tempt the Savior? Yet no Christian can admit the existence of an evil deity on a par with God the Father—that would be Manicheanism. Martensen therefore described evil as an impersonal principle in the cosmos, the origin of which is not clearly explained. This evil tendency is in a sense unreal, but it is striving after reality and, above all, after personality. Evil first entered into the free personalities of certain angels, just as later it took possession of human souls: by this means impersonal evil becomes personal. The Satan of Scripture is the being who is so completely identified with the cosmic principal of evil as to have become its perfect embodiment and expression.[12]

Such a doctrine seems to a non-Christian to be, if not Manichean, at least decidedly Gnostic. Yet Bishop Martensen's ideas met with considerable respect and some acceptance.[13] Such speculations, however, had a limited vogue prior to World War I and were entertained by individuals rather than by schools of thought. For most Protestants, the choice was between a literal, Scriptural Devil and a theology in which he played no important part.

CHAPTER THIRTY

Epilogue

This book was begun as a purely scientific inquiry into the beliefs of an earlier age. But as the study progressed, I became more and more aware that the issues involved are still current. Our world is not only wrestling with the problems treated herein, but is increasingly turning back to the old solutions of these problems. My presentation would therefore be incomplete if I did not indicate its present-day implications. But here the rigorous objectivity for which I have striven will no doubt be breached. One cannot be cool and detached about living issues. What follows is admittedly colored by personal convictions.

Our historical study has yielded definite findings. Jewish thinkers, in seeking an answer to the problem of evil and suffering, have from time to time experimented with dualistic myth. They suggested that sin and pain originated in the revolt of angelic beings against the authority of God. But such explanations have not been accepted as authoritative in Judaism. The classic expositions of the Jewish faith have implicitly or explicitly rejected the belief in rebel angels, and in a Devil who is God's enemy. The enormous influence of the rabbis of the Talmud and of the medieval Jewish philosophers is on the anti-mythical side. The Hebrew Bible itself, correctly interpreted, leaves no room for belief in a world of evil powers arrayed against the goodness of God. Even the Cabalists, some of whom adopted a rather extreme dualistic position, usually declared that the emergence of the destructive forces was somehow part of the divine scheme; and this dualism had been largely liquidated by the Hasidic teachers even before modern influences had undermined the prestige of the Cabala.

Historical Christianity, on the other hand, has consistently affirmed the continuing conflict between God and Satan. A doctrine which Jews took up hesitantly and which was repudiated by their most respected teachers, has been universally upheld by the Church, often in radically mythological forms. The Church, moreover, acted on the logical consequences of this notion by executing witches; and its consciousness of diabolic powers made even more horrible the hatred and persecution of the Jews. The issue of belief in a malignant Devil may therefore be regarded as one of the basic differences between Judaism and Christianity.

Seventy-five years ago this distinction might have seemed relatively unimportant. True, Christian fundamentalists, both Catholic and Protestant, still clung to the belief in the Devil; but they did so defensively, by uncritical adherence to the traditions of the past; and most of them had ceased to draw practical consequences for conduct from the doctrine. Enlightened rationalism had discarded such ideas; historical scholarship had shown them to be survivals of pagan mythology. The more advanced and liberal among Protestant thinkers had quietly disregarded the concept of the Devil, where they had not explicitly rejected it.

This was the heyday of optimistic faith in progress through science, technology and education. Men looked to the future with assurance and hope. But the twentieth century has disappointed the rosy expectations of the nineteenth. Science, far from opening the way to salvation, has given mankind the instruments of self-destruction. Tragedy has piled upon tragedy until most of us have grown morally numb, callous to the suffering of others. The killing of forty-five Jews at Kishinev in 1903 aroused more active indignation among Americans than the slaughter of six million Jews during World War II.

As the lights of humanity and hope went out all over the world, dark and dangerous beliefs again became popular. In Europe, where the shadows gathered first, these ideas gained favor sooner than in America. Their influence has been growing here as well. The change in spiritual climate may be summed up simply. A brilliant popular essay published in 1871 by a French Protestant was entitled *The Devil: His Origin, Greatness, and Decadence.* In 1946, E. Langton issued a useful booklet, entitled *Satan: A Portrait.* Its final chapter, dealing with contemporary trends, is headed "The Return of the Devil." Satan has once again come to the fore of human consciousness.

Before examining evidences of this trend in religious thought proper, we may note some curious resemblances between the ideas we have been studying and certain elements in modern secular culture. It is possible, without denying the importance of Karl Marx's analysis of social and economic phenomena, to speak also of the Marxist scheme as a kind of apocalyptic myth. The revolutionary pattern is presented not as an objective to be achieved but as an inevitable destiny. The will of God (read: dialectic materialism) cannot be resisted or changed. Apocalyptic likewise is the mounting course of evils under the sway of capitalism, the "god of this world," until the cataclysmic revolution after which the new heavens and new earth shall appear.

Certainly popular radicalism sees in the struggle for the dictatorship of the proletariat a simple schematized myth. The war between capitalism and communism is the war between God and Satan, with Lenin and Stalin in messianic roles, and with a series of Antichrists—Trotsky, for example—who are the incarnation of everything abominable. Whereas to many modern Catholics, communism is the Antichrist, in communist theology the dignitaries are interchanged. Just so, the ancient Gnostics identified the God of Judaism and the Devil, while the Catholics saw in the Gnostic doctrine the very breath of Satan.

Again, one need not deny the scientific importance of Freudian psychology to note some of its mythological overtones—a situation fostered by the fantastic terminology which Freud himself invented, drawing in many cases upon classical myth. It must be remembered that analytic psychology has permeated many levels of modern culture and has influenced, not only the intellectuals, but plain people as well. Whatever may be intended by the disciplined psychoanalyst, in the popular version of Freudianism the "complex" behaves like an independent being with purposes of its own. Beneath the mind of the individual, the self he knows, lurks the "unconscious," savage, primitive, seeking an outlet for its destructive energies—as in the figurative descriptions which the rabbis gave of the evil inclination trying to encompass man's ruin.[1] The current mythological temper has certainly been colored by the Freudian approach with its determinism, its account of dark subterranean forces beyond the control of intelligence or moral power and its generally pessimistic estimate of man's nature.

The foregoing observations may seem unconvincing to some and may evoke the indignation of others. But few will doubt the mythological character of the National Socialist creed. Its chief theoretical expositor, Alfred Rosenberg, liked to use the term "mythos." Incidentally, the Nazi doctrines emerged in a milieu which was influenced, if not by the actual teachings of Marx and Freud, at least by the folklore of communism and psychoanalysis. The apocalyptic expectation of a revolution which should not merely reshape the structure of government but fundamentally transform the character of human life was derived from socialism. The stress on the basically irrational quality of human behavior and the low evaluation of the worth of the individual were influenced in some degree by the Viennese psychologists. It must be added that whatever the Nazis borrowed from any source, they distorted and defiled.

The essential Nazi myth, however, is a neo-Gnosticism. Ironically enough, no one has stated it more clearly than the Jew, Walther Rathenau: "The epitome of the history of the world, of the history of mankind, is the tragedy of the Aryan race. A blond and marvellous people arises in the north. In overflowing fertility it sends wave upon wave into the southern world. Each migration becomes a conquest, each conquest a source of character and civilization. But with the increasing population of the world, the waves of the dark peoples flow ever nearer, the circle of mankind grows narrower. At last a triumph for the south: an oriental religion takes possession of the northern lands. They defend themselves by preserving the ancient ethic of courage. And finally the worst danger of all: industrial civilization gains control of the world, and with it arises the power of fear, of brains and cunning, embodied in democracy and capital." [2]

Rathenau himself, in his maturer years, freed himself intellectually—if not altogether emotionally—from this racism of Gobineau and Chamberlain. But it had meanwhile acquired an unparalleled power in Germany. The Nazis adopted it in the most extreme and vulgar forms, identified even more sharply the Germans with the noble blond folk of Ahura-Mazda, and the Jews with the sly, dark, corrupt minions of Ahriman. Six million Jewish dead testify to the destructive force of a mythological fantasy.

We need not study more deeply this most horrible of all dualistic philosophies. Yet it helps us better to understand certain recent trends in Christian thought. For Hitler revealed with a fullness never before attained the possibilities of human depravity. It is the consciousness of this vileness in man that obsesses current Christian theology.

The reaction against the rationalism and optimism of liberal thought did not indeed have to wait for the emergence of National Socialism. It goes back at least to Sören Kierkegaard (1813–1855), the Danish critic of Hegel. In his time he was an isolated figure, but the number of his followers has grown until today he is the patron saint of the new theology. Kierkegaard discovered through his own inner experience the superficiality of the belief in progress. Less searching intellects have learned the same thing through the massive, tangible events of outer history. Mankind has not been made happier and better by science and popular education. Economic disasters, class hatreds, wars of unparalleled savagery—these brute facts are not to be denied. The more sensitive religious thinkers of our age had faced them, even before the threat of atomic annihilation gave pause to the dullest spirit.

A characteristic reaction to these realities in present-day Christianity has been to repudiate liberalism and to adopt some form of neo-orthodoxy. We shall mention only a few representatives of this trend, and of their doctrine we shall supply only such items as are germane to our theme. None of them—and they differ greatly among themselves—is an old-fashioned fundamentalist, clinging with unsophisticated simplicity to the teachings of the past. They are permeated by modern scientific culture and have repudiated its presuppositions out of knowledge, not out of ignorance. They are convinced that the rationalistic, scientific, liberal foundations of modern society have collapsed, had to collapse because of their inherent insufficiency. They agree that man lacks both the intellectual and moral strength to solve his own urgent problems.

In some respects, the most moderate of these thinkers is Jacques Maritain, a Protestant who entered the Church of Rome and has devoted his great philosophic gifts to the defense of the Catholic faith. In accordance with Catholic tradition, he assigns a place of some dignity to the intellect. But he insists that valid and constructive results can be achieved only through the insights of Aristotle, as modified and interpreted by St. Thomas Aquinas and guided by the revealed doctrine of the infallible Church. The secular, independent, atomized intellectualism of our time can only lead us into ever deeper confusion. As long as he is criticizing contemporary culture, Maritain is a modern of the moderns. But this criticism is only a preliminary. It leads back, by a new route, to changeless and inscrutable Catholic dogma, including the pronouncement of the Fourth Lateran on the nature of Satan.

A parallel trend is to be noted in the Protestant theologians, whose most eminent representative in Europe is Karl Barth, and whose best known spokesman in the United States is Reinhold Niebuhr. Out of their disappointment with modernism, they have made their way back to the tradition of Paul, Augustine, Luther and Calvin. This is a more extreme position than that of the Roman Church, which allows some room within its scheme for the achievement of intellectual and moral gains. The radical Protestant doctrine, however, has no confidence in either the mind or the soul of man, affirms more or less bluntly the total depravity of human nature, and sees no hope whatever for man save through the spontaneous working of divine grace. Depicting man as so thoroughly diabolic, this kind of thinking leads to a revival of belief in the Devil.

Of special interest for our study is a little book by Gustaf Aulén, written about two decades ago, and published in English under the title *Christus Victor*. The author, who later became a Bishop of the Swedish Church, was at one time a professor of theology; and in form the work is an historical inquiry into theories of the atonement.

For centuries, conservative theologians have held to the doctrine of legal satisfaction, associated with Anselm, though its origins are earlier. This theory holds that Jesus paid by his suffering for the sins of mankind, the payment being due God for the violation of His law. Liberal theologians have preferred a "subjective" theory of the atonement—the thought of the self-sacrifice of Jesus inspires moral and spiritual regeneration in the soul of the individual. Aulén, however, draws attention to what he calls the "classical" theory of the atonement—that which we found taught by Irenaeus, Origen and Gregory the Great. According to this doctrine, the death of Jesus was a ransom paid to the Devil, or a device by which the Devil was in some way entrapped or outwitted. The expressions of the doctrine vary: what is common to them all is the dramatic element. The atonement is a divine conflict and victory: Christ fights and subdues the evil powers, the tyrants who hold mankind in bondage and suffering; and in Christ, God reconciles the world to himself.[3]

Scholars have been too quick, Aulén holds, to brush aside this view because of the grotesque imagery in which it has been clothed. Even the latter, on careful examination, proves to be significant. The chief concern, however, is the basic concept—the atonement as the victory of Christ over evil. Bishop Aulén argues that this doctrine was widely held by the greatest Fathers of the Church prior to the rise of the "legalistic" theory; that it is in accord with Scripture; and that it was maintained by Luther, though not by his successors. While the form of his presentation is that of historical scholarship, Aulén does not conceal his predilection for the "classic" view. Anselm's doctrine is too rationalistic and moralistic to suit him, the "subjective" theory too superficial. Without taking literally the mythical tales of Origen and Gregory, Aulén clings to the belief which those tales symbolize—that through the Cross, Jesus triumphed over the power of darkness.

In one passage of this work, the dualism of historical Christianity is admirably characterized. It is not "a metaphysical Dualism between the infinite and the finite, or between spirit and matter; nor again ... the absolute Dualism between good and evil typical of the Zoroastrian and Manichean teaching, in which Evil is treated as an eternal principle opposed to Good. It is ... the opposition between God and that which in His own created world resists His will; between the Divine love and the rebellion of created wills against Him. This dualism is an altogether radical opposition; but it is not an absolute Dualism, for in the Scriptural view, evil has not an eternal existence." [4] To which one may add, that it may make a difference to philosophers that evil is not eternal; but to the plain man, this doctrine means that the Devil exists *now*, in "radical opposition" to God.

Aulén's book reached only a specialized audience. Much more widely read is Reinhold Niebuhr's *Nature and Destiny of Man*, which will serve us as an excellent sample of the new Christian orthodoxy. Like Barth, Niebuhr is not concerned to defend the literal inerrancy of Scripture. The findings of biblical criticism may be correct; but the underlying truth of the Bible, as Niebuhr apprehends it, is vindicated both by logic and experience. Niebuhr speaks of the Garden of Eden story as "the myth of the Fall," and admits that Christian satanology has drawn on Persian and Babylonian sources. "The story of the Fall," he concedes, "is innocent of a fully developed satanology; yet" he insists, "Christian theology has not been wrong in identifying the serpent with, or regarding it as an instrument or symbol of, the devil. To believe that there is a devil is to believe that there is a principle or force of evil antecedent to any evil human action. Before man fell the devil fell. The devil is, in fact, a fallen angel. His sin and fall consists in his effort to transcend his proper state and to become like God." And characteristically, Niebuhr cites at this point Isaiah 14.11 ff., though he knows it refers primarily to Babylon.

Two points, he continues, are to be stressed. "(1) The devil is not thought of as having been created evil. Rather his evil arises from his effort to transgress the bounds set for his life, an effort which places him in rebellion against God. (2) The devil fell before man fell, which is to say that man's rebellion against God is not an act of sheer perversity, nor does it follow inevitably from the situation in which he stands. The situation of finiteness and freedom in which man stands becomes a source of temptation only when it is falsely interpreted. This false interpretation is not purely the product of the human imagination. It is suggested to man by a force of evil which precedes his own sin. Perhaps the best description or definition of this mystery is the statement that sin posits itself, that there is no situation in which it is possible to say that sin is either an inevitable consequence of the situation nor yet that it is an act of sheer and perverse individual defiance of God." [5]

This means—put crudely—that the source of moral evil is outside man. Though the biblical Devil be only a symbol of the abstraction that "sin posits itself," sin is not regarded merely as the personal failure of the individual or the collective failure of the group or nation. "Before man fell the devil fell." Niebuhr is particularly fond of the adjective "daemonic" to describe man's behavior, individual and collective. "Contemporary history," he writes, "is filled with the manifestations of man's hysterias and furies; with evidences of his daemonic capacity and inclination to break harmonies of nature and defy the prudent canons of rational restraint." [6]

Denis de Rougemont is a young man of Swiss birth, who fought Hitlerism as a publicist in Paris and later served with the French underground. He now lives in the United States, where in 1944 he published a new version of his book, *La Part du Diable*. (Soon after it appeared in English as *The Devil's Share*.) It is an incisive critique of modern life, written out of deep religious conviction. For de Rougemont, the Devil is not merely a literary device. De Rougemont is concerned that the reader take him seriously. He is not to be put aside by accounts of the historical development of the concept of the Devil: they explain only the externals of the matter. "If someone tells me: the devil is only a myth, therefore he does not exist—a rationalistic formula —I answer: the devil is a myth, therefore he does exist and is unceasingly active . . . For a myth is a story which describes and illustrates, through a dramatic form, certain profound structures of reality." [7]

These structures are literally fundamental, prior to our distinction between matter and spirit. "To speak of the devil will not be in this book an easy means of illustrating ideas. Reality is not composed of ideas and matter. I conceive it to be governed by structures of force or dynamic combinations anterior to every material form, to every idea which we can elucidate. The specific dynamism which I should like to describe in this book bears the traditional name of the devil." Freedom and its consequences imply "the existence of a good, and of something other than good. Otherwise, where could there be choice, tragedy, liberty? When this not-good, this evil acquires significance, we call it the devil—and I accept this name." [8]

In describing the Devil's activity, de Rougemont makes many penetrating observations on morals and manners, which are worth considering even though we do not accept his fundamental assumption. He has, moreover, a shrewd explanation of our skepticism, derived from a remark of Baudelaire: "The cleverest trick of the devil is to persuade us that he does not exist."

Aulén's book was read chiefly by professional theologians. The writings of Maritain, Niebuhr, de Rougemont and their fellows reach a somewhat larger, but still restricted, circle of intellectuals. But the kind of thinking they represent is being made more and more accessible to the plain man, as a few random examples will show.

A recent * radio broadcast over a nation-wide network was entitled "The Supreme Sorrow." The speaker was the Rev. John C. Murry, S. J., professor of theology in Woodstock College; the subject, the inward struggle of Jesus in the Garden of Gethsemane. The radio preacher pictures Satan as renewing his temptation of the Savior; and here is the climax of his narrative: "At this point, perhaps, Satan struck into our Lord's mood of loathing and disgust with his last desperate blow. It was the Accuser's hour, in which to use the darkest of his powers. He, then, the Accuser, drew up his pitiless indictment of the human nature whose enemy he is . . . And at the end he appeals to the justice of God and claims the verdict that is his own triumph and man's eternal despair: Guilty, unforgivably guilty, worthy of death. Give up, then, he says to our Blessed Lord, give up . . . You who are innocent, save yourself and let them die." And the preacher adds: "Only the intelligence of a fallen angel could have conceived such a temptation." [9]

A different phase of the matter appears in a story which reached the vast public of *The Reader's Digest*. (It was first

---

* The present work was completed several years before publication, so that "recent" items are no longer brand new. But the instances cited are typical of an outlook still the same in 1952.

published in a periodical of the Passionist Missions.) Written by
the well known journalist Fulton Oursler, it tells how Bishop
Fulton J. Sheen, when a young priest, succeeded in reaching
the heart of a bitter and rebellious young sinner. Our interest
is in her story as she first told it defiantly to the priest. She had
been sent to the State Reformatory and wanted above everything else to be released. She went to the chapel and prayed to
God for help in gaining her liberty; but nothing happened. Thereupon she turned to the Devil, promising "that if he would only
get me out of that place, I would make nine sacrilegious com-
munions. I did, too. I took communion and I cursed God! Plenty!
And you know what? After the eighth time I got paroled." [10]
We see, then, how vivid is the reality of the Devil to plain un-
educated Catholics. The notion of Devil-worship—the kind of
thinking that produced the Black Mass—still persists. We see,
moreover, that the leaders of the Church feel that such materials
are not unsuitable for presentation to the non-Catholic public, in
the present state of the world's mind.

Our final item likewise is drawn from a highly popular mass
medium—the magazine *Life*. When it appeared in February 1948,
the author had to be identified as one of the editors of *Time*.
Since then he has attained national notoriety. He is Whittaker
Chambers. Called simply "The Devil," his article relates a conversation between Satan and a pessimist, during the New Year's
Eve celebration in a swanky night club. The conversation turns
rather fully on de Rougemont, Niebuhr, and C. S. Lewis, and
more briefly on other contemporaries who are interested in the
Devil. The style is satiric and self-consciously clever; but the
author clearly wants us to believe in his essential seriousness.
Scientific liberalism has dulled men's minds to the enormity of
evil. The Devil's cleverest ruse is to make us doubt his existence.
He is the spirit of sterility and death. He cannot love and he
cannot create, because he cannot suffer. His envious desire is
the extinction of mankind; and to judge by present indications,
he has an excellent chance of success.[11]

One wonders how the readers of *Life* reacted to this extraordinary performance. Many of them must have found it baffling. But
the very fact that it was published, not in one of the "little" reviews, but in a magazine designed for mass circulation, indicates
how much times have changed.

I cannot attempt here a thoroughgoing critique of the new Christian theology. The effectiveness of the attack on modern positivism and rationalism cannot be disputed. The reality of evil, in particular of human wickedness, must be fully recognized. We are no longer convinced by the easy confidence of the meliorists that social evil can be eliminated by increased industrial production and by governmental reforms, or that personal sin can be dissolved by psychiatry and education. But the neo-orthodox substitutes for liberal theology, for all their fascination, are extremely dangerous. Just so, the totalitarians of right and left have made telling criticisms of economic liberalism and political democracy—and have offered us something much worse instead.

Through the centuries Judaism has had to struggle with two basic realities: the absolute oneness of God and the existence of evil in His universe. Sometimes Jewish thinkers, in their devotion to the belief in God's unity, have minimized the extent of the problem of evil. Sometimes their experience of the world's wickedness has tempted them to mythological explanations. But by and large they have avoided both traps. The Bible, for all its keen awareness of sin and wrong, will not derive them from an area of reality remote from and opposed to all-pervading God.

This, indeed, is the tragedy and the heroism of Job, who will neither blink the facts of actual experience nor surrender his confidence in God's goodness. Job's challenge to God is rooted in faith: he appeals, so to speak, from God to God himself. This phenomenon has been repeated many times in Jewish history. One thinks of Honi, the Circle-Drawer, bluntly demanding that God send rain to His suffering people; of the Hasid Levi Yizhak of Berditchev berating the Almighty because He is too severe with Israel.[12] Like Job, these saints of later days would not abate one jot of their faith in God, yet they would not distort the facts to reconcile them with that faith. As the Talmud puts the matter in another similar instance: "Because they knew that the Holy One (blessed be He!) is a true God, therefore they would not lie on His behalf." [13]

This is a difficult, paradoxical kind of faith. Men like to have things neatly explained and ticketed and systematized. It takes spiritual grandeur to admit that we cannot synthesize the deepest realities of our experience, and yet cling to all of them.

Surely the Jewish people, more than any other, has beheld the daemonic in man. It seems impossible that all the hate, the ingenious devices of torture and mechanized extermination, the shameless espousal of sub-feral brutality, should emerge from simple human reactions. In the face of this massive wickedness, the belief in some malignant deity or rebel angel is not implausible. Yet, to my knowledge, nothing of this sort has manifested itself among present-day Jews. The teachers of Judaism have learned their lesson. They see in such doctrines a surrender to fear. The doctrine of the Devil is too easy an excuse for human failure; it tempts us to leave this world to the control of the "god of this world," and to wait for salvation through some super-earthly power. Or else it sunders the unity of mankind, the children of God. Those who recognize a Devil often hold that some group or nation or sect are the Devil's own—the witches, the heretics, the Jews, the capitalists, the communists—and these enemies of God are no longer entitled to the rights, the just dealing, the simple humanity which are the heritage of all created in the divine image.

It remains for the "remnant of Israel" to uphold with unflagging zeal the basic intuition that ours is a moral universe. To make truth and right prevail in human affairs is not arrogant meddling with things beyond our competence; for man is God's partner in the work of creation.[14] His distinction should not make him proud, but it should save him from inertness, sloth and despair.

This ancient Jewish message has come to us with renewed power out of the concentration camps. It has been made visible in creative deeds on the soil of Palestine. It has been voiced with moving eloquence by Rabbi Leo Baeck, the saint of our generation, tested in the crucible of affliction, who calls on the Jewish people to give vision and courage to a world that has lost both. In the glow of such a faith, the Devil and his hosts fade and disappear.

Fallen Angels

Bibliography

Abbreviations.

This list does not include the customary abbreviations of the names of biblical books and other familiar and obvious abbreviations. For the abbreviations used in citing Midrashim and other aggadic works see the Bibliography, section B. 3.

Ant.	Antiquities
Bar.	Baruch
Bel. Jud.	The Wars of the Jews (Bellum Judaicum)
CE	Catholic Encyclopedia
Ecclus.	Ecclesiasticus
En.	Enoch
HUCA	Hebrew Union College Annual
ICC	International Critical Commentary
JBL	Journal of Biblical Literature
JE	Jewish Encyclopedia
JQR	Jewish Quarterly Review
Jub.	Jubilees
JZWL	Jüdische Zeitschrift für Wissenschaft und Leben

Mac.   Maccabees
MGWJ   Monatsschrift für Geschichte und Wissenschaft des Judentums
ns.   new series
os.   old series
PG   Patrologia Graeca
PL   Patrologia Latina
RB   Revue Biblique
REJ   Revue des Études Juives
RSPT   Revue des Sciences Philosophiques et Théologiques
SCG   Summa Contra Gentiles
ST   Summa Theologica

A. Works constantly cited by the author's name.

CAHANA = CAHANA, A., ed. Sefarim Hizonim. 3 v., Tel Aviv, 1936–1937.

CHARLES = CHARLES, R. H., ed. The Apocrypha and Pseudepigrapha of the Old Testament in English. 2 v., Oxford, 1913.

GINZBERG = GINZBERG, L., The Legends of the Jews. 7 v., Philadelphia, 1909–1938.

GRÜNBAUM = GRÜNBAUM, M., "Beiträge zur Vergleichende Mythologie aus der Hagada," in *Gesammelte Aufsätze zur Sprach- und Sagenkunde*, ed. F. Perles. Berlin, 1901.

JUNG = JUNG, L., Fallen Angels in Jewish, Christian and Mohammedan Literature. Philadelphia, 1926. (Originally in *JQR*, ns. XV and XVI.)

LODS = LODS, A., "La Chute des anges. Origine et portée de cette spéculation," in *Revue d'Histoire et de Philosophie Religieuses*, VII, 295-315. Strasbourg.

ROBERT = ROBERT, C., "Les Fils de Dieu et les Filles de l'Homme," in *RB*, IV, 340-373, 525-552.

SCHOLEM = SCHOLEM, G. G., Major Trends in Jewish Mysticism. Jerusalem, 1941.

B. Ancient and Medieval Sources.

JEWISH

1. *Apocrypha and Pseudepigrapha.*
See above, under Cahana and Charles.

THE APOCALYPSE OF ABRAHAM, trans. G. H. Box and J. I. Landsmann. London, 1918.

THE TESTAMENT OF ABRAHAM, trans. G. H. Box. London, 1927.

THE BIBLICAL ANTIQUITIES OF PHILO, trans. M. R. James. London, 1917.

THE BOOK OF ENOCH, ed. R. H. Charles. Oxford, 1912.

DOCUMENTS OF JEWISH SECTARIES, ed. S. Schechter. v. I: Fragments of a Zadokite Work. Cambridge (England), 1910.

III ENOCH, OR THE HEBREW BOOK OF ENOCH, ed. H. Odeberg. Cambridge (England), 1928.

DIE HEBRÄISCHE ELIAS–APOCALYPSE, ed. M. Buttenwieser. Leipzig, 1897.

2. *Hellenistic Writings.*
SEPTUAGINTA, ed. A. Rahlfs. 2 v. 3rd ed., Stuttgart, 1949.

JOSEPHUS, WORKS, trans. W. Whiston. N.Y., n.d.

PHILO, trans. F. H. Colson and J. E. Whittaker (Loeb Classical Library). 9 v., London, 1929–1941.

3. *Rabbinic Writings.*
The Mishnah and the Babylonian and Palestinian Talmuds are cited in the usual manner from the standard editions.

TOSEFTA, ed. M. S. Zuckermandel. Passewalk, 1881. Cited by ch. and halakah.

ABBA GORION. In SIFRE DE-AGGADATA AL MEGILLATH ESTHER, ed. S. Buber. Vilna, 1886. Cited by p.

AGGADATH ESTHER, ed. S. Buber. Krakau, 1897. Cited by p.

ARN. ABOTH D'RABBI NATHAN, ed. S. Schechter. Vienna, 1887. Cited by ch. and p.

BM. BATTE MIDRASHOTH, ed. S. Wertheimer. New ed., Jerusalem, 1950.

BR. BERESHIT RABBA, ed. J. Theodor and Ch. Albeck. Berlin, 1912–1929. Cited by parashah and paragraph.

BETH HAMIDRASCH, ed. S. Jellinek. 7 v., Leipzig, 1853–1857. (*N.B.* The small pieces originally published in this collection are usually cited from OM—see below.)

ER, EZ. SEDER ELIAHU RABBA V'SEDER ELIAHU ZUTTA, ed. M. Friedmann. Vienna, 1902. Cited by ch. and p.

MHG. MIDRASH HAGADOL, ed. S. Schechter. Cambridge (England), 1902.

MEKILTA. MEKILTA D'RABBI ISHMAEL, ed. J. Z. Lauterbach. 3 v., Philadelphia, 1933–1935. Cited by Massekta and Bible verse.

MEKILTA RS. MECHILTA D'RABBI SIMON B. JOCHAI, ed. D. Hoffmann. Frankfurt a. M., 1905. Cited by p.

MISHNATH R. ELIEZER, ed. H. G. Enelow. N.Y., 1933. Cited by p.

OM. OZAR MIDRASHIM, ed. J. D. Eisenstein. 2 v., N.Y., 1915. Cited by p. and column.

PK. PESIKTA D'RAB KAHANA, ed. S. Buber. Lyck, 1868. Cited by ch. and p.

PR. PESIKTA RABBATI, ed. M. Friedmann. Vienna, 1880. Cited by ch. and p.

TEHILLIM. MIDRASH TEHILLIM, ed. S. Buber. Vilna, 1891. Cited by ch. and p.

PRE. PIRKE D'RABBI ELIEZER, ed. D. Luria. Warsaw, 1852. Cited by ch.

——, English trans. By Gerald Friedlander. London 1916.

BaR.   BEMIDBAR RABBA
DR.   DEBARIM RABBA
ESTHER R.   ESTHER RABBA
KOHELETH R. KOHELETH RABBA
SHIR.   SHIR HA SHIRIM RABBA
shR.   SHEMOTH RABBA
WR.   WAYIKRA RABBA

In: Midrash Rabba, 2 v. Vilna 1921. Midrashim to the Pentateuch cited by ch. and paragraph, those to the Scrolls by Bible verse.

SOR. SEDER OLAM RABBA, Amsterdam, 1711. Cited by ch.

MIDRASH SAMUEL, ed. S. Buber. 2nd ed., Vilna, 1925. Cited by ch. and paragraph.

SIFRA, ed. I. H. Weiss. Vienna, 1862. Cited by Bible verse and p.

SIFRE D. SIPHRE ZU DEUTERONOMIUM, ed. L. Finkelstein. Berlin, 1935–1938. Portions still unpublished in this edition are cited from the Malbim Pentateuch, Vilna, 1923.

SIFRE N.
SIFRE Z.
SIPHRE AD NUMEROS ADJECTO SIPHRE ZUTTA, ed. H. S. Horowitz. Frankfurt and Leipzig, 1917. Sifre N. is cited by section, Sifre Z. by Bible verse or p.

TAN B. Midrash Tanhuma, ed. S. Buber. Vilna, 1913. Cited by v. and p.

TAN N. Midrash Tanhuma (*Nidpas*). Berlin, 1924. Cited by parashah and paragraph.

TANNAIM. Midrash Tannaim zum Deuteronomium, ed. D. Hoffmann. Berlin, 1909. Cited by p.

TARGUM YERUSHALMI (1) Pseudo-Jonathan, ed. M. Ginsburger. Berlin, 1903. (2) Das Fragmenthargum, ed. M. Ginsburger. Berlin, 1899.

YALK. Yalkut Shimoni. 2 v., Warsaw, 1876–1877. Cited by v. and section.

YASHAR. Sefer Hajaschar, ed. L. Goldschmidt. Berlin, 1923. Cited by parashah, sometimes by p.

4. *Medieval Commentaries and Treatises.*

AARON B. JOSEPH, Sefer haMibhar. Goslow, 1835.

ABRABANEL, ISAAC, Perush al haTorah. Hanover, 1710.

ANATOLI, JACOB, Malmad haTalmidim. Lyck, 1866.

ARAMA, ISAAC, Akedath Yizhak. 4, v., Pressburg, 1849.

BAHYA B. ASHER, Biur al haTorah. (P. references to 5th ed., Venice, 1566.)

———, Kad haKemah. Warsaw, 1872.

BERESHIT RABBATI, ed. Ch. Albeck. Jerusalem, 1940.

EPSTEIN, A., Eldad haDani. Pressburg, 1891.

HADAR ZEKENIM. Photostat of original ed. (Livorno, 1840) in *Ozar Perushim al haTorah.* N.Y., 1950.

HEBREW ETHICAL WILLS, ed. Israel Abrahams. 2 v., Philadelphia, 1926.

HILLEL B. SAMUEL, Tagmule haNefesh, ed. S. Halberstamm. Lyck, 1874.

JACOB DI ILLESCAS, Imre Noam. Cremona, 1565.

JOSEPH BEKOR SHOR, Perush haTorah, ed. A. Jellinek. Leipzig, 1856.

MAIMONIDES (MOSES B. MAIMON), Biur Shemoth Kodesh v'Hol. ed. M. Gaster. In *Debir*, I, 191 ff.

——, Mishneh Torah. 4 v., Vilna, 1900.

——, Moreh Nebukim. Warsaw, 1872.

MANN, J., "Early Karaite Bible Commentaries." In *JQR*, ns., XV.

MASNUTH, SAMUEL B. NISSIM, Ma'yan Ganim, ed. S. Buber. Berlin, 1889.

MIDRASH AGGADAH, ed. S. Buber. Vienna, 1894.

SAADIA B. JOSEPH, HaEmunoth v'haDeoth. Josefow, 1885.

R. SAADIA BEN JOSEF AL-FAYYOUMI, Oeuvres Completes de., v. I, ed. J. Derenbourg. Paris, 1893.

SIDDUR OZAR HATEFILLOTH. Vilna, 1923.

TOBIAH B. ELIEZER, Midrash Lekah Tob., v. I, ed. S. Buber. 2nd ed., Vilna, 1924.

YERAHMEEL. The Chronicles of Yerahmeel, trans. M. Gaster. London, 1899.

Other Rabbinic Commentaries are cited from Pentateuch (*Humash*), Lemberg, 1909; Malbim Pentateuch, Vilna, 1923; Rabbinic Bible (*Mikraoth Gedoloth*), Warsaw, 1902.

5. *Cabala and Hasidism.*

ABULAFIA, TODROS, Ozar haKabod. Novyvdor, 1808.

AZULAI, ABRAHAM, Hesed l'Abraham. Amsterdam, 1685.

BACHARACH, JACOB ELHANAN, Emek haMelek. Amsterdam, 1648.

ELIJAH B. SOLOMON ABRAHAM, Shebet Musar. Lublin, 1881.

SEFER HASIDIM, ed. J. Wistinetzki. 2nd ed., Frankfurt, 1924.

HAVDALAH SHEL R. AKIBA. See Ch. XVIII n. 31.

HORODETZKY, S. A., Torath haKabbalah shel R. Mosheh Cordovero. Berlin, 1924.

HOSHKE, REUBEN, Yalkut Reubeni. Amsterdam, 1700.

ISRAEL B. ISAAC SIMHAH, Esser Zahzahoth. Pietrkow, 1909.

JACOB JOSEPH OF POLONOYE, Toledoth Jacob Joseph. Medziboz, 1811.

KAIDANOVER, ZEBI HIRSCH, Kab haYashar. Vilna, 1888.

SEFER HaKANEH. Koretz, 1784.

KETHER SHEM TOB. Pietrkow, 1912.

LIKKUTE HaSHAS ME-HAARI. Livorno, 1790.

NAHMAN OF BRATZLAW, Sefer haMiddoth. Warsaw, 1927.

——, Sippure Maasiyoth, ed. A. Cahana. Warsaw, 1922.

SEFER PELIAH. Przemysl, 1843.

SEFER RAZIEL HAMALAK. Salonica, 1843.

ROKEAH, ELEAZAR, Sode Razayya, ed. I. Kamelhar. Bilgoraj, 1936.

SABA, ABRAHAM, Zeror haMor. Warsaw, 1879.

SCHOLEM, G. G., "Kabbaloth R. Jacob v'R. Yizhak B'ne R. Jacob haKohen." In *Mada'e haYahaduth*, II, 164-262.

SHIBHE HABESHT, ed. S. A. Horodetzky. Berlin, 1922.

VITAL, HAYYIM, Ez Hayyim. Korzec, 1784.

ZOHAR. 3 v., Vilna, 1922.

ZOHAR HADASH. Berditchev, 1825.

CHRISTIAN

ANSELM, Opera. v. II, Cologne, 1583.
The Ante-Nicene Fathers, ed. A. Roberts and J. Donaldson. American
    ed., revised A. C. Coxe. 10 v., N.Y., 1899.
The Apostolic Fathers, trans. Kirsopp Lake. (Loeb Classics Series).
    2 v., 1914.
AUGUSTINE, The City of God, trans. J. Healey. Edinburgh, 1909.
The Book of Common Prayer (American ed.).
CALVIN, J., Institutes of the Christian Religion, trans. J. Allen. 2 v.,
    Philadelphia, 1936.
MIGNE, J.-P., Patrologiae Latinae Cursus Completus. 221 v., Paris,
    1844–1864.
——, Patrologiae Graecae Cursus Completus. 166 v., Paris.
A Select Library of the Nicene and Post-Nicene Fathers of the Chris-
    tian Church.
    First Series, ed. P. Schaff, 14 v., Buffalo and N.Y., 1886–1890.
    Second Series, ed. P. Schaff and H. Wace, 14 v., N.Y., 1890–1900.
Die Schatzhöhle, trans. C. Bezold. Leipzig, 1883.
ST. THOMAS AQUINAS, Basic Writings of, 2 v., ed. A. Pegis, N.Y., 1945.
    Includes:
    Summa Theologica, cited by Part, Quaestio, and Article.
    Summa Contra Gentiles, cited by Book and Ch.

MOSLEM

The Koran, trans. G. Sale (1734), N.Y., n.d.
MUHAMMAD ALI, Translation of the Holy Quran. Lahore, 1934.

C. *Other works consulted.*

ALBRIGHT, W. F., From the Stone Age to Christianity. Baltimore, 1940.
APTOWITZER, V., "Mélanges IV; Sur la Légende de la Chute de Satan
    et des Anges. In *REJ*, LIV, 59 ff.
——, "Untersuchungen zur gäonischen Literatur." In *HUCA*, VIII-
    IX, 373 ff.
AULÉN, G., Christus Victor: An Historical Study of the Three Main
    Types of the Idea of the Atonement, trans. A. G. Herbert. Lon-
    don, 1931.
BAMBERGER, B. J., "A Messianic Document of the Seventh Century."
    In *HUCA*, XV, 425 ff.
BENTWICH, N., Josephus. Philadelphia, 1914.
BERKHOF, L., Reformed Dogmatics. Grand Rapids, 1923.
BLAKE, WILLIAM, Poetry and Prose of William Blake, ed. G. Keynes.
    N.Y. and London, 1927.
BONSIRVEN, J., Le Judaisme palestinien au Temps de Jésus-Christ. 2
    v., Paris, 1934–1935.
BUBER, M., "Myth in Judaism." In *Commentary*, June 1950.

BÜCHLER, A., "Review of Schechter's 'Documents of Jewish Sectaries.'" In *JQR*, ns., III.

BUNYAN, JOHN, The Pilgrim's Progress (Everyman's Library). London and N.Y., 1945.

BUTTENWIESER, M., An Outline of the Neo-Hebraic Apocalyptic Literature. Cincinnati, 1901. (The author's own version of the art. in *JE*, I, 675 ff., which was printed with changes he did not accept.)

CARUS, P., The History of the Devil and the Idea of Evil. Chicago, 1900.

CASSUTO, U., "Maaseh B'ne haElohim uV'noth haAdam." In: *Essays in Honour of the Very Rev. Dr. J. H. Hertz*. London, 1945.

Catholic Encyclopedia, The. 15 v., N.Y., 1913.

CHAMBERS, W., "The Devil." In *Life*, February 2, 1948.

CHARLES, R. H., A Critical and Exegetical Commentary on the Revelation of St. John (ICC). 2 v., N.Y., 1920.

Contemporary American Philosophy, ed. G. P. Adams and W. P. Montague. 2 v., N.Y., 1930.

CONYBEARE, F. C., "The Demonology of the New Testament." In *JQR*, os., VIII-IX.

DILLMAN, C. F. A., Genesis Critically and Exegetically Expounded, trans. W. B. Stevenson. 2 v., Edinburgh, 1897.

ELBOGEN, I., Der jüdische Gottesdienst in seiner geschichtlichen Entwicklung. 2nd ed., Frankfurt a. M., 1924.

The Empire State Baptist, October 1948.

Encyclopaedia Britannica. 25 v., 1951.

Encyclopedia of Islam. 5 v., London and Leyden, 1913–1938.

Encyclopedia of Religion and Ethics, ed. J. Hastings. 12 v., N.Y., 1908–1922.

FASCHER, E., Jesus und der Satan (Hallische Monographien nr. 11). Halle, 1949.

FINKELSTEIN, L., The Pharisees. 2 v., Philadelphia, 1940.

FRANKEL, Z., Ueber den Einfluss der palästinensischen Exegese auf die alexandrinische Hermeneutik. Leipzig, 1851.

——, Vorstudien zu der Septuaginta. Leipzig, 1841.

FREY, J.-B., "L'Angélologie juive au temps de Jésus-Christ." In *RSPT* (Kain, Belgium), V, 75-110.

GEBHARDT, O., "Die 70 Hirten des Buches Henoch." In Merx, *Archiv für wissenschaftliche Erforschung des Alten Testaments*, Band II, Heft II.

GEIGER, A., "Einige Wörter über das Buch Henoch." In *JZWL*, III, 196 ff.

GIBBON, EDWARD, The Decline and Fall of the Roman Empire. 3 v. (Modern Library), N.Y., n.d.

GOODENOUGH, E. R., "John a Primitive Gospel." In *JBL*, LXIV, 145 ff.

GRAETZ, H., Gnosticismus und Judenthum. Krotoschin, 1846.

GUTTMANN, J., "Über Jean Bodin in seiner Beziehungen zum Judentum." In *MGWJ*, XLIX, 315 ff., 459 ff.

HELLER, B., "La Chute des Anges: Schemhazai, Ouzza, et Azaël." In *REJ*, LX, 202 ff.

HACKSPILL, L., "L'Angélologie juive à l'époque néo-testamentaire." In *RB*, XI, 527-550.

HUSIK, I., A History of Medieval Jewish Philosophy. N.Y., 1918.

JASTROW, M. A., A Dictionary of the Targumim, The Talmud Babli and Yerushalmi, and the Midrashic Literature. 2 v., London and N.Y., 1903.

The Jewish Encyclopedia. 12 v., N.Y., 1901-1906.

KESSLER, H., Walther Rathenau; His Life and Work. N.Y., 1930.

KOHUT, A., Aruch Completum. 8 v., 2nd ed., Vienna, 1926.

——, Über die jüdische Angelologie und Dämonologie in ihrer Abhängigkeit vom Parsismus. Leipzig, 1866.

KROCHMAL, N., Kithbe RNK, ed. S. Rawidowicz. Berlin, 1924.

LANGTON, E., Satan: A Portrait. London, 1946.

LAUTERBACH, J. Z., "A Significant Controversy between the Sadducees and the Pharisees." In *HUCA*, IV, 173 ff.

——, "The Origin and Development of Two Sabbath Ceremonies." In *HUCA*, XV, 367 ff.

Lexikon für Theologie und Kirche. 10 v., Freiburg, 1930-1938.

LITTMAN, E. "Harut und Marut." In *Festschrift Friederich Carl Andreas zur Vollendung des Siebzigsten Lebensjahres*. Leipzig, 1916. 70 ff.

MCGIFFERT, A. C., A History of Christian Thought. 2 v., N.Y., 1932-1933.

MANN, J., The Bible as Read and Preached in the Old Synagogue. v. 1., Cincinnati, 1940.

MAUNDER, MRS. A. S. D., "The Date and Place of Writing of the Slavonic Book of Enoch." In *The Observatory, A Monthly Review of Astronomy* (London), LXI, 309 ff.

MIESES, M., "Hebräische Fragmente aus dem jüdischen Urtext des Apocalypse des heiligen Johannes." In *MGWJ*, LXXIV, 345 ff.

MONTGOMERY, J. A. and HARRIS, Z. S., The Ras Shamra Mythological Texts. Memoirs of the American Philosophical Society, IV (1935).

MOORE, G. F., Judaism in the First Centuries of the Christian Era. 3 v., Cambridge (U.S.A.), 1927-1930.

——, History of Religions. 2 v., N.Y., 1925-1926.

MORGENSTERN, J., "A Chapter in the History of the High Priesthood." In *AJSL*, LV, 1 ff.

——, "The Mythological Background of Psalm 82." In *HUCA*, XIV, 29-126.

MURRAY, M. A., The Witch-Cult in Western Europe. Oxford, 1921.

NEWMAN, L. I. and SPITZ, S., The Hasidic Anthology. N.Y., 1938.

NIEBUHR, R., The Nature and Destiny of Man. v. I, N.Y., 1943.

OURSLER, F., "A Bargain in Brimstone." In *The Readers Digest*, June 1947.

PALMER, A. S., "The Fall of Lucifer." In *Hibbert Journal*, XI, 766 ff.

PEAKE, A. S., A Commentary on the Bible. N.Y., 1919.

PORTER, F. C., The Yeçer Hara. Yale Biblical and Semitic Studies, 1902.

RABBINOVICZ, R. N., Dikduke Soferim. Variae Lectiones in Mischnam et in Talmud Babylonicum. 16 v., Munich and Przemysl., 1867–1897.

REICKE, B., "The Law and This World According to Paul." In *JBL*, LXX, 259 ff.

REVILLE, A., The devil: his origin, greatness, and decadence. Trans. H. A. London, 1871.

ROSKOFF, G., Geschichte des Teufels. 2 v., Leipzig, 1869.

ROUGEMONT, D. DE, La Part du Diable. Nouvelle Version, N.Y., 1944.

SCHÄRF, R., "Die Gestalt des Satans im Alten Testament." In Jung. C. G., *Symbolik des Geistes*. Zürich, 1948.

SCHOEPS, H. J., Theologie und Geschichte des Judenchristentums. Tübingen, 1949.

SCHAFF, P., The Creeds of Christendom. 3 v., N.Y., n.d.

SCHOLEM, G. G., "L'Heker Kabbalath R. Yizhak b. Jacob HaKohen." In *Tarbiz*, II-V.

——, "L'Maaseh R. Joseph della Reyna." In *Zion*, os., V, 124 ff.

SMITH, P., The Life and Letters of Martin Luther. Boston and N.Y., 1911.

——, The Age of the Reformation. N.Y., 1920.

SPIEGEL, S., "Noah, Daniel, and Job, Touching on Canaanite Relics in the Legends of the Jews." In *Louis Ginzberg Jubilee Volume* (N.Y. 1945), English Section, 305 ff.

STRONG, A. H., Systematic Theology. 2 v., Philadelphia, 1907.

TRACHTENBERG, J., The Devil and the Jews, New Haven, 1943.

——, Jewish Magic and Superstition. N.Y., 1939.

WOLFSON, H. A., Philo. 2 v., Cambridge (U.S.A.), 1948.

ZEITLIN, S., "The Book of Jubilees." In *JQR*, ns, XXX, 1 ff.

——, "The Hebrew Scrolls: Once More and Finally." *Ibid.*, XLI, 1 ff.

——, "The Legend of the Ten Martyrs and Its Apocalyptic Origins." *Ibid.*, XXXVI, 1 ff.

Notes

Cross references are always given by chapter and note. They often refer, however, not to the note only, but also to the corresponding passage in the text.

NOTES TO CHAPTER TWO
Pp. 7-13

1. See Job 1.6, 2.1, 38.7; Ps. 29.1, 89.6 f. and the full discussion by Robert, *RB*, IV, 341-8. See also U. Cassuto, 'Ma'aseh B'ne haElohim uV'noth haAdam,' in *Essays in Honour of . . . Hertz*, Hebrew section, 35 ff. Cassuto's views are similar to those presented in the text. Gen. 6 relates not angelic sin, but the origin of the giants. It is not so much a survival of mythology as a reply to it. It is not a fragment: the biblical author disposes of a distasteful subject as quickly as he can. The title "sons of God," applied in Ugaritic to various deities, here designates a grade of angels inferior to those called "messengers of God."

2. So Lods, 304-5. He holds that Gen. 6.3 refers to the *gibborim*, not to mankind (reading *bam* instead of *ba-adam*) and means: Though there is a divine strain in these beings, they will not live forever, since they are of part human descent. This parallels the Gilgamesh epic, whose hero, though of partly divine parentage, seeks immortality in vain. Cassuto (*op. cit.*), 41 f., contends that the traditional rendering of *yadon* has good philological justification. The v. means that angelic paternity will not make the giants immortal, since they are partly flesh. (But this does not fit the phrase "My spirit.") "His days shall be 120 years," C. holds, means that the life span of men will gradually dwindle to that maximum. Cf. the view of Abrabanel cited below, Ch. XX.

3. Montgomery and Harris, 76 f.
4. Morgenstern, *HUCA*, XIV, 85. Cf. Num. 13.33; Deut. 2.20 ff.
5. Cf. Ch. XIV n. 20; Ch. XXIX n. 1.
6. So also Ez. 28.11 ff.
7. Morgenstern, *op. cit.*, 29-40, 114 ff.
8. *Ibid.* 76-83, 114 ff. M. supposes further that the author of Ps. 82 knew both myths, the rebellion of Helel b. Shahar and the marriage of angels and men. The *nefilim* were Helel and his followers, the fallen ones who were already on earth in the days when the angels sought mortal consorts. For the difficult half-verse "as one of the princes (*ha-sarim*) ye shall fall," he would read "as Helel b. Shahar ye shall fall." Though ingenious, this seems to me unfounded. It assumes that the myths contained in II En. and the Adam Books (below, Ch. VII and VIII) are implied in the biblical texts; in fact, these stories are midrashic elaborations on the biblical words. M. even supposes (*ibid.*, 95) that the first star which fell to earth in I En. 86.1 was Satan-Helel, and the stars which followed were the angels that took mortal wives: the more natural explanation is that the first star was Azazel, setting an example to his followers. Below, Ch. V, n. 2.
9. PR 43, 179b; Midrash Samuel 2.4; Mishnath R. Eliezer 29.
10. The imprisonment and ultimate punishment of sinners resembles the judgment on Azazel and his host (below, Ch. III, nn. 7 f.), but Is. 24.22 may refer to human sinners. Morgenstern (*op. cit.*, 124 f.) overlooks the difference between rebel angels and national *sarim*.
11. Montgomery and Harris, 78.
12. Is. 30.7; Ps. 87.4. Cf. Is. 51.9; Ps. 74.4, 89.11; Job. 9.13, 26.12.

NOTES TO CHAPTER THREE
Pp. 16-21

1. Charles, II, 171 ff.
2. *Ibid.*, 170-1.
3. "Heaven" is a substitute for the name of God: the phrase is equivalent to "sons of God," Gen. 6.2.
4. But the roster of the "chiefs of tens" includes only 19 names; Samiazaz is first, Asael tenth: I En. 6.7.
5. The rabbis also taught that animals became immoral before the Flood: Ginzberg, I, 160 and n. 32.
6. Here the story is interrupted by a variant account of the wicked practices taught by the angels, including the manufacture of weapons and jewelry and the cosmetic arts. The chief malefactor is Azazel, Semjaza takes second place. On the names of the fallen angels, see Ginzberg, V, 152-3.
7. See Dan. 4.14.
8. I En. 65-7; see Charles, II, 168. The fragments in Ch. 54-5 and 60 yield nothing for our purpose. Ch. 106-7 state explicitly that the flood resulted from the intermarriage of angels and mortals and the engendering of the giants.
9. I En. 69. 1-13. The mention of Gadreel is the only ref. in I. En. to the Eden story. The author disregarded the problems raised by his statement, which other writings of the sort treat at length. See below Ch. VIII.
10. I En. 69.13-25. The sinful angel is named Kasbeel; according to Charles, the oath is called Biqa and Akae. Cahana and Faitlovitch take Biqa as the original name of the angel (it means "a good person" in Amharic); after his fall he was named Kazbiel, "he who lies to God." This faintly suggests a medieval version, below, Ch. XIX n. 7.

11. Lods, 298 and Charles, II, 168 n. 1 speak of a "conflation" of myths: this overstates the case.

12. Mishnah Yoma 6.8, but the text is not certain: Jastrow, *Dictionary*, 333 top. The identification was first suggested by Geiger, *JZWL*, III, 200 f.

13. So explicitly I En. 15.3-7; below, Ch. IV n. 1.

14. Writing was one of the marvels created by God on the eve of the first Sabbath: Abot 5.9. Before Creation, the Torah was written in black fire on a scroll of white fire: Tehillim 90, 91, etc.

15. See the excellent analysis of Lods, 304 ff. Though written before the Ras Shamra lit. was known, this account recognizes the close connection of the tale with the Palestinian terrain.

NOTES TO CHAPTER FOUR
Pp. 21-23

1. I En. 12-16, the direct quotations from 15.3-7.

2. *Ibid.*, 68.4, a Noah passage.

3. *Ibid.*, 15.8 ff., 16.1-2, 19.1-3. Lods, 311, remarks that the ref. to sirens in 19 does not prove Greek influence. It may be only the Greek rendering of *lilin* or a similar word. Zohar, III, 76b (Ch. XXIII n. 9 below) is too late to be a useful parallel. On the characteristics of demons, see Ch. XVI n. 68.

4. I En. 18.12-6.

5. Grünbaum, 67-8; independently A. Smythe Palmer, *Hibbert Journal*, XI, 766 ff. Lods, 309, says that I En. closely associates fallen angels and rebel stars. In fact, the two topics are mentioned in the same ch., but are in no way combined. The punishment of the stars is more like the rabbinic story of the punishment of the moon: Ginzberg, V, 34-5.

NOTES TO CHAPTER FIVE
Pp. 23-26

1. I En. 85-90. Preceding this is a vision in which the sin of the angels seems to be the cause of the Flood and of continuing human guilt. See esp. I En. 84.4.

2. I En. 85-8. On the identification of the stars, above, Ch. II n. 8.

3. The biblical story, ibid., 89.1-50. The appointment of the shepherds, vv. 51-67. The reports, v. 70 f., at the end of the exile; vv. 76 ff., probably at the end of the Persian period; 90.5, perhaps at the beginning of the Seleucid rule over Palestine (Charles).

4. *Ibid.*, 90.13 ff.

5. O. Gebhardt, "Die 70 Hirten des Buches Henoch;" Charles, especially in his separate ed. of I Enoch (Oxford, 1912). Cf. Ch. II n. 10.

6. I En. 54.1-6, 55.3-56.4. Ch. 64 is out of place.

7. *Ibid.*, 92.1-5, 91.1-10, 18, 19. "All those who brought down sin" (100.4) could refer to human tempters; if to the fallen angels, it may be a harmonistic insertion.

8. Satan is a person only *ibid.*, 54.6. "Instruments of Satan" (53.3) means simply instruments of torture. In 40.7 an archangel is to fend off the "satans," preventing them from accusing mankind before God.

NOTES TO CHAPTER SIX
Pp. 26-32

1. Zeitlin has recently argued (*JQR*, ns, XXX, 1 ff.) that it is the oldest of the Pseudepigrapha, composed in the Persian period. Albright, *From*

the Stone Age to Christianity, 266 f., places it at the beginning of the 3rd cent. B.C.E., perhaps a little earlier. I am still inclined to accept the dating of Charles in the 2nd cent. B.C.E., a data accepted by Kohler (*JE, sv,* Jubilees, Book of) and Finkelstein, *The Pharisees,* 600 f.

2. Charles, II, 289.

3. Controversy on this subject has recently flared up, because this work is undeniably related to some of the newly discovered "Dead Sea Scrolls." Zeitlin, who regards the latter as medieval, maintains the view first advanced by Büchler that the "Zadokite" Work is actually Karaitic: see *JQR,* ns, III and XLI, 35 ff. But a pre-Christian date was maintained by Charles, E. Meyer, Kohler, Ginzberg, and other important authorities. See Charles, II, 788; Moore, *Judaism,* I, 201-4, III 58-9. The fact that this document calls the fallen angels "Watchers" (below, n. 14) seems to me strong evidence for an early date; this term for the fallen angels does not appear in medieval Hebrew literature.

4. Jub. 4.15-5.10. See also 7.20 ff., acc. to Charles taken from an old Noah-book. The statement that the giants were "all unlike" may have originally meant "they were of monstrous form" (*meshunim*). *Naphidim* and *Naphil* are variants of *Nephilim;* what *Eljo* means is unknown. Cf. also Jub. 20.5.

5. *Ibid.,* 8.1-4. Parallels, Ginzberg, V, 149-50.

6. Jub. consistently avoids the use of angelic names, hence it never specifically mentions Shemhazai and Azazel.

7. Jub. 10.1-14, according to Charles from a Noah-book. This passage appears almost verbatim in a medieval Hebrew Noah-book (Jellinek, *Beth haMidrasch,* iii—not iv, as Charles has it—p. 155) Eisenstein, *OM,* 400. Cf. Ginzberg, V, 196.

8. Jub. 17.16-18.12; 12.19 f. Cf. below, Ch. XVI n. 22, Ch. XIX nn. 24-28.

9. Jub. 49.2. Cf. below Ch. XVI n. 84, Ch. XIX nn. 39-41.

10. Above, n. 7; cf. Ch. XIV nn. 10 f.

11. Jub. 15.31 f. Charles explains "to lead them astray from Him: the ultimate result treated as if it were the immediate purpose of God's action." Cf. Ecclus. 17.17: "For every nation He appointed a ruler, but Israel is the Lord's portion."

12. Fragments of a Zadokite Work 6.9 f., 9.12.

13. *Ibid.,* 7.19 (cf. II Timothy 3.8, Menahot 85a), 14.5, 20.2.

14. *Ibid.,* 3.4 f.; above, n. 3.

15. Cf. below, Ch. XVII n. 8.

16. E.g., Reuben 2-3, which Charles considers an addition composed under Stoic influence.

17. Simeon 3.1 ff.; Judah 13.3, 14.2, 16.1; Issachar 4.4; Dan 1.6-7, ch. 2-4, 5.5; Naphtali 3.3; Gad 1.9, 6.2; Asher 1.9, 6.2; Benjamin 5.2.

Other allusions to Beliar, Satan, and the evil spirits: Reuben 4.7, 11; Issachar 6.1, 7.7; Zebulon 9.8; Dan 1.6 f., 3.6, 5.1-6, 6.1 ff.; Naphtali 8.6; Gad 4.7, 5.2; Asher 1.8, 3.2; Joseph 7.4; Benjamin 3.3 f., 3.8 (is this passage Christian?), 6.1, 7; 7.1 f.

18. Further: Simeon 6.6; Judah 25.3; Dan 5.10 f., 6.4; Levi 4.1. Asher 7.3, where the Most High breaks the head of the dragon upon the water, may be a Christian interpolation, even though the slant serpent is very ancient. Cf. Ch. II n. 11 and XIV n. 3 ff.

19. Levi 5.6; Dan 6.2; cf. above, n. 11. But the medieval Hebrew Testament of Naphtali emphasizes that only the Gentiles have guardian angels; the destinies of Israel are directly supervised by God.

NOTES TO CHAPTER SEVEN
Pp. 32-35

We shall cite II En. from Charles' texts A and B, and from the Sokolow text (C) used by Cahana for his translation. Where necessary, we shall render Cahana's Hebrew into English.

1. A-B 7; C 4.1-7. Note A 7.3: "took counsel with their own will, and turned away with their prince, who is fastened in the fifth heaven;" C 4.5: "followed the stubborn impulses of their hearts, they and their prince and they who are set in the fifth heaven." See next n. and Ch. IV n. 1.

2. A 18; C 7.1-13. A speaks of only 3 angels who descended on Hermon, C of 2 million! All the sources state that the gloomy beings in the fifth heaven are also sinful angels. But there are many difficulties. Why should some of the Watchers be punished in the second and others in the fifth heaven? A 7.3 places Satanail in the fifth heaven, but Enoch does not find him there; later we learn that he is flying about at liberty (see next n.). Not all the Watchers sinned; but if those in the fifth heaven were culprits, no place is left in the scheme of II En. for the loyal members of the order. Why moreover should En. have urged those who were already undergoing eternal punishment to hymn Gods praise, lest His wrath against them increase? What more could they have feared? Besides, it has been already stated that God would not accept the prayer of the fallen angels.

The error must have arisen out of confusion over the meaning of "Watchers." Because the sinful angels were of this category, the scribes began to take the word "Watcher" itself to mean "fallen angel."

3. A 29; C 11.34-40. The creation of the angels on the second day, BR 3.8.

4. A 31.3-8 (very corrupt text); C 11.73-8. Cf. esp. A 31.7 f., "I cursed ignorance, but what I had blessed previously, those I did not curse, I cursed not man, nor the earth, nor other creatures, but man's evil fruit, and his works;" C 11.76-7: "And because of their ignorance I cursed them. But what I had blessed previously, those I did not curse; and even what I had not blessed previously, I did not curse. And I did not curse man or the earth or the other creatures, but the evil seed of man; and therefore a good creation is the fruit that follows upon labor."

5. A 30.16; C 11.66.

6. A 33.7 ff.; C 11.90 ff.

7. As Charles did in his n. on 29.5.

NOTES TO CHAPTER EIGHT
Pp. 35-37

1. On the various texts, see the intro. of Wells *ap*. Charles, II 123 ff. Wells agrees that it is difficult to determine how much of the extant material belongs to the original Jewish kernel, and suggests some doubt as to the soundness of Ginzberg's method (*JE*, *sv* Adam, Book of) of reconstructing the story. According to Jagic, editor of the Slavonic version, Ch. 33-5 of this text are an insertion by a Bogomil; but this section is not strikingly different from the rest of the work.

2. Vita Adae et Evae 5-10; in the Slavonic, Eve recognizes the Devil and does not respond to his blandishments.

3. *Vita* 12-17.

4. Below, Ch. XVII n. 2.

5. Apocalypsis Mosis 15-6.

6. Apoc. Mos. 17.1-3, Satan waits till the angels have left Paradise to hymn God's praise on high (so also Vita 33), then appears outside the wall in the guise of an angel chorister and Eve does not recognize him. In 17.4 and Ch. 18, the serpent (or the Devil speaking through the serpent) urges Eve to eat the forbidden fruit. In 19.1 Eve opens the gate to Satan, which seems needless if his agent were already successful.

7. *Ibid.*, 19.3. Cf. Ch. XVI n. 55 below.

8. *Ibid.*, 21.3.

9. *Ibid.*, 23.5; 25.1, 4; 26; 28.4.

10. *Ibid.*, 39.

NOTES TO CHAPTER NINE
Pp. 37-42

1. For bibliographical details see Cahana's Intro. and Kohler, *JE*, sv Job, Testament of. James doubted that the work is entirely Jewish; Charles did not include it in his ed. of the Pseudepigrapha. But Kohler, Cahana, and Ginzberg accept it as Jewish; the latter (V, 383 f.) cites parallels in the later aggada. The book seems to be in the Palestinian tradition—note esp. the emphasis on resurrection—but the figure of the wrestler (4.11; 27.3, 4) suggests Hellenistic influence. The original language and date remain uncertain.

As to the purpose of the book, Cahana, II, 516, regards it as propaganda, showing how the power of Judaism could transform an Edomite into a saint. But Job is a saint while still an idolater; he becomes a monotheist, but is not formally converted to Judaism. Nor would a book addressed to the heathen world have stressed the injunction against intermarriage (45.3). Kohler considered the book an exposition of Hasidic ideals. But Job, fabulously wealthy, gives charity on a scale much too lavish to serve as an example to ordinary people. Other important aspects of Hasidic piety, notably Sabbath observance, go unmentioned. Our author most likely had no clear intent except to write an interesting and edifying tale.

2. Other instances are the stories by Artapanus about Moses (Ginzberg, V, 407 ff.), the Testament of Abraham, and the Martyrdom of Isaiah. The pseudo-Philonic Biblical Antiquities (below, Ch. X) provide an even closer parallel: here much traditional lore is combined with inventions of the author. The Psalm there ascribed to David is analogous to the poetical insertions in the Test. of Job.

3. "Satan as a beggar occurs frequently in Jewish legends:" Ginzberg, V, 384 n. 15. But usually he entraps someone in an act of indifference or unkindness to the poor. Here Job defeats Satan by *refusing* him hospitality!

4. Assumptio Mosis 10.1; cf. above, Ch. VI n. 18. For the legend about the body of Moses, see Jude 9; Charles, II, 408 n. 2; Ginzberg, VI, 159.

5. Similar legends in rabbinic lit.: Ginzberg, VI, 373 f.

6. Martyrdom of Isaiah 1.

7. *Ibid.*, 2.1-4.

8. See below, Ch. XVI n. 15.

9. II Cor. 4.4; below, Ch. XIV nn. 15, 31; Ch. XV n. 35.

10. Above, Ch. VI n. 11.

11. Test. of Abraham 16-17 describes the Angel of Death in gruesome terms; some of the details may have been of Egyptian origin and added by the Greek translator (so Box in his ed. p. xxi f.). In any case, the Angel is God's agent, not a wicked being.

12. Morgenstein, in *HUCA*, XIV, 93, refers to Wisdom of Solomon 14.6;

Judith 16.7; III Mac. 2.4; I Baruch 3.26 ff. These passages mention God's defeat of the giants; but they do not mention the ancestry of the latter, nor is there reason to assume that these authors accepted the story of the fallen angels. Quite the contrary is true of Judith, which never mentions angels. Sybilline Oracles 5.512 ff. is probably not pertinent to our theme.

NOTES TO CHAPTER TEN
Pp. 42-45

1. This notion is foreshadowed in Jub. 4.20 ff.; Test. Reuben 5; above, Ch. VI nn. 4, 15. The fact that fallen angels are mentioned in II Bar. only in this section supports Charles' view that the work is composite and the vision in Ch. 56 a separate unit.

2. Ginzberg, V, 197 f.; VI, 184 n. 19.

3. James, *The Biblical Antiquities*, Intro. 58-9. For a radically new approach to this work, see A. Spiro, in *Proceedings of the Amer. Academy for Jewish Research*, XX, 279 ff.

4. *Ibid.*, 18.5, 32.1: the sacrifice of Isaac was suggested craftily by angels who were jealous of Abraham. This view is not related to the idea of rebel angels and is found also in rabbinic lit. Below, Ch. XVI n. 19.

5. *Ibid.*, Ch. 34.

6. *Ibid.*, 11.12, 13.6, 15.5, 59.4.

7. *Ibid.*, 45.6, where the Latin reads *Anticimus*. James thinks this may correspond to Mastemah in the original, but Satan is more likely.

8. *Ibid.*, 25.9.

9. *Ibid.*, 53.3, 4.

10. *Ibid.*, Ch. 60. See James' n., citing parallels from Christian and magical texts. On the time when the demons were created, below, Ch. XVI nn. 58, 67. The offspring of David who is to rebuke the demons may be Solomon (so James) or the Messiah: cf. above, Ch. VI n. 18.

NOTES TO CHAPTER ELEVEN
Pp. 46-49

1. It is not included in the collections of Kautsch, Charles, or Cahana; Jung disregards it.

2. See Ginzberg in *JE, sv* Abraham, Apocalypse of. Rationalistic elements also appear in the apocalypse proper: the discussions ch. xx, xxiii-xxv, and especially the prayer ch. xvii.

3. This is a midrash on Gen. 15: Abraham and Jaoel ride on the dove and pigeon which A. did not split (15.10); Azazel is the bird of prey that swooped down, v. 11.

4. Cf. above, Ch. VIII n. 10.

5. Cf. below, n. 8, and Ginzberg, V, 97 n. 70.

6. Cf. Ch. VIII nn. 5 ff.

7. Box, *Apoc. of Abraham* 77 n. 5.

8. The computations of the end of days can no longer be interpreted with assurance, but seem to indicate that the Messiah was expected at a date early in the Christian era. Ch. xxix contains an odd Christian interpretation, in which Azazel worships and kisses Christ. A passage in ch. xix (see Box, 64 n. 3) seems to deny the reality of angels, but probably should not be so interpreted.

The small book known as III Baruch must date from about the same time as II Bar. and Apoc. Abr. Note the following passages from it: Baruch sees Hades and a dragon that consumes the bodies of the wicked. He learns that the forbidden fruit of Paradise was the vine, which Samael had planted and which God cursed along with Samael (above, n. 5): 4.4-9. The moon saw Samael taking the serpent as a garment; she should have hidden herself because of the crime, but instead she increased—therefore God reduced her original splendor: 9.5-7, cf. Ginzberg, V, 34 n. 100. The guardian angels of wicked men seek to be relieved of their painful responsibility, but Michael keeps them at their posts "in order that the enemy may not prevail to the end": 13.3. By Michael's ordinance the demons afflict the wicked: 16.3.

NOTES TO CHAPTER TWELVE
Pp. 51-54

1. See Rahlfs' ed. *ad loc.*, and below, n. 7. Frankel *Ueber den Einfluss*, 46, regards the reading "sons" as primary. He suggests that *toutois*, v. 3 (which corresponds to no word in the Heb.), was added to suggest that the sons of God were not angels but mortals; but he admits that other explanations are possible. Sept. Deut. 32.8 reads: "He set the boundaries of the peoples according to the number of the sons of God," which has generally been interpreted as a reference to the guardian angels of the nations, whose number equals that of their protégés. But cf. Frankel, *Vorstudien*, 66 f.

2. Josephus, *Ant.* 1.3.1; Ginzberg, V, 177-8.

3. *Ant.* 6.8.2.

4. *Ibid.*, 8.2.5.

5. *Bel. Jud.* 7.6.3.

6. Bentwich, *Josephus*, 114, 131.

7. Philo, *De Gigantibus* 6-11; cf. *De Somniis*, I, 133 f. On the Septuagint text, cf. n. 1 above.

8. *De Gig.* 12-18.

9. *Ibid.*, 58-60.

10. Frey, in *RSPT*, V, 100. But Wolfson, *Philo*, I, 383 ff., ascribes to Philo a more realistic notion of fallen angels.

11. *De Gig.* 12-15; cf. Plato, *Phaedrus* 246 ff.

NOTES TO CHAPTER THIRTEEN
Pp. 54-59

1. Scholem, *Major Trends*, 34 ff. For a different view, Buber, "Myth in Judaism" (English trans. in *Commentary*, June 1950).

2. The literature on Gnosticism is endless. See Moore, *History of Religions*, II, 154 ff., McGiffert, *History of Christian Thought*, ch. IV. The Jewish aspect, Scholem, ch. II; Graetz, *Gnosticismus u. Judenthum*.

3. Scholem, 49.

4. "The prince of the world," Hullin 60a; "the prince of the presence," Tan. N. Mishpatim 18; "Metatron," Hagigah 15a, Sanhedrin 38b; "Jaoel," above, Ch. XI. See, further, Scholem, 67 ff., Ginzberg, V, 28-9.

5. Ginzberg, V, 163: "The Babylonian Nebo, the heavenly scribe, gave Enoch to the Palestinian Jews, Metatron to the Babylonian Jews, and nothing could be more natural than the final combination of Enoch-Metatron." But if, as is possible, the name Metatron comes from the Greek, it would have come to Babylonia via Palestine. Moreover, Jaoel, who differs from Metatron only in name, is doubtless of Palestinian origin.

6. Ginzberg, V, 156-7.

NOTES TO CHAPTER FOURTEEN
Pp. 61-72

1. So Kohler in *JE, sv* Revelation, Book of. See also the radical theory of M. Mieses that the original apocalypse was composed by R. Johanan b. Zakkai: *MGWJ*, LXXIV, 345 ff. and LXXV, 67 f. I prefer the view of Charles in his commentary on *Revelation* (ICC).

2. The visions are preceded by letters to seven churches in Asia Minor. The angel who dictates them mentions a "synagogue of Satan" in Smyrna and Philadelphia (2.9, 3.9) and a group at Thyatira who professed to fathom the deep mysteries of Satan (2.24).

3. Ch. 13 speaks of 2 beasts, one from the sea, the other from the land. The first beast derives his power from the dragon, and transmits power to the second beast. Elsewhere Rev. mentions only one beast. Andrews (Peake, *Commentary ad loc.*) suggests that the first beast is the Roman power, the second the spirit of idolatry, esp. emperor-worship. But he admits that the first beast may be a direct ref. to Nero, to whom the cipher at the end of the ch. probably alludes. Also baffling is the symbolism of the froglike spirits in 16.13 ff., and the relation of this passage to the conflict in ch. 19 is obscure.

4. The reader should clearly distinguish between the Dragon—Satan—and the Beast—the Antichrist. On the Antichrist see below, n. 7. This concept appears clearly for the first time in these NT passages. Ginzberg (*JE, sv* Antichrist) points to the biblical and other Jewish components of the idea and concludes that the concept is of Jewish origin. But the *combination* of these elements into the new figure of the Antichrist is not found in Jewish lit. of this period. The only exceptions are the Sybillines (IV, 119 ff.; V, 28 ff., 363 ff.), and from this source no safe conclusions can be drawn. The books in question are predominantly Jewish and date from the beginning of the Christian era; but they contain additions by many later hands, Jewish and Christian.

5. Cf. nn. 15, 31.

6. This consciousness is almost entirely absent from the early letter to Galatia, much more marked in the letters to Thessalonica (which are probably next in order), at its height in the correspondence with Corinth. Romans lacks this element, except for the personification of sin in 7.14 ff. If genuine, Colossians, Ephesians, and Philippians are Paul's latest extant writings; references to the world of evil spirits are mild in Col., vehement in Eph., totally absent in Phil. It is not surprising that Paul mentions the Antichrist only in II Thess., for this is the only Pauline work which deals with the future of mankind as distinguished from the future of the individual soul.

7. II Thess. 2; above, nn. 4, 6.

8. Rom. 16.20. Cf. above, Ch. VI n. 18.

8a. There is voluminous scholarly discussion on "elemental spirits" in Paul. See the commentaries, and for a recent viewpoint *JBL*, LXX, 259 ff.

9. Eph. 1.20 f., 3.10. Cf. Yerushalmi Rosh haShanah 1.3, 57b and parallels.

10. Mk. 1.23-8 (Luke 4.33-7); Mk. 1.32-4 (Mat. 8.16; Luke 4.40-1); Mk. 1.39, 3.11-12; Mk. 5.1-20 (Mat. 8.28-34; Luke 8.26-39); Mk. 7.25-30 (Mat. 15.22-8); Mk. 16.9 (Luke 8.2).

11. Mk. 3.22-9 (Mat. 12.22-9; Luke 11.14-22 add the argument "If I cast out demons by Beelzebul, by whom do your sons cast them out?").

12. Mk. 3.15; 6.7, 13; Mat. 10.1; Luke 9.1. An unauthorized man cast out demons in Jesus' name: Mk. 9.38-40 (Luke 9.49-50).

13. Mk. 16.17.

14. Mk. 9.14-29 (Mat. 17.14-20; Luke 9.37-42).

15. See Mark 16 in Moffatt's translation.

16. Mk. 1.12 f.; Mat. 4.1-11; Luke 4.1-13.

17. Mat. 11.18 (Luke 7.33). Ref. to exorcism in Mat. 4.24, 7.22, 9.32-3.

18. Mat. 25.41. Cf. 13.38-9 and Mk. 4.15 (Mat. 13.19; Luke 8.12). Jesus calls Peter "Satan," i.e., tempter: Mk. 8.33 (Mat. 16.23).

19. Mat. 12.43-5 (Luke 11.24-6). Instead of "dry places," the text should probably read "ruins," for the latter are the usual abode of demons (Berakot 3ab). The Aramaic *horba* can have either meaning.

20. Luke 10.17-20, obviously referring to Is. 14.12. Cf. below Ch. XXIX n. 1.

21. Luke 22.3; below, n. 30.

22. Luke 22.31; cf. above, n. 5.

23. Acts 19.13-17. Other ref. to demons and exorcism: 5.16, 8.7, 10.38, 16.16.

24. Jude 6 (cf. 8). It is improbable that the passage refers to the rebellion and downfall of Satan, as argued by Robert, *RB*, *IV*, 546 ff., all the more since Jude 14 f. cites I En. 1.9. Paul (I Cor. 11.10) ordered women to veil themselves in church "because of the angels." Some expositors (so Peake, *Commentary, ad loc.*) suppose this was to prevent angels present in the church from being attracted by female worshippers as their forebears had been tempted. But this is doubtful; by all accounts, the angels who withstood the original temptation are immune. Conybeare, "The Demonology of the NT" (*JQR*, os, VIII, 579) thinks Paul's rule was intended as protection against evil spirits.

25. Jude 9; above, Ch. IX n. 4.

26. Heb. 11.5 ff.; above, Ch. XIII nn. 4-6.

27. I Peter 3.19. The insertion of Enoch's name was suggested by Rendel Harris and adopted by Moffatt in his translation; but many scholars question the emendation. See commentaries. On the harrowing of hell, below, Ch. XV n. 45.

28. For a different view, see Goodenough in *JBL*, LXIV, 145 ff.

29. John mentions demons only in passages where the enemies of Jesus say "He has a demon," i.e., is insane: 7.20, 8.48, 10.20 ff.

30. John 13.2, 21-30; above, n. 21.

31. Cf. above, nn. 5, 15.

32. I John 2.18 ff. Cf. above, nn. 3, 4, 7.

33. Cf. above, Ch. XIII n. 4. Baal Zebub appears as the god of Ekron, II K. 1.2 ff., but I do not know any Jewish source that applies this name to Satan.

NOTES TO CHAPTER FIFTEEN
Pp. 73-86

1. Cf. Ch. XIV n. 24 f.

2. *I Apology* 5, 14, 57; cf. *Dialogue* 18.

3. *II Apology*, 5, makes the demons offspring of fallen angels; *ibid.*, I, 5, angels and demons seem to be identical.

4. *I Apology* 5, 64; *Dialogue* 30.

5. *I Apology* 54 ff., 65-7; *Dialogue* 69 f.

6. *Dialogue* 76, 88, 141.

7. *Ibid.* 79.
8. Tatian, *Cohortatio ad Graecos* 7-9, 14.
9. Athenagoras, *Legatio pro Christianis*, 24-6.
10. Irenaeus, *Adv. Haereses* IV, 16.2, 36.4.
11. *Ibid.*, I, 15.6.
12. Clemens Alexandrinus, *Paedagogus* 3.2 end, *Stromata* 3.7, 5.1, 7.7. Cyprian, *De Disciplina et Habitu Virginum* 14; *De Singularitate Clericorum* (Migne, *PL*, IV, 857c). Minucius Felix, *Octavius* 26; Commodian, *Instructiones* 3; Methodius, *De Resurrectione* III 7.
13. Tertullian, *Adv. Marcionem* 5.18 end.
14. *De Cultu Feminae* 1.2; cf. *ibid.*, 2.10; *De Virginibus Velandis* 7. *De Idolatria* 9 ascribes the invention of astrology to fallen angels.
15. *De Cultu* 1.3, referring to *IV Esdras* 14.37 ff.
16. *Apologia* 22.
17. Lactantius, *Instituta* 2.15 ff., 4.27.
18. For the status of the "higher criticism" of the Clementina, see Schoeps, *Theologie u. Geschichte*, 37 ff.
19. *Clementine Homilies* 8.12-18; cf. *Recognitiones* 4.26. *Recog.* 1.29 tells of the downfall of righteous men who had hitherto led lives of angelic purity: the text here may have been changed slightly to bring it into consonance with the view that became standard later: below, nn. 23 ff.
20. *Homilies* 9.10.
21. *Recognitiones* 4.24-5. According to the analysis in Schoeps, *op. cit.*, 52, this passage is the only one we have cited which belongs to the later strata of the Clementines; the others are from a second century Ebionite source.
22. Eusebius, *Praeparatio* 5.4 end. Sulpitius Severus, *Historia Sacra* 1.2. Ambrosius, *De Noe* 4.8; *De Virginibus* I, 8.53; *In Ps. CXVIII Expositio*, 8.58; but *ibid.*, 4.8, he seems to think the ref. is to men who led angelic lives.
23. Julius Africanus, *Chronographia* fragment 2 (*Ante-Nicene Fathers*, VI, 131). The expression "by whose power the giants were conceived," avoiding the actual statement that there was intercourse between angels and humans, is significant; cf. above, Ch. VI n. 15.
24. Josephus, *Ant.* 1.3.1, mentions the erstwhile virtues of the Sethites, later corrupted; but goes on at once to tell of the fallen angels. For Gnostic glorification of Cain, cf. Moore, *History of Religions*, II, 156; of Seth, Ginzberg, V, 149.
25. Origen, *Contra Celsum* 5.55; cf. *In Joannem* 6.25.
26. *De Principiis* I, 3.3; IV, 35.
27. *Contra Celsum* 5.54-5.
28. *Opp.* II, 477; Grünbaum 88; cf. above, n. 19.
29. Hilarius, *In Ps.* 132.2 (Migne, *PL*, IX, 748-9).
30. Hieronymus, *Lib. Hebraicarum Quaestionum in Gen.* 6.2; *Breviarum in Ps.* 132; *De Viris Illustribus* 4; *In Epist. ad Titum I*, 12 (*PL*, XXIII, 573-4).
31. Philastrius, *De Haeresibus* 108; John Chrysostom, *Hom. in Gen.* 22; Cyril of Alexandria, *Glaphyra in Gen. II* (Migne, *PG*, LXIX, 51 ff.). *In Julianum* beg.; *Adv. Anthropomorphitas* 17. Caesarius, *Dialogus I, Interrogatio XLVIII* (apparently not in Migne) is cited by Robert, *RB*, IV, 365.
32. Augustine, *In Gen. Quaestionum* 3.
33. *De Civitate Dei* XV, 22-3, XVIII 38; cf. IX, 4.
34. John Cassian, *Collatio* VIII (denies that incubi exist). Theodoret, *Quaestiones in Gen. Interrogatio* XLVII. A Syriac work probably of the

sixth cent., *The Cave of Treasure*, narrates in great detail the gradual corruption of the Sethites and their final downfall, then explicitly rejects the older interpretation of Gen. 6. This author denies that demons have sex; since their apostasy they have not multiplied. Could they consort with women, they would not leave a single virgin undefiled. *Schatzhöhle*, pp. 14 ff., esp. 18.

34a. Dillmann, *Genesis*, I, 234.

35. Ignatius, Ephesians 10.3, 13.1, 17.1, 19.1; Trallians 4.2, 8.1; Smyrneans 9.1; Philadelphians 6.2; Magnesians 1.2; Romans 5 end, 7.1.

36. Barnabas 18.1-2; cf. 2.1, 4.9, 15.5, 21.3. See also Shepherd of Hermas, Mandate IV 3.4, 6; V 1.3; VII; XII 4.6, 7.

37. *Dialogue* 69 f.; above, n. 5.

38. *Ibid.*, 103 (Justin explains Satanas as derived from *sata*, "apostate," and *nas*, i.e., *nahash*, "serpent"); cf. 124. See above, Ch. VIII nn. 5 ff. Justin, *ibid.*, 100, states that Eve "conceived the word of the serpent and bore disobedience and death." Cf. below, Ch. XVI n. 55; Ch. XIX n. 16.

39. *Cohortatio* 7.

40. Above, Ch. VII nn. 3 f.

41. *Legatio* 24-5.

42. What follows is based on McGiffert, *Christian Thought*, I, 134 ff.

43. *Ibid.*, 136.

44. *Ibid.*, 226 n. 1, 212.

45. Text in *Ante-Nicene Fathers*, VIII, 436-7. Cf. above, Ch. XIV n. 27.

46. McGiffert, II, 154.

47. Below, Ch. XXX nn. 3 f.

48. McGiffert, I, 297.

49. *De Civ. Dei*, Book IX, discusses devils in general, esp. heathen views. Book XI, ch. 11 ff., treats of fallen angels. Ch. 12-15 argue against the Manicheans that Satan was created good. The serpent was Satan's tool: XIII, 10. A very clear exposition is given by John Cassian, *Collatio* VIII: Satan fell originally through pride, and again through envy of Adam and Eve.

50. *De Civ. Dei*, XXII, 1; *Enchiridion* 29. See Jung, 160 f.; and for Anselm, McGiffert, II, 196.

51. *CE*, XI, 310.

NOTES TO CHAPTER SIXTEEN
Pp. 89-111

1. Yoma 67b (Tannaitic); Ginzberg, V, 170.

2. Niddah 61a.

3. So also Sifre N. 86; cf. BR 26.5, WR 23.9, Tan. B. I 23 f. For the Palestinian Targumim, below, Ch. XIX n. 4.

4. BR 26.5. I find no basis for Finkelstein's notion (*The Pharisees*, 182) that R. Simeon rejected the belief in "personalized angels." He held the usual opinions of his age. See Sifre Z. to Num. 6.26 (p. 249), BaR 11.7, Shir 2.5. If R. Simeon had a specific target in view, it may have been Aquila, who—as Jerome and others attest—translated with his slavish literalness *hyioi tōn theōn*, "sons of the gods."

5. Tan. B. I 30, BR 27.4.

6. Above, Ch. XV n. 7.

7. Sabbath 88b-89a.

8. Tehillim 8, 74; PR 25, 128a; Shir 8.11.

9. Above, Ch. XIII nn. 4-6; Ginzberg, V, 156. Actually, Enoch is mentioned (but just mentioned) in SOR 1 beg.

10. BR 25.1.

11. Hagigah 4b, BR 50.9.

12. Sanhedrin 38b, etc.; Ginzberg, V, 69.

13. Ginzberg, *ibid.;* Philo, *De Opificio Mundi* 72 ff.

14. BR 8.10; Kohelet R. and Z. 6.10. Below, Ch. XVII n. 2.

15. See Conybeare, *JQR,* os, VIII, 576 ff. On Samael, see above, Ch. IX, nn. 7 f. Samael is a name for Satan, e.g., Sotah 10b and regularly in PRE; for the Angel of Death, Ch. XIX nn. 29 f.; for the guardian angel of Rome, Ch. XVIII nn. 23 f.

16. Ginzberg, V, 94 n. 60, regards the rabbinic *nahash hakadmoni* as only a verbal parallel to "the old serpent" of the NT. It means, not "the primeval dragon," but merely "the original snake." Bonsirven, *Judaisme palestinien,* I, 246 n. 4, asserts the contrary view, but without proof.

17. Baba Bathra 16a.

18. *Ibid.* Kohut, *Jüdische Angelologie,* 62 ff., tries unsuccessfully to prove from this passage that Satan has the qualities of Ahriman. See Grünbaum, 116.

19. Cf. Sanhedrin 89b with BR 55.4. In Tan. N. Vayera 18, God before creation foretells Abraham's faithfulness. An unknown Midrash, Yalk. I 96, has the *Middath haDin* arguing with God: "All the trials to which Thou has subjected him involved only his wealth: now try him personally, tell him to sacrifice his son!"

20. Cf. BR 67.2; Tan. B. I 131 and 136 with Tan. N. Toledoth 11. The tale of the attack on Moses at the inn (Ex. 4.24 ff.) was a source of perplexity to the rabbis. In defiance of the Bible text, rabbinic sources usually explain that the attacker was an angel: Mekilta Amalek on Ex. 18.3; ShR 5.8; Yerushalmi Targumim Ex. 4.24 ff.; Yerushalmi Nedarim 3.14.38b; R. Judah b. Bizna in Nedarim 32a. But the printed text of Nedarim 31b-32a makes Satan the attacker. See Rabbinovicz, *Variae Lectiones, ad loc.*

21. Abba Gorion 32-3; Esther R. 7 (on Esth. 3.9); Aggadath Esther 38; OM 52a, 55b, 58a.

22. BR 56.4, 5; Tan. B. I 114; Tan. N. Vayera 22-3 (and see the Intro. to Tan. B. p. 166); PR 40, 170b; Sanhedrin 89b; Mann, *The Bible as Read . . .,* Hebrew sec., p. 63.

23. Sotah 10b. Cf. below, Ch. XIX n. 36.

24. BR 57.4; cf. ShR 21.7.

25. Baba Bathra 15b-16a.

26. Tan. B. II 113; Tan. N. Tissa 19; ShR 41.7; Sabbath 89a. The last source contains a legend in which Satan, after the Revelation at Sinai, comes first to God, then to Moses, inquiring where the Torah is to be found. He is put off with evasive answers; but it is not clear what harm Satan could have done had he known the whereabouts of the Torah. Tosafot, *ad loc.,* cite a Midrash that God exiled the Angel of Death (i.e., Satan) before giving the Torah, lest the Angel object that Israel would soon worship the Golden Calf. This would fit with the statement (Sanhedrin 26b; Kallah Rabbati 8) that the Torah is called *Tushiah* because it was given in secret (*behashai*) on account of Satan.

27. Sanhedrin 95a, 107a. The Palestinian parallels do not mention Satan.

28. Sifre D. 218; Sifre N. 42 (cf. BR 38.6); Pesahim 112b and Rashbam, *ad loc.*

29. Yoma 67b; Sifra on Lev. 18.4

30. Yerushalmi Berakot 1.2.2d.

31. BR 38.7; cf. Sifre N. 131; Sifre D. 43; ShR 41.7.

32. BR 84.3. *Ibid.*, 17.6, states that the letter *samek* is not used in the Torah until Gen. 2.21; for when woman was created, Satan (beginning with *samek*) was created with her: this is probably a clumsy witticism.

33. Tosefta Sabbath 17(18).2, 3 and Abodah Zarah 1.17-8; Tan. N. Vayishlah 8. "Angels of Satan" are not, to my knowledge, mentioned elsewhere by the rabbis; the expression was probably used for literary symmetry.

34. Sabbath 32a.

35. "Break Satan" is the version of Rab Amram (cited in *Ozar haTefillot*, 544); the second version is that of recent prayerbooks. See Mishnah Berakoth 1.4; Yerushalmi, *ibid.*, 4.5.8c; Elbogen, *Jüdische Gottesdienst*, 101-2.

36. Berakoth 46a. In Rabbi's personal prayer, *ibid.*, 16b, bot., the phrase, "from the destructive Satan," does not appear in the Munich ms. and other sources cited by Rabbinovicz.

37. Yerushalmi Sabbath 2.6.5b (Babli Sabbath 32a suggests that our sins catch up with us in times of danger, but does not mention Satan); BR 91.9; Tan. N. Vayiggash 1. *Ibid.*, Vayishlah 8: "If one lives in a rickety house, Satan accuses him and his record book is opened," but in the parallel case of one who reneges on a vow, it is angels who demand his punishment.

38. Berakoth 19a, 60a; Ketuboth 8b.

39. Morgenstern, *AJSL*, LV, 1 ff.

40 Sifra Shemini 1 on Lev. 9.2 (Weiss 43c).

41. Lauterbach, *HUCA*, IV, 173 ff.

42. Rosh Hashanah 16ab.

43. Yoma 20a; cf. PRE 46.

44. PR 45, 185b-186a.

45. Kiddushin 81a.

46. *Ibid.*, 81ab.

47. Gittin 52a.

48. Yoma 69b.

49. Baba Bathra 16a; Kiddushin 30b; BR 9.7; Mishnah Berakot 9, end. See, in general, Porter, *The Yeçer Hara.*

50. Kiddushin 81a.

51. Sukkah 52a; Grünbaum, 117.

52. Sukkah 52ab; cf. ER 4, 20.

53. Above, Ch. VIII nn. 5 ff.; Ch. XI n. 6; Ch. XV n. 38.

54. Ginzberg, I, 71 f., V, 124.

55. Sabbath 145b-146a; Yebamoth 103b; Abodah Zarah 22b; above, Ch. VIII n. 7.

56. Ginzberg, V, 133.

57. Sabbath 146a. The statement (*ibid.*, 55b; Baba Bathra 17a) that 4 men died only by the counsel of the serpent means that they were of spotless character and would not have died but for the fall of Adam. In this the serpent—as serpent—had a part.

58. Abot 5.9.

59. Mishnah Sabbath 2.5. No ref. to this point in Tosefta or Gemaras: is this significant? Maimonides (Mishnah Commentary, *ad loc.*, explains "evil spirit" rationalistically as mental illness.

60. Mishnah Gittin 6.8; Yerushalmi *ibid.*, 48b.

61. Berakot 6a.

62. Gittin 68a; see Grünbaum 46 ff., refuting Kohut.

63. Berakoth 6a; Sabbath 67a; etc. A few passages state that witchcraft is performed with the aid of demons: Sanhedrin 67b; ShR 9.11.

64. Sifre N. 40; Sifre Z. on 6.24.

65. PK 4, 40ab; PR 14, 65a; Tan. B. IV, 118-9; Tan. N. Huk. 8; BaR 19.8. Other references to possession: Sifre D. 318, 321 (Finkelstein 364, 368); Tannaim 195; below, n. 81.

66. Tosefta Sabbath 7(8).23.

67. Above, n. 58; BR 7 end; *ibid.*, 11.9 in name of later teachers. The demons are here called *meriim* (so London ms. in both places; modern prints have *shedim* in 7, *meriim* in 11.9), the meaning of which is not entirely certain. See Kohut, *Aruch Completum*, V, 237b. Tan. B. I 12 (R. Benaya) gives the legend followed by statements implying that demons have bodies: see next n.

68. Hagigah 16a; ARN 37, 55a adds that they can change shape or become invisible. Cf. second recension 43, 60b.

69. "One who has intercourse with a female demon has demon children. Whence do you learn this? From Adam, who had children from the spirits": Tan. B. I 12.

70. BR 20.11; Tan. B. I 20; Erubin 18b.

71. Below, Ch. XIX nn. 52 ff.

72. Berakot 43b; Pesahim 112b bot.; Sabbath 151b; and n. 74.

73. Berakot 33a; Pesahim 112b; n. 78.

74. Berakot 62a.

75. Sifre N. 40; Sifre Z. on 6.24; BaR 11.5. In Mekilta RS 116, 164; Tosefta Baba Kama 7.6 (cf. Sifra Kedoshim *perek* 11) *mazzikin* probably means dangers in general, not excluding danger from demons.

76. BR 20.11, 24.6. From the readings given by Theodor, I have adopted the one that makes the best sense.

77. *Ibid.* 36.3. Shamdan is elsewhere regarded as the father of Ashmedai.

78. Pesahim 112b. Agrat uses the same language as Satan, above, n. 45.

79. Yerushalmi Berakot 5.1.9a; Babli Pesahim 110a.

80. WR 24.3; Tan. B. III 77; Tan. N. Kedoshim 9; Tehillim 20, 176.

81. Meilah 17b. Demons and spirits aided in the building of the Temple; Shir 1.1; ShR 52.4.

82. Sifra Behukkothai, *perek* 2, on 26.6. The beginning of this passage refers to wild beasts; the latter part, citing Ps. 92, may refer to demons. Cf. Tehillim 92, 405 and above, n. 75; Ch. VI n. 18. Demons disappeared when the Tabernacle was built (PK 1, 6b; PR 5, 21b; Tan. B. IV 39) but apparently only for the time being.

83. Above, Ch. II n. 10; Ch. V nn. 3-5.

84. Mekilta Shiratha 2, on 15.1; Mekilta RS 58-9; Tan. N. Beshallah 13.

85. DR 1.23. See further ShR 15.15, 21.5 (which states that the guardian of Egypt is named Mizraim; in later sources he is generally called Uzza: below, Ch. XIX nn. 39 ff.), 23.15; DR 1.22; Tan. N. Mishpatim 18; Shir 8 end. Tehillim 82, 369, very exceptionally, applies Ps. 82.7 to the national *sarim*.

86. Yoma 77a; Ginzberg, VI, 434.

87. Above, Ch. VI nn. 11, 19. Ginzberg's remarks on this point (V, 204-5) are not entirely clear.

88. PK 23, 150b, WR 29.2; Tan. N. Vayeze 2; in Tehillim 78, 347, this view is confused with that of R. Samuel b. Nahman. A similar interpretation of Jacob's dream BR 68 end, is found only in modern prints and in one Yemenite ms., but not in Theodor's other sources.

89. Shir 2.1.

90. BR 56.5.

91. *Ibid.* 77.3, 78.3 (without the parable). The opponent was Samael the guardian angel of Edom: Tan. N. Vayishlah 8; below, Ch. XIX n. 34.
92. Makkoth 12a.

NOTES TO CHAPTER SEVENTEEN
Pp. 111-117

1. Above, Ch. XVI n. 12; below, Ch. XIX n. 14.
2. Koran 7.11-24; more briefly 2.30-6, 15.28-44, 17.61-5, 18.50, 20.116-23, 38.71-8. Cf. *Schatzhöhle,* 4.
3. But Muhammed Ali translates: "But the devils disbelieved, teaching men enchantment, and it was not revealed to the two angels Harut and Marut at Babel, nor did they teach (it to anyone), so that they should have said: We are only a trial, therefore do not disbelieve." In his n., Muhammed Ali states that the story of Harut and Marut was derived by the Jews from Persian sources; the Koran discredits the tale, denying both that the methods of sorcery were revealed to the angels in question, and that they taught these secrets to men. But strongly apologetic motives seem to color his interpretation.
4. Jung, 131 f.
5. Grünbaum, 44.
6. The ensuing presentation is derived from E. Littmann, "Harut und Marut," in *Andreas Festschr.,* 70-87. See, further, Grünbaum, 61 ff.; Jung, 124 ff.; B. Heller, in *REJ,* LX, 202 ff.; and *Encyclopaedia of Islam,* II, 272-3 (Wensinck).
7. Littmann, 85.
8. Cf. Ch. VI n. 15; Ch. XV nn. 20, 23.
9. Cf. Ch. XV nn. 9; 19 end.
10. Cf. Ch. IV n. 1; Ch. VII n. 1.
11. Littmann, 80-1.
12. Heller, *op. cit.,* 209 ff. The Persian poet Schahin calls the leader of the fallen angels Azazel; the Jews of Persia apply this name to the angel who refused to bow before Adam and who was henceforth called "accursed Satan."
13. Littmann, 70-2.
14. *Ibid.,* 79, 82; Jung, 128 f.

NOTES TO CHAPTER EIGHTEEN
Pp. 117-127

1. Bamberger, *HUCA,* XV, 425 ff.
2. PR 36, 161b.
3. Below, n. 23; Ch. XIX nn. 32 ff.
4. PR 34, 159a.
5. Buttenwieser, *Outline of the Neo-Hebraic Apocalyptic Literature,* is still the best account of this material. Buttenwieser (p. 30) dates the Book of Elijah in the 3rd century, but it is hard to believe it so much earlier than the other works it so closely resembles. Ginzberg (VI, 331) places it in the middle of the eighth century.
6. Buttenwieser, *Die Hebräische Elias-Apocalypse;* OM 26b. B's ms. reads *Gigith sh'mo;* but I think it likely that Gigith is properly the name of the king's mother, not of the king. The form of the noun is feminine; and another source tells that Ishmael's wife was named Gigit: Ginzberg, V, 146.

7. OM 466a. The date of this work is fixed by recognizable allusions to the Caliphs Hisham and Walid II (reigned 724-743 and 743-744). A similar account in the Book of Zerubbabel, OM 160a, 161b. Here the mother of the true Messiah, Menahem b. Amiel, escapes to the wilderness, as in Apoc. John 12.1 ff. A date in the present text indicates that this work is from the 11th century; but it may be an interpolation: Buttenwieser, *Outline*, 33.

8. Sukkah 52a, which does not specifically name Gog and Magog; but so Rashi interprets, no doubt correctly.

9. OM 556a. Buttenwieser's emendation (*Outline*, 34) does not seem an improvement.

10. OM 155b.

11. OM 554b. The text refers to the Crusades: Buttenwieser, *Outline*, 41.

12. The two texts, OM 390 and 394, are essentially the same; they provide little evidence to determine the date. The Persian Daniel Apocalypse (OM 102a) mentions a false Messiah, but he is not the Antichrist, not being sufficiently ferocious.

13. Targum Yerushalmi, Deut. 34.3; Targum Is. 11.4; *Emunot veDeot*, VIII, 5-6.

14. See *JE*, II, 119-120. Several of the Jewish scribes identify Armilus with him "whom the Gentiles call Anticristo": OM 390-1; Buttenwieser, *Outline*, 38; Ginsburger's n. to Targum Yerushalmi, Deut. 34.3.

15. OM 84-94, 212.

16. Perek R. Josiah, OM 203a; Pirke Mashiah, OM 392b. *Ibid.*, 392a, states that God will flog the *sar* of Edom and then turn him over to Israel.

17. III En., ed. Odeberg; excerpts in OM 183 ff. Odeberg, following Buttenwieser (*Outline*, 9 ff.) assigns this part of the book to the third century. But the arguments are weak and are rejected by Scholem, 354 n. 14. The florid style is that of the Gaonic period. The use of *pulsa* as a Hebrew word (III En. 16.5, 20.2, 28.10) is without parallel and indicates direct dependence on the Aramaic story in Hagigah 15a.

18. III En. ch. 1-15 and 48c.

19. Hagigah 15a; Sanhedrin 38b.

20. III En. ch. 4; cf. ch. 6. Azza and Azzael appear quite exceptionally as the angels who reveal secrets to Solomon in OM 530a. Abkir, in Yalk. I, 166, explains Ex. 2.6 to mean: The angel who accompanied Moses wept; from Zech. 2.8 we learn that an angel may be called "lad."

21. III En. ch. 5. On the generation of Enosh, Ginzberg, I, 122 ff.

22. III En. ch. 13; above, n. 17.

23. *Ibid.*, ch. 14; Ginzberg, V, 164.

24. *Ibid.*, ch. 26. The ref. to Dobiel and the failure to mention a prince of Ishmael imply a pre-Islamic date. Satan is mentioned among the winds in ch. 23. Ch. 30 speaks of 72 angelic patrons of the nations. Ch. 40 and 47 relate the dire punishment that befell certain angels because they did not chant the *Kedushah* properly: this probably has nothing to do with our main theme.

25. Text in OM 111b ff.; Batte Midrashoth 63 ff. See Scholem, 44.

26. Scholem, 49.

27. OM 121a; BM 111.

28. OM 113 f.; BM 74-81.

29. OM 121a bot.; BM 113.

30. OM 440b ff. gives four versions. The most familiar poetic form is the *piyyut* mentioned in the text, found in the Yom Kippur *Mussaf* according to the Ashkenazic rite. See Zeitlin, *JQR*, ns, XXXVI, where previous

discussions of the legend are cited in connection with a somewhat new viewpoint.

31. Scholem, 67, 361 n. 100. I have used the Jewish Theological Seminary Ms. Maggs 419. Dated 1413, it is a beautifully written ms. from North Italy, containing various cabalistic items. The *Habdalah shel R. Akiba* comprises pp. 66-70. The blessing over the spices is omitted, probably by scribal error.

32. Ms. p. 68a.

33. *Ibid.*, 67b, a list of angelic names ends:

מרניואל זה הוא מטטרון מרנותיאל זה מטטרון ויוה זהו מטטרון המטטט עילאה ותחתאי ומאהבה שאוהבין אותו קורין אותו ויותיאל. עבד בזבוריאל יהוה אלהי ישראל בין (דין .r.)
רוא רז רזיא לאינש הדיוט לא יתמסר ולא יתקרי בפרהסיא לחכים חכימין ימסור יתיה חנוך בן ירד כתיבת יתיה בשבעין שנין לעלמותי אות(?!) שבעין ושבעה מלאכים כפיתיה יתהון במניהון וחתימת יתהון במניניהון יהבת ואשתכלית ברזא דנא וכ'

34. *Ibid.*, 69a: עחא ועזאל רוא דמריהון גליין ונקוב יתההון מן נוריהון ויתלה יתהון
קבל שמשא לא חזין ורוחא מנשבא(?!) על אפיהון כל שעה חמן מי דתבר עצתיה דעחא ועזאל
הוא יתכו (יתבר.r.) עצתיה דכל בני אדם וחוה דקיימין לקבלו ולהרע לו א א א א ט ט ט

Recanate, Gen. 6.1 reads: עזא ועזאל רזי דמריהו' גליין ונקב יתהו' מן נחיריהון
ותלא יתהון בטורי קבל דשמשא לא חזיין ורוחא לא נשבא אל אפיהון כל זמן וכל שעה

This reading means that the prisoners were deprived of a refreshing breeze; the ms. suggests that a constant wind blows on them as torment. See Grünbaum, 72.

35. See Lauterbach, *HUCA*, XV, 367 ff. and cf. Ch. XVI n. 78.

NOTES TO CHAPTER NINETEEN
Pp. 128-145

1. Pirke d'Rabbi Eliezer, Intro., p. xiii.
2. Ch. XVIII n. 4; cf. Ch. XVI n. 1.
3. DR 11 end; the version in OM 368a is briefer; other versions make no mention of the two angels.
4. Cf. Ch. XVI n. 3.
5. EZ 25, 49.
6. Aggadath Bereshith p. 30 f. Cf. Ch. XV, nn. 9, 19; Ch. XVII nn. 6 ff. Hadar Zekenim Gen. 6.2 and 28.12 cites from a Midrash the story of the angels who sued for the favors of "a righteous virgin." She demanded first that they give her their wings, and by these made good her escape to heaven, where she became the constellation Virgo. The angels could not return to heaven until they found the ladder which Jacob saw in his dream.
7. Yalk. I 44 (in early editions cited as "Midrash," only later prints mention Abkir), Bereshith Rabbati 29-30; Yerahmeel ch. 25.
8. Cf. Ch. XVII nn. 6-13.
9. *Ginzberg Jubilee Volume*, English Section, 341 ff.
10. PRE 22; brief ref. *ibid.*, 7.
11. *Ibid.*, 22; cf. above, Ch. III n. 8.
12. Yashar Bereshit, end, p. 15.
13. Yerahmeel 24. Cf. above, Ch. XV nn. 23 ff.
14. PRE 13. Cf. above, Ch. VIII nn. 5 ff.
15. PRE 14, 27.
16. PRE 21, the source of Targum Yerushalmi Gen. 4.1, 5.3. The earlier

sources cited by Ginzberg, V, 133 n. 3, do not refer to Satan or the paternity of Cain. Only MHG I, 88-9, states that the serpent defiled Eve and Cain was the offspring; *ibid.*, 105, states that Cain was born after both the serpent and Adam had relations with Eve. The child had a heavenly rather than an earthly appearance. A variant reading of Targum Job. 28.7 implies that Samael was responsible for Eve's fall.

17. ARN p. 164. This very late document shows Christian influence. It is dependent on the Babylonian Talmud (above, Ch. XVI n. 25). See also Ginzberg V, 389 f.

18. Bereshith Rabbati 24-5; Epstein, *Eldad haDani,* 66 ff.

19. Cited in *Eldad haDani,* 68 f.

20. Yerahmeel 23.6; Hadar Zekenim Gen. 4.26; cf. Ch. XVIII n. 21.

21. PRE 45.

22. Abkir in Yalk. I, 61; Tan. N. Noah 13. Cf. Ch. XVI n. 77. The legend is examined in Grünbaum, 435 ff.

23. OM 3b, 6ab.

24. Above, Ch. XVI n. 19. Divergent opinions are given in Abkir and an unknown Midrash, both cited in Yalk. I, 96.

25. Yashar Vayera p. 74-5.

26. *Ibid.* 75-80, unknown Midrashim in Yalk. I 98-9, OM 147a.

27. PRE 31; Yashar, p. 81.

28. PRE 32; Yashar, p. 81-2. See also Ginzberg, V, 256 top.

29. OM 367-8.

30. OM 369a-370b. DR 11.10 combines elements from this and the preceding citation. Further details, ARN, pp. 156 ff.; Ginzberg, VI, 159 f.

31. Abkir in Yalk. I 161; OM 457b. Cf. Ginzberg, V, 147 n. 45. MHG I, 118, states that Naamah's beauty led the angels astray. Schechter, *ad loc.,* infers from Nahmanides, Gen. 4.22, that a similar statement was contained in N.'s text of PRE. Targum Yerushalmi, Gen. 4.22, merely says Naamah was adept at laments and joyous songs.

32. PRE 46; above, Ch. XVI n. 43.

33. Above, Ch. XVIII nn. 14, 23.

34. Tan. N. Vayishlah 8; Yalk. Machiri, Prov. 20.25. Cf. Mann, *The Bible . . . in the Old Synagogue,* Hebrew section, 325.

35. See Aptowitzer in *HUCA,* VIII-IX, 410 ff.

36. Rashi, Sotah 10b and Makkot 12a (above, Ch. XVI n. 23) identifies Samael as the *sar* of Edom, following the later view; it is not implied in the Talmud.

37. Abkir, in Yalk. I, 110.

38. *Ibid.,* 234. See also Abkir, Yalk. 133; Ginzberg, V, 311-2; above, Ch. XVI n. 92.

39. Above, Ch. VI n. 9; Ch. XVI n. 84.

40. Abkir, Yalk. I, 243; Vayosha, OM 148. In Jellinek's ed. of Vayosha, Beth HaMidrasch, I, 46 f., Rahab, the Prince of the Sea, protests that the Egyptians should not be drowned. God smites Rahab and his host: it is their corpses which give the sea its peculiar smell.

41. Abkir, *ibid.*

42. Abkir, Yalk. I, 120.

43. Hullin 91b; BR 68.12; above, Ch. XVI nn. 11 ff.

44. Abkir, Yalk. 132; cf. BR 78.2; Ginzberg, V, 306 n. 249.

45. OM 451.

46. OM 418b.

47. OM 259ab, 492a.

48. OM 191-2 and 193b.

49. PRE 8 and 40; OM 461b.
50. Aggadath Bereshith p. 30.
51. OM 421b; cf. 410a, 417a, 494a.
52. Above, Ch. XVI nn. 69-71.
53. OM 47a.
54. Blau, in *JE*, VIII, 88.

NOTES TO CHAPTER TWENTY
Pp. 147-161

1. See Husik, *Jewish Philosophy*, 53 ff., 124, 148 f., 394; below, n. 16.
2. *Oeuvres . . . de R. Saadia*, I, 8-9; Lekah Tob and Midrash Aggada Gen. 6.1 ff.; Joseph Bekor Shor, *Torah Commentary*, p. 14; Maimonides, *Moreh Nebuchim*, I, 14; *Biur Shemot Kodesh v'Hol, Debir*, I, 196. Cf. *Moreh*, I, 7: Seth was the first son of Adam created in his likeness, i.e., with intellectual and moral perfection. The earlier sons lacked these qualifications, hence the Midrash calls them spirits (above, Ch. XVI n. 70). On Bahya, see below, Ch. XXII n. 7. The other commentators mentioned deal with the matter in their remarks on Gen. 6.
3. Aaron b. Joseph, *Sefer haMibhar*, Gen. 6; Mann, "Early Karaite Bible Commentaries," in *JQR*, ns, XV, 365, 378-9. This author mentions Shemhazai and Azzael and argues that they could not have been angels.
4. See Albeck, *Bereshith Rabbati*, intro., 6 ff.
5. Abrabanel mentions the Talmud, Midrash and PRE. What Midrash he had in mind is not known—perhaps Bereshith Rabbati.
6. Anatoli, *Malmad haTalmidim*, 4b-6b.
7. *Akedath Yizhak*, I, 86b f.
8. Above, Ch. VI n. 10. The controversy of R. Akiba is not mentioned in any classic source.
9. See previous n. and Ch. XIX n. 50.
10. Ch. XVI n. 40.
11. Ibn Ezra, Lev. 16.8.
12. See Solomon haKohen of Lissa, *Abi Ezer, ad loc.* (in Pentateuch Lemberg, 1909). Krochmal adopted the explanation of Nahmanides: *Kitbe RNK*, 341.
13. BR 65.9; PRE 46.
14. Cited by Ibn Ezra, *ad loc.*; Bahya (below n. 17) and, without mentioning his name, by Masnuth, *Ma'yan Ganim, ad loc.*
15. *Moreh*, III, 22-23; above, Ch. XVI n. 18.
16. *Ibid.*, 10-12. Cf. n. 1, above.
17. Bahya, *Kad haKemah*, 27a ff.
18. *Tagmule haNefesh*, 52b-55a.
19. *Moreh*, II, 26, 30.
20. BR 10.6. Cf. Tehillim 104, 440.
21. Above, Ch. XV n. 50.

NOTES TO CHAPTER TWENTY-ONE
Pp. 163-168

1. Scholem, 79-82.
2. *Sefer Hasidim*, par. 11, 31, 305.
3. *Ibid.*, 361.
4. E.g. *Sefer Hasidim*, 327.

5. *Ibid.*, 324-327.
6. *Ibid.*, 381.
7. *Ibid.*, 939.
8. *Ibid.*, 733, 1763. Cf. 1648: the angels and demons that accompany man do not sing the *Kedushah* at night.
9. *Ibid.*, 371.
10. *Ibid.*, 1871.
11. *Ibid.*, 210-212, 1983.
12. *Ibid.*, 1452.
13. Scholem, 89 ff., stresses the dualistic character of the doctrine taught by Eleazer of Worms, citing among other things the statement: "Man is a rope whose two ends are pulled by God and Satan, and in the end God proves the stronger." (Cf. below, Ch. XXVIII n. 2.) But a careful examination of the passage (*Sode Razayya*, 39) shows that its real subject is *man's free will*, and Satan's weakness in the tug of war is especially stressed. This is not to deny an occasional dualistic touch in Eleazer's thought; it may have been strengthened by his experience of the horrors of that age of persecution.
14. Trachtenberg, *Jewish Magic*, ch. 2, esp. pp. 15 f. On p. 14 ref. is made to a few Jewish writers, notably Menasseh ben Israel, who borrowed the idea of a compact with Satan from the Christian environment. See Ch. XXVII, below.

NOTES TO CHAPTER TWENTY-TWO
Pp. 168-176

1. Scholem, 74. *Masseket Azilut*, formerly regarded as one of the earliest cabalistic documents, has now been assigned to the post-Zoharitic period by Scholem, *Tarbiz*, III, 61 ff.
2. Cf. above, Ch. XIII.
3. *Bahir*, par. 53-55. Par. 53 also tells that Satan tried to seduce Israel at Marah. The end of this work reproduces almost verbatim the Eden story of PRE: above, Ch. XIX n. 14.
4. Bahya, Gen. 3.21 end, p. 14d ff.
5. *Ibid.*, Gen. 3.6, p. 14a; cf. Job 4.18; Tan. B. II 88; Tan. N., Mishpatim 18.
6. *Ibid.*, Gen. 3.14, 15, p. 14c.
7. *Ibid.*, Gen. 5.1 ff., p. 17a; the non-mythical interpretation *ibid.*, Gen. 6.2, p. 17c. On Num. 13.33 (p. 179a), Bahya explains that the Nefilim were heads of the family called "sons of God." They were so called because terror fell on those who saw them. As the virility of the stock declined, they were called Anakim and later Refaim. *Ibid.*, Hukkat, end, p. 192a, he cites a Midrash that Sihon and Og were children of Shemhazael, who were of the sons of God. Shemhazael assaulted the wife of Ham just before she entered the ark, and Sihon was born during the flood. Cf. above, Ch. XVI n. 2.
8. Bahya, Gen. 4.22, p. 16d.
9. *Ibid.*, Gen. 3.22 (p. 15d); 4.2 (p. 16a).
10. Scholem, 175.
11. Cited in *Yalk. Reubeni*, Gen. 6.2, p. 27a.
12. Scholem, "Kabbalot R. Jacob vR. Isaac B'ne R. Jacob haKohen," in *Mada'e haYahadut*, II, 164 ff.
13. *Ibid.*, 248-252, a different version, 260.

14. *Ibid.*, 252.

15. *Ibid.*, 254-5.

16. *Ibid.*, 262 f., cf. 258.

17. *Ibid.*, 259.

18. Scholem, "L'Heker Kabbalat R. Isaac b.R. Jacob haKohen," in *Tarbiz*, II-V. Text of Moses' *Amud haS'moli*, in IV, 208 ff.

19. *Ozar haKabod*, 17b. See Scholem, in *Mada'e haYahadut*, II, 185 ff., citing unpublished writings of Abulafia.

NOTES TO CHAPTER TWENTY-THREE
Pp. 176-186

1. Scholem, Major Trends, Lecture 5.

2. *Zohar Hadash*, Midrash haNeelam, Bereshith, end. *Zohar*, I, 117b-118a (also Mid. haNeelam) seems to refer to human sinfulness; cf. I 62b.

3. *Zohar*, I, 25ab, 37a, 58a (the fallen angels teach magic); III, 159a. More cryptic ref., *Zohar*, II, 178b-179a; III, 60b, 144a.

4. *Zohar*, I, 23a.

5. *Zohar Hadash*, Ruth, 95c.

6. *Zohar*, III, 212ab; another version, 208a, displays the exegetical virtuosity of the author.

7. *Zohar*, III, 233ab.

8. *Zohar*, I, 19b.

9. *Zohar*, I, 55a; III 76b-77a.

10. See previous n. and cf. *Zohar*, III, 19a, Ginzberg, V, 87. Yalk. Reubeni, Gen. 4.8, cites from *Mishkan haEduth* (an unpublished work of Moses de Leon) that Adam consorted with Naamah and Lilith: They are the two "women" who appeared before Solomon (I K. 3.16). See *Zohar*, II, 111a.

11. *Zohar*, I, 9b; Ginzberg, V, 143.

12. Above, Ch. XIX n. 16.

13. *Zohar*, I, 125a-127a. The passage also reports various means used by Balaam (aside from meeting the fallen angels) to obtain magical knowledge "from the side of the primeval serpent."

14. *Zohar Hadash*, Shir haShirim, cited in Yalk. Reubeni, Gen. 4.1, p. 20ab. Cf. *Zohar*, III, 76b.

15. *Zohar*, I, 126b. Ps. 82.9 refers to the reinfection of Israel with the filth of the serpent when they worshipped the Golden Calf: *Zohar*, I, 131b, 228a; II, 236b.

16. *Zohar*, I, 10b-11a.

17. *Zohar*, I, 35b.

18. Cited in Yalk. Reubeni, Gen. 32.25, p. 56d.

19. *Zohar*, I, 146a, cf. 170a. But *Ra'ya Mehemna* (*Zohar*, II, 41b-42, by a later author) says Jacob wrestled with Gabriel, who is identified with the good impulse.

20. *Zohar*, II, 51ab.

21. *Zohar*, I, 161b; see Scholem, in *Tarbiz*, III, 276. According to Ginzberg, *JE*, III, 468, the theory of double emanation is also found in *Sefer Temunah* and in another major work of this period, *Maareket haElohut*. Because scholars still debate the relation of this massive work to the *Zohar*, I have not considered it further.

22. This concept is generally expressed in metaphorical allusions to the "kings of Edom" (Gen. 36.31) who reigned before there was a king in Israel: *Zohar*, I, 177a, 223b etc. Cf. II, 242-244b, which seems to reflect the

symbolism of R. Isaac haKohen, and see Scholem, in *Mada'e haYahadut,* II, 193 ff.

23. Horodetzky, *Torat haKabbalah,* 215 f.

24. *Zohar,* I, 17a-18a; Scholem, *Major Trends,* 232, 398, n. 108.

NOTES TO CHAPTER TWENTY-FOUR
Pp. 186-194

1. Saba, *Zeror haMor,* 8a, states that the sin of Adam, who prior to his fall was immaterial, was identical with that of the evil angels: ambition to rise above their proper station caused them to fall below it; but on p. 11a he gives the traditional explanation of Gen. 6. See, further, *Kaneh,* 102d, the story of Shemhazai and Azzael, but also the statement that the "mighty men" were Cainites; *Peliah,* 68b, gives a more sophisticated mystical coloring to the translation of Enoch and the fall of the angels. For another instance of post-Zoharitic dualism, Ch. XXIII n. 19.

2. *Imre Noam,* Ahare, end. Jacob's antagonist was Salmael (sic): *ibid.,* Gen. 32.25. This work also quotes an unknown Midrash that Satan seized the High Priest by the throat as he entered the Holy of Holies on Yom Kippur: to Ex. 28.32 (not 38.32, as in Ginzberg, VI, 78).

3. Above, Ch. XXIII n. 23.

4. Horodetzky, *Torat . . . R. Mosheh Cordovero,* 216.

5. *Ibid.,* 222.

6. *Ibid.,* 219-220.

7. *Ibid.,* 218 f.

8. *Ibid.,* 220.

9. *Ibid.,* 216-18 and 223 ff.

10. Scholem, 261-5. The followers of Luria combine his new explanation of the origin of the Kelipot with the Zoharic teachings. Hayyim Vital, his chief disciple, gives a rather technical and sophisticated account of the subject in *Ez Hayyim,* Shaar 48 and 49. The Zoharic material is reproduced more simply by Azulai, *Hesed l'Abraham,* Ma'yan 7. Azza and Azzael are mentioned in *Kanfe Yonah* (ascribed to Azariah da Fano), Yalk. Reubeni, 27a, and in several passages of *Emek haMelek* by Jacob Elhanan Bacharach. This work states (107c, cf. 68a) that the two angels accused Adam and were sent down to earth for testing. They fell prey to the beauty of women; having remained on earth 7 days, they could not divest themselves of the materiality they had put on. (None of the ten orders of angels can become so material as those known as *ishim* and sons of God. Cf. above Ch. XV n. 9.) They could not return to heaven even when they pronounced the divine Name and were banished by the forces of strict justice to the mountains of darkness. Azza has one eye open and one eye shut. He is constantly falling but never touches the earth: his one eye remains open that he may perceive his plight and suffer the more. Azzael is suspended by his eyelids. Balaam derived his prophetic powers from them. Another passage (cited Yalk. Reubeni, 20b) states that when Eve ate of the tree of knowledge, good and evil were confounded. Abel was born from the spark of goodness, Cain from evil. But since all holiness was intermingled with husk, this paradox resulted: Jethro the convert was descended from the element of holiness in Cain, Balaam the wicked from the husk in Abel!

11. Lauterbach, in *HUCA,* XV, 404 ff., especially n. 74.

12. Scholem, "LeMaaseh R. Joseph della Reyna," in *Zion,* os, V, 124 ff.

13. Scholem, *Major Trends,* 295-320.

NOTES TO CHAPTER TWENTY-FIVE
Pp. 194-199

1. *Kav haYashar*, 69.
2. *Shevet Musar*, ch. 1, p. 10 f.
3. *Zavaot haBesht*, in Abrahams, *Hebrew Ethical Wills*, II, 299.
4. *Kether Shem Tov*, 8ab.
5. Israel b. Isaac Simhah, *Esser Zahzahot*, 94.
6. *Kether Shem Tov*, 58a.
7. Jacob Joseph, *Toldoth Jacob Joseph*, Vayera, 14b.
8. *Esser Zahzahot*, 29.
9. *Shibhe haBesht*, p. 13.
10. *Sippure Maasiyoth*, no. 4.
11. *Sefer haMiddoth*, 139 f.

NOTES TO CHAPTER TWENTY-SIX
Pp. 201-208

1. *CE*, IV, 764.
2. McGiffert, II, 197.
3. *CE*, IV, 767; cf. above, Ch. XV nn. 42 ff.
4. Anselm, *Opera*, II, 94 ff.; Langton, *Satan*, 65 f.
5. Above, Ch. XX nn. 15 f.
6. Aquinas, *ST*, I. 48.1, 2 = *SCG*, III, 4-15.
7. *ST*, first of II. 18.1 = *SCG*, III, 15.
8. *SCG*, III, end of Ch. 7, 15, and 107.
9. *ST*, I. 61.2.
10. *Ibid.*, 59.3, 4.
11. *Ibid.*, 62.1, 2, 5, 8.
12. *Ibid.*, 68.1, 2 = *SCG*, III, 109.
13. *ST*, I. 68.7.
14. *Ibid.*, 68.3.
15. *Ibid.*, 68.8 f.= *SCG*, III, 109. The demons are not bad by nature: *ST*, I. 68.4 = *SCG*, III, 107.
16. *ST*, I. 64.1.
17. *Ibid.*, 59.4.
18. *Ibid.*, 68.2.
19. *Ibid.*, 51.3. Here St. Thomas states that Gen. 6 refers to the Sethites and Cainites.
20. *Ibid.*, 64.2, 3.
21. *Ibid.*, 64.4.
22. *Ibid.*, 114.1, 2.
23. *Ibid.*, 109.1, 2.
24. *Ibid.*, 114.3, first of Part II. 76-79.
25. *ST*, first of Part II. 80.1, 2, 4.
26. *Ibid.*, 74.1.
27. *ST*, I. 114.4 = *SCG*, III, 101-3.
28. *CE*, IV, 765.

NOTES TO CHAPTER TWENTY-SEVEN
Pp. 208-220

1. Carus, *History of the Devil*, ch. 13, esp. pp. 282 ff., citing Abbot Richelmus and Caesarius of Heisterbach (13th cent.). The *Ingoldsby*

Legends retell these stories in a facetious tone foreign to their original character.

2. Below, n. 17.

3. Cited by Langton, *Satan*, 72, from G. G. Coulton, *Five Centuries of Religion*.

4. Carus, 416 ff.; *Lexikon für Theologie und Kirche*, X, 85.

5. Mishnah Sanhedrin 7.11.

6. *Ibid.*, 6.4; Yerushalmi, *ibid.*, 23c.

7. Mishnah Sabbath 6.10; Tosefta 6(7); Yerushalmi 8cd; Babli 67ab.

8. Carus, 275 ff.

9. Maimonides, *Mishneh Torah*, Hilkoth Avodah Zarah 11.16.

10. *SCG*, III, 104 ff.

11. *CE*, XV, 675 ff.

12. Carus, 318.

13. *Ibid.*, 310 ff.

14. *Ibid.*, 317, 321 f.

15. *Ibid.*, 322 ff.

16. *Ibid.*, 325 f.

17. M. A. Murray, *The Witch-Cult in Western Europe;* but this view has been challenged by other scholars.

18. *Encyclopaedia Britannica*, sv. "Rais, Gilles de."

19. Carus, 364 f.

20. Trachtenberg, *The Devil and the Jews*, esp. 22 ff.

21. *Ibid.*, 32 ff.

22. *Encyclopaedia Britannica*, sv. "Albigenses." Gibbon's treatment of the subject, *Decline and Fall*, ch. XIV, can still be read with profit.

23. *Encyclopaedia Britannica*, sv. "Bogomils"; *Encyclopaedia of Religion and Ethics*, II, 784 f.

24. *Encyclopaedia Britannica*, sv. "Cathars."

25. *Ibid.*, sv. "Waldenses."

NOTES TO CHAPTER TWENTY-EIGHT
Pp. 220-232

1. Smith, *Martin Luther*, 125 f.

2. *Ibid.*, 208. Cf. above, Ch. XXI n. 13.

3. *Ibid.*, 393.

4. *Ibid.*, 324. Cf. above, Ch. XXV n. 3.

5. *Ibid.*, 339; Carus, *History of the Devil*, 342 f.

6. Text and translation in Smith, *Martin Luther*, 232.

7. *Ibid.*, 340 f. Cf. Smith, *Age of the Reformation*, 655 f.

8. *JE*, VIII, 213 ff. Smith does not discuss this aspect of Luther's career, except for a reference to some "beautiful" letters to Katie; in one of these Luther announces his decision to unleash vigorous attacks against the Jews: Smith, *Martin Luther*, 418 f.

9. Calvin, *Institutes*, Book I, ch. XIV, par. IX.

10. *Ibid.*, par. XIX.

11. *Ibid.*, par. XIII.

12. *Ibid.*, par. XIV f.

13. Is this "other purpose" witchcraft?

14. *Ibid.*, par. XVI.

15. *Ibid.*, par. XVII f.

16. Smith, *Age of the Reformation*, 656.

17. Langton, *Satan*, 91-96.
18. Cf. Revelation 9.11, and above, Ch. XIV, after n. 2.
19. *Pilgrim's Progress* (Everyman's Library ed.), pp. 65-70. This theme is developed more systematically by Bunyan, in *The Holy War;* but we have quoted the book which has been more widely read.
20. *Contemporary American Philosophy,* I, 385.
21. Guttmann, "Ueber Jean Bodin" etc., in *MGWJ,* XLIX.
22. Carus, *History of the Devil,* 360; Smith, *Age of the Reformation,* 657 ff.; Langton, *Satan,* 76, 82 f.
23. Carus, 367 ff.
24. Smith, *op. cit.,* 656.
25. Carus, 371; Smith, 660.
26. Carus, 370 ff., 374 ff.
27. *Ibid.,* 373.
28. *Ibid.,* 378 f.; Smith, 659.
29. Carus, 381 ff.
30. *Ibid.,* 398.
31. *CE,* XV, 677.

NOTES TO CHAPTER TWENTY-NINE
Pp. 235-239

1. *CE,* IV, 764.
2. *Ibid.,* XV, 675.
3. *Ibid.,* II, 273; *The Book of Common Prayer:* The Ministration of Holy Baptism.
4. Carus, *History of the Devil,* 401.
5. *Ibid.,* 397.
6. Berkhof, *Reformed Dogmatics,* I, 135 f.; Strong, *Systematic Theology,* II, 443 ff. and esp. 460 ff.
7. Printed in *The Empire State Baptist,* October 1948. The Rev. Kenneth G. Ohrstrom of Yonkers, editor of this periodical, writes me that this document is a development of the so-called "New Hampshire Confession," adopted in 1833 and revised on several subsequent occasions. "The article on the devil was evidently added after 1900 to clarify our position on this subject."
8. Carus, 395.
9. Langton, *Satan,* 96 ff.
10. The fullest study is still Roskoff, *Geschichte des Teufels.* See also Reville, *The Devil: His Origin, Greatness and Decadence.* In the present work we have constantly cited the more popular volume of Carus. Langton's brief outline is extremely valuable so far as Christian sources are concerned; his treatment of rabbinic materials is altogether unsatisfactory.
11. Langton, *Satan,* 110 ff. esp. 113-4.
12. *Ibid.,* 100 ff.
13. *Ibid.,* 109.

NOTES TO CHAPTER THIRTY
Pp. 239-251

1. Above, Ch. XVI n. 52.
2. Kessler, *Walther Rathenau,* 37.
3. Aulén, *Christus Victor.* Above, Ch. XV nn. 43-7. In addition to the Fathers there discussed, Aulén quotes also from Gregory of Nyssa.

4. *Op. cit.*, 20, footnote.
5. Niebuhr, *Nature and Destiny of Man*, I, 180 f.
6. *Ibid.*, 94; cf. 51, 59, 80 etc.
7. De Rougemont, *La Part du Diable*, 27. The translation is mine.
8. *Ibid.*, 30. A curious error occurs on p. 34 n. 2. Referring to the myth of the fallen angels, De R. cites the book of Enoch as "anterior to Genesis." Characteristically, the advocate of myth overstates the age and importance of a work where such myths may be found.
9. "The Supreme Sorrow," broadcast on the "Hour of Faith," March 21, 1948, over the network of the American Broadcasting Co.
10. "A Bargain in Brimstone," in *Reader's Digest*, June 1947, pp. 8 ff.
11. "The Devil," *Life*, February 2, 1948, pp. 77 ff.
12. For Honi, see Mishnah Taanith 3.8. Levi Yizhak's complaint is found in his *Kaddish*, one of the classics of Yiddish folksong.

ADDITIONAL NOTE:
THE DATE OF II ENOCH

Jung (p. 93 and n. 144) dismisses II En. from consideration on the authority of Mrs. Maunder, who regards it as a Bogomil work composed between the 12th and 15th centuries. (On the Bogomils, cf. Ch. XXVII.) The exact ref.—kindly furnished me by Dr. Jung—is to an article, "The Date and Place of Writing of the Slavonic Book of Enoch," which appeared in a British journal of astronomy, *The Observatory*, XLI, 309 ff. One might cite against this lady the impressive authority of Charles, Kohler, Ginzberg and Cahana, all of whom held the book to be pre-Christian. But since it is unlikely that these savants saw her article, it seems proper to examine her argument.

She argues first that the Slavonic text cannot, for linguistic reasons, have originated till long after the 9th century. She finds it hard to believe that a Greek text could have been in existence for a thousand years, then disappeared completely. But *habent sua fata libelli*. The same considerations apply likewise to the Apocalypse of Abraham, which also survived only in Slavonic. (The Christian interpolations in the latter work make its original Jewish character all the plainer.) Mrs. M. herself recognizes that this argument is not conclusive.

The decisive evidence, to her mind, is the astronomical material in the description of the 4th heaven. The author follows the Julian calendar, which a Jewish author would not have regarded as divine. He mentions the lunar epacts, to which there is no reference before 243 C.E., and describes the Great Cycle of 452 years, which was first proposed about the year 457. (Charles had already held this reference to be interpolated, and Mrs. M. challenges this explanation.) II En. makes frequent reference to the Bogomil myth of Satanel.

These arguments are not as impressive as they seem. Of the astronomical evidence, only the ref. to the Great Cycle is important. The lunar epacts (i.e., the excess of the solar over the lunar year) are a regular part of Jewish calendation.

Both linguistic and astronomical aspects were complicated by the publication of a fuller Slavonic text by Sokolow, which differs much from the version used by Morfill and Charles, on which Mrs. Maunder based her arguments. (Cahana's translation was made from this text.) This version (ch. 24.7, 9) mentions the months of Iyyar and Nisan by their Hebrew names. Cahana (I, 103) adduces other reasons for assuming a Hebrew original.

Despite occasional references to Satanel, there is nothing of Christian thought in general, or Bogomil thought in particular, in the book. The defeat of Satanel by Michael-Christ is nowhere foreshadowed. The anticlericalism of the Bogomils is entirely lacking. The long ethical section is thoroughly Jewish in spirit, devoid of Bogomil asceticism. The doctrine of the heavenly throne and the apotheosis of Enoch belong to the quasi-Gnostical development in Judaism, not to Bogomilism. The work implies that the Temple was still in existence.

Our present texts of II En. surely contain some later additions. Because some passages make sense only on the assumption of a Greek original, Charles inferred that the entire work was composed in Greek; but Cahana's view that these passages were additions to the Greek translation of a Hebrew original is just as plausible. The reference to the Great Cycle, as Charles argued, may well be the interpolation of a Christian scribe. The Satanel passages, whatever their origin, seem to have been inserted awkwardly into their present place.

There is, in short, no good reason to doubt that II En. was composed shortly before the Christian era, probably in Palestine. It contains some later insertions, a few of which may possibly come from Bogomil scribes.

Index

(Names or titles of angels and demons are marked by an asterisk *.)

Abraham, 29, 46 ff., 95 f., 110, 129 f., 136 f., 183.
Abrabanel, Isaac, 150 f., 153, 155 f.
Abulafia, Todros, 176.
Adam, 34-37, 43 f., 48, 83, 94, 102, 112 f., 132, 142 f., 150, 170 f., 174, 178, 180, 182, 219, 278.
*Adversary, 36, 45, 48.
*Afrira and *Kastimon, 181 f.
Agobard, 213, 231.
Agrippa of Nettesheim, 211 f.
*Agrat bat Mahlat, 106 f., 171, 181.
*Akteriel, 192.
Albertus Magnus, 203, 217.
Albigenses; *see* Cathari.
Ambrose of Milan, 78.
*Ammon of No, 191.

Amram Gaon, 98.
Anahid, 115, 131.
Anatoli, Jacob, 151 f.
*Angel of Death, 93-5, 102, 137 f., 156, 268, 275.
Anselm of Canterbury, 84 f., 202 f., 204 f., 245.
Antichrist, 63 f., 66, 72, 120-3, 139, 217 f., 241. *See* Armilus.
*Appolyon, 63, 227 f.
Aquinas, Thomas, 203-8, 212 f., 217, 236, 244.
Arama, Isaac, 152.
*Armilus, 121-3, 139. *See* Antichrist.
*Asbeel, 19.
Ashamdon; *see* Shamdan.
*Ashmedai, 104, 170 f., 174.

*Asmodeus, 42.
Athenagoras, 75 f., 82.
Atonement, Day of (*Yom Kippur*), 20, 91, 99 f., 127, 131 f., 139, 154-6, 186 f.
Attribute of Justice (*Middat haDin*), 95 f., 126, 136, 141, 165, 275.
Augustine of Hippo, 80 f., 84 ff., 201, 205 f., 244.
Aulén, Gustaf, 244-6, 248.
*Azazel, 17-21, 24, 26, 46-9, 56, 75, 91, 116, 130 f., 139, 154-6, 186 f., 278.
Azriel, 169.
*Azza and *Azzael, 91, 120, 124, 127, 129, 131, 133, 150, 174, 178-81, 282, 285 f.
*Azziel, 124.

Baal Shem Tov (Besht), 196-8, 222.
Bahya ben Asher, 150, 157 f., 169-72.
Balaam, 179 f., 285.
Baptism, 76, 236 f.
Barth, Karl, 244, 246.
Baudelaire, Pierre C., 248.
Beduht, 115.
*Beelzebub (Beelzebul), 67, 72, 83 f., 94, 227 f.
Bekker, Balthasar, 231.
Bekor Shor, Joseph, 150.
*Belial (Beliar), 28, 30 f., 41, 72, 94.
Benét, Stephen Vincent, 210.
Berlioz, Hector, 210.
*Biqua and *Kasbiel, 264.
Blake, William, 228.
Bodin, Jean, 229-31.
Bogomils, 218 f., 267, 289 f.
Boehme, Jakob, 185 f.
Boito, Arrigo, 210.
Browning, Robert, 143 f.
Bunyan, John, 226-8.
Buxtorf, Johannes, 143.

Caesarius of Arles, 80.
Caesarius of Heisterbach, 287.
Cain, 48, 132, 134, 171, 180-2, 219.
Calvin, John, 220, 223-5, 244.
Cathari, 218-20.
Chambers, Whittaker, 249.
Clement of Alexandria, 84.
Conrad of Marburg, 213.
Cordovero, Moses, 185-9, 196.
Crescas, Chasdai, 148.

Demiurge, 58, 86, 194, 218.
Demons, 22, 26, 28-30, 32, 42, 45, 52 f., 58, 67 ff., 71, 74-8, 103-8, 113, 125, 127, 134, 143 f., 155, 166 f., 174 f., 180 f., 190 f., 195 f., 201, 203, 206-8, 213, 224, 270, 274.
*Devil, 26, 31, 42, 52, 56 f., 62-71, 76, 81-5, 131 f., 134, 197, 201-32, 236-41, 244-9. See Satan.
Dionysius (Pseudo-), 84, 203.
*Dobiel, 109 f., 124.
Dragon, 63 f., See Leviathan, Serpent.
Dudael, 18, 20.
Duns Scotus, 203, 208.

*Edom, Guardian angel of, 183. See Rome, Guardian angel of.
*Egypt, Guardian angel of, 108 f., 139-41, 184, 277. See Mizraim, Uzza.
El, 8 ff.
Eleazar Rokeach of Worms, 165.
Elemental Spirits, 66.
Elijah b. Solomon Abraham, 195 f.
Elijah di Vidas, 194.
Elimelech of Lesiensk, 198.
Elyon, 9 ff.
Enoch, 17 f., 21-3, 28, 33 f., 59, 70, 75 f., 92 f., 114, 123-5, 142, 152-4.
Ephraem Syrus, 79.
Erasmus, Desiderius, 220, 230.
Erskine, John, 144.
Eugene IV, Pope, 214.
Eve, 19, 34-7, 48, 82, 102 f., 112 f., 134, 143, 150, 170 f., 174, 178, 180, 182, 219.
Evil Inclination, 92, 95, 97, 101 f., 130, 156, 170 f., 183, 197 f., 242.
*Evil One, 66, 72, 94.

Faust, 4, 193, 210.
France, Anatole, 4 f.
Frank, Jacob, 194.
Freud, Sigmund, 242.

*Gabriel, 12, 18, 96, 109 f., 137, 140-2, 285.
*Gadreel, 19.
Gersonides (Levi ben Gerson), 150 f., 153, 155, 157.
Ghosts, 53, 166.
Giants, 17, 22, 24, 31, 44, 52, 75, 77-

80, 105, 131, 133, 266. *See* Gibborim.
Gibborim, 9, 152.
Gigith, 120 f., 278.
Gilgamesh, 263.
Gilles de Rais, 216.
Gnosticism, 46, 57 ff., 75, 77, 79, 83, 85, 93, 125, 169, 172 f., 194, 218, 228, 239, 241 f.
*God of this world, 65, 237 f. *See* Ruler of this world.
Goethe, Johann W. von, 143, 210.
Gog and Magog, 121 f.
Gore, Bishop, 238.
Gounod, Charles, 210.
Gregory the Great, Pope, 84 f., 205, 245.
Gregory of Nyssa, 289.
Guardian angels, 7, 12 f., 24 f., 32, 42, 108-11, 120, 124 f., 139-41, 159 f., 183.

*Harut and Marut, 113-7, 129.
Hasidism, 196-9.
*Hayyot, 134.
Helel ben Shahar, 9 f.
Hell, Harrowing of, 70, 83 f.
Hermon, Mount, 17, 19, 21, 33.
Hiva and Hiyya, 131 f.
Hillel ben Samuel of Verona, 149, 158-61.
Hizkuni, 150.
Hilary of Tours, 79.
Hocking, W. E., 228.
Horowitz, Isaiah, 195.
Hugo de Beniols, 214.
*Husk(s) (*Kelipah, Kelipot*), 180, 185, 187-90, 195, 198 f.

*Iblis, 36, 94, 112 f.
Ibn Ezra, Abraham, 148, 150, 153 f., 156.
Ignatius, 81.
*Incubi and *Succubi, 80, 106, 181, 195, 206, 236, 273, 277.
Innocent VIII, Pope, 214.
Irenaeus, 57, 75, 82 ff., 86, 245.
Isaac haKohen, 173-6, 185.
*Ishim, 285.
Israel b. Eliezer; *see* Baal Shem Tov.
Istahar, 131.

Jacob, 110 f., 139, 141, 183 f., 277, 281.

Jacob di Illescas, 187.
Jacob Joseph of Polonoye, 197.
*Jaoel (Jahoel), 46, 58 f., 270.
Jared, 17, 27, 152.
*Jekon, 19.
Jerome, 79, 207.
Job, 6, 37, 39-41, 96, 134 f., 156-8, 250.
Joseph della Reyna, 191-3, 196, 199.
Judah the Pious, 163, 165.
Julius Africanus, 78 f.
Justin Martyr, 74 f., 82.

*Kafkefoni, 174.
*Kafzefoni, 174.
Kaidanover, Zevi Hirsch, 195.
Kant, Immanuel, 237.
*Kasdaye, 19.
*Kelipot; *see* Husk (s)
Kierkegaard, Sören, 243.
Kimhi, David, 150, 153.
Kirkisani, 118.

Lactantius, 76, 81.
*Lahash, 138.
Langenfeld, Friederich Spee von, 220.
Left Side, 168 f., 172-6, 178, 181 f., 184 f., 187.
Leo XIII, Pope, 237.
Leviathan (Lothan), 12 f., 47; Clean and unclean L., 175.
Lewis, C. S., 249.
*Lilith, 106, 142-4, 171, 174-6, 181, 189, 192; Lesser L., 174.
Luria, Isaac, 187, 189-91, 193-6.
Luther, Martin, 220-3, 228, 244.

Maimonides, Moses (Maimuni, Moses ben Maimon), 129, 148-50, 153, 156 f., 158, 203, 212 f.
*Malchira, 41 f.
Mani, Manichaeism, 86, 204, 218, 239, 246.
Maritain, Jacques, 244, 248.
Marlowe, Christopher, 210.
Martensen, H., 238 f.
Martini, Raymundo, 135.
Marx, Karl, 241 f.
*Mastema, 28-31, 94, 140.
*Matanbuchus, 41 f.
Mather, Increase and Cotton, 229 f.
*Mazzikin; *see* Demons.

Messiah, 23, 32 f., 48, 63 f., 103, 119-
23, 190, 193 f., 199, 269.
Messiah son of Joseph, 121-3.
*Mesukiel, 173.
*Metatron, 59, 123, 125, 127, 131,
142, 153, 188, 270.
*Michael, 12, 18 f., 22, 25, 32, 36, 41,
63, 70, 109 f., 122, 134, 137, 139-
42, 219, 227, 270.
Michelet, Jules, 238.
Middath haDin; see Attribute of Jus-
tice.
Milton, John, 4, 220, 226, 228.
*Mizraim, 277.
Montaigne, Michel de, 230.
Moses, 30 f., 41, 70, 97 f., 137 f., 275.
Moses of Burgos, 175 f., 184.
Moses haDarshan, 135, 150.
Moses de Leon, 177.
Moses ben Maimon; see Maimonides.
Mujahid, 115 f.
Murry, John C., 248.
Mushtari, 116.

*Naamah, 138, 170 f., 178, 180 f.
Nahman of Bratzlav, 198 f.
Nahmanides (Moses ben Nahman),
148-51, 154 f., 169 f., 173.
Naphtali Zevi of Ropshitz, 197.
Nathan of Nemirov, 199.
Navarro, Solomon, 191.
*Nefilim (Nephilim), 8 f., 20, 129 f.,
151 f., 178.
Niebuhr, Reinhold, 244, 246-9.
Noah, 4, 17 ff., 28, 52, 107, 136, 142,
170 f.

Origen, 79, 81, 83 ff., 245.
"Other Side"; see Left Side.
Oursler, Fulton, 249.

Paterines, 218.
Paul, 43, 55, 64-6, 69 ff., 81, 245.
Paulicians (Paulinians), 218.
*Penemue, 19.
*Persia, Guardian angel of, 109 f. See
Dobiel.
Persian religion, 5, 100, 122, 246.
Philastrius of Brescia, 80.
Philo, 44, 53 f., 79, 93.
*Power of darkness, 65.
*Prince of the air, 65, 72.

*Prince of the sea, 139 f.
*Prince of this world; see Ruler of this
world.
Prometheus, 3, 20.

Rahab, 13; *R., Prince of the sea,
282.
*Raphael, 18.
Rashi (R. Solomon Yitzhaki), 148-50,
152, 154, 157.
Rathenau, Walther, 242 f.
Recanati, Menahem, 186 f.
Richelmus, 287.
*Rome, Guardian angel of, 110 f.,
124, 126, 139. See Edom.
Rossi, Azariah dei, 44.
Rougemont, Denis de, 247-9.
*Ruler of this world, 41 f., 68 f., 71 f.,
76, 81 f. See God of this world.

Saadia ben Joseph, 118, 122, 148 f.,
154, 156 f.
Saba, Abraham, 187.
Sabbatai Zevi, 193 f.
*Salmael, 285.
*Samael, 41 f., 94, 96, 124, 126 f.,
132, 134, 136-9, 171, 173-6, 183 f.,
191 f., 270, 275, 281.
Samuel ibn Hofni, 154.
Samuel b. Masnuth, 157.
*Sandalfon, 192.
*Sar, Sarim; see Guardian angels.
*Sar haOlam (*Sar haPanim), 58 f.
Sartorius, 237.
*Satan, 4, 6, 9, 12, 18, 30 ff., 34-7,
39-41, 47 f., 55-7, 63-72, 74-6, 78,
81-6, 94-100, 102, 104, 108 f.,
112 f., 116, 119 f., 121-4, 133-9,
156-8, 165, 169 f., 172, 182, 183 f.,
187, 195 f., 198, 201-32, 237, 265.
See Beelzebub, Beliar, Devil, Mas-
tema, Ruler of this world.
*Satanel (Satanail), 34, 219, 267,
290.
Schahin, 278.
Schleiermacher, Friederich, 237.
Scot, Reginald, 230.
Sefiroth, 168, 171-3, 175 f., 189.
*Semjaza (Semiazaz, Shemhazai),
17, 19, 24, 26, 91, 116, 129-31, 133,
282, 285.
*Seraphim, 125, 134, 171.

Serpent, 12, 27, 35-7, 48, 82, 94, 102 f., 134, 170 f., 246, 266, 274-6, 181-3.
Sethites and Cainites, 78 ff., 130, 132 f., 150-2, 274, 286.
*Shamdan (Ashamdon), 107, 170 f.
Shahar, 9 f.
*Shedim; *see* Demons.
Shekinah (Divine Presence), 135, 178.
Sheen, Fulton J., 249.
Shemhazael, 284.
Shemhazai; *see* Semjaza.
Sin, original, 43 f., 65, 102 f.
Solomon, 113 f., 171, 178, 180.
*Sons of God, 8, 37, 51, 53, 78, 80, 91, 129 f., 149-52, 156-8, 170 f., 177 f., 186 f., 264, 270, 285.
Spirits, evil; *see* Demons.
Sprenger, Jacob, 214.
Stars, falling, 23 f.

Tabari, 114-6.
Tatian, 75, 82.
*Temalyon, Ben, 107.
Ten Martyrs, 126 f.
Tertullian, 75 f., 81, 84, 86, 208.
Theophilus, 210.
Thomasius, Christian, 231.

Tiamat, 13, 238.
Trithemius, Johann, 214 f.

*Uriel, 18.
*Uzza (Uzzi), 91, 124, 127, 129, 130, 140 f.
*Uzzael, 130.

Vigny, Alfred de, 4.

Waldenses, 220.
*Watchers, 18, 20 f., 27 f., 31, 33 f., 45, 75, 266 f.
Weier, Johannes, 229 f.
Wesley, John, 230 f.
William of Edelin, 213.
Witchcraft, 5, 45 f., 75 f., 113-6, 127, 129 f., 166-8, 179 f., 182, 198, 207 f., 209-16, 222, 225, 228-32, 277.

Yezer, Evil (Yezer hara); *see* Evil Inclination.
*Yofiel, 174.
Yom Kippur; *see* Atonement, Day of.

*Zanzagiel, 137.
*Zefonith, 174.
Ziuni, Menahem, 187.
Zuhra, 115 f., 131.